AUTISM AND THE
DEVELOPMENT OF MIND

Three Week L

To Jacqui

Autism and the Development of Mind

R. Peter Hobson

*Developmental Psychopathology
Research Unit, Adult Department,
Tavistock Clinic
and Department of Psychiatry,
University College, London*

Psychology Press

An imprint of Erlbaum (UK) Taylor & Francis

Reprinted in paperback 1995, 1997

Psychology Press, Publishers
27 Palmeira Mansions
Church Road
Hove
East Sussex, BN3 2FA
UK

British Library Cataloguing in Publication Data
A catalogue record for this book is available from the British Library

Hobson, R. Peter
    Autism and the Development of Mind.—
    (Essays in Developmental Psychology, ISSN 0959-3977)
    I. Title II. Series
    155.4

    ISBN 0-86377-239-0

Printed and bound in the United Kingdom by Redwood Books, Trowbridge

Contents

Preface

As its title suggests, this book is about two things. The first is early childhood autism. The second is the growth of normal children's awareness of "self" and others, and their developing capacity for creative imagination and thought—in short, the development of mind. The two topics are intricately linked. I believe that childhood autism reveals how a normal infant's experience of affectively co-ordinated interpersonal relations is critical for the subsequent emergence of a range of cognitive capacities that are distinctive to the human mind. If this is the case, then much of our perplexity about the psychology of autism may reflect inadequacies in contemporary theories of child psychology. Correspondingly, progress in our understanding of autism may promote a re-evaluation of the patterning and mechanisms of normal child development.

This book is intended to represent the unfolding of a line of thought about these matters, not an exhaustive and critical review of empirical research nor a survey and critique of contemporary theoretical perspectives. Rather than erring on the side of caution or being overly circumspect in analysing the interpretative options, I shall take risks in what I say. I can only hope that my mistakes and oversights will be partly offset by the significance of the issues concerning infant psychological development with which I need to deal: the partial replacement of traditional cognitive/conative/affective categories of psychological functioning with the concept of "modes of relatedness" in infancy, the personal–emotional origins of social life, the social-developmental contribution to the emergence of symbolism and to the development of "self", and the earliest stages in acquiring and understanding the representational mind. In order to get a purchase on such weighty matters, I shall draw on the work of philosophers. In order to acknowledge some neglected sources of insight into the issues, I shall make occasional reference to psychoanalytic studies—although I have decided to defer a treatment of psychoanalytic approaches until another time. Alongside all of this, I shall present a formulation on the nature of autism in an interpersonal frame of reference. I hope to keep my bearings by returning time and again to three amongst several sources of psychological understanding—clinical observation, controlled experiment, and last but not least, the nature of one's own personal experience of being in relation with autistic and non-autistic individuals.

I wish to acknowledge some personal and intellectual debts. Foremost is what I owe to my wife Jacqui and to our children, James and Joe—and I owe a very great deal. My primary intellectual acknowledgments, coupled with deeply personal indebtedness, are to my father Bob Hobson and my mentor and friend Beate Hermelin. I thank those who have read and commented on all or parts of the essay, especially Frankie Happé, Cathy Lord, Jim Russell, and Mike Tomasello, and also David Hamlyn, Alan Leslie, Michael Rutter, and Lorna Wing. I am grateful to my colleagues in the Developmental Psychopathology Research Unit of the Tavistock Clinic, Martin Bishop, Tony Lee, Derek Moore, and Matthew Patrick, not least for putting up with The Book. Finally, for a variety of very important things, I give special thanks to Tony Lee, Janet Ouston, Catherine Buckley, David Hamlyn, Gillian Hudson, and (first rather than last) my mother, Marjorie Hobson.

CHAPTER ONE

Prolegomena

INTRODUCTION

In writing this book, I have tried to integrate an account of early childhood autism with a perspective on the development of mind in normal young children. In a way, nothing could be more natural than addressing these issues together. It is only by locating the source of autistic children's "particular mode of existence" (Bosch, 1970: p. 3) and by charting the developmental implications of this abnormality with reference to the normal (non-autistic) course of development, that we shall apprehend the nature of the perplexing and tragic condition we call "autism".

In another respect, however, the task is far from simple. This is only partly because the issues are too difficult for me to tackle—although too difficult they certainly are. A more technical problem is that I need to move back and forth between descriptions and theories of development in autistic children on the one hand, and accounts of development in normal young children on the other. Too close an integration of these viewpoints would result in an unhelpful muddle, too rigid a compartmentalisation would probably seem sterile and defeat my purpose. I have settled on an uneasy compromise, boxing and coxing as I go. This first chapter is intended to reveal that what follows subsequently is not quite as haphazard as it may seem.

I shall begin by saying something about autistic children.

THE AUTISTIC INDIVIDUAL

It is very difficult to convey what autistic children are like. The reason is that one needs to convey what it is like to relate to an autistic individual, how it feels to try to communicate or otherwise become engaged with the child. In such a situation, it is not uncommon to feel that one is faced with a strangeling who moves on some other plane of existence, a person with whom one cannot connect. This experience of being with an autistic child seems to correspond with something essential that is lacking in the child's own experience of other people. A central purpose of this essay is to argue that autistic children's deficient capacity for and experience of personal relatedness is the cardinal feature of their disorder.

On the other hand, it is not simply that autistic children have striking impairments in their interpersonal relations—they also speak and think in unusual ways, they frequently suffer from generalised intellectual deficits, and they commonly engage in stereotyped activities or pursue idiosyncratic preoccupations. In order to illustrate both the consistency and diversity of the clinical picture, as this essay proceeds I shall offer condensed versions of several published accounts of autistic individuals. I hope that the cumulative effect may be to give the reader a sense of how we need to understand and explain a "form of life" that differs fundamentally from our own.

It is fitting to begin with a case vignette from the classic account of autism, a beautiful clinical paper of 1943 in which the American psychiatrist Leo Kanner first described 11 children with "autistic disturbances of affective contact". Here are some edited excerpts from one of Kanner's descriptions:

> Case 9: Charles was brought to the clinic at the age of four and a half years, his mother complaining how "the thing that upsets me most is that I can't reach my baby". As a baby, this child would lie in the crib, just staring. When he was one and a half years old, he began to spend hours spinning toys and the lids of bottles and jars. His mother remarked: "He would pay no attention to me and show no recognition of me if I enter the room … The most impressive thing is his detachment and his inaccessibility. He walks as if he is in a shadow, lives in a world of his own where he cannot be reached. No sense of relationship to persons. He went through a period of quoting another person; never offers anything himself. His entire conversation is a replica of whatever has been said to him. He used to speak of himself in the second person, now he uses the third person at times; he would say, "He wants"—never "I want"…When he is with other people, he doesn't look up at them. Last July, we had a group of people. When Charles came in, it was just like a foal who'd been let out of an enclosure…He has a wonderful

memory for words. Vocabulary is good, except for pronouns. He never initiates conversation, and conversation is limited, extensive only as far as objects go."

In this moving account by a mother who felt she could not reach her baby, we can register the force of Kanner's (1943: p. 250) suggestion that autistic children "have come into the world with innate inability to form the usual, biologically provided affective contact with people". The sense of emotional connectedness that we feel when relating to other people, whether the people are infants, children or adults, seems to have been tragically lacking in this mother's relationship with her own son. Charles was "inaccessible" to her. For his own part, Charles seemed not to attend to his mother nor to other people, nor even to recognise them as persons with whom he could become emotionally engaged: "...it was just like a foal who'd been let out of an enclosure". Such unengagement was at the same time physical and mental, and was expressed on a number of levels. On the level of non-verbal communication, there was a virtual absence of co-ordinated, reciprocal bodily expressive exchanges; on the linguistic level there was a dearth of conversational interchange; and on all levels, there was the pervasive sense of the missing intersubjective, personal contact. Where was the meeting of hearts and minds that this mother yearned for with her child? There even seemed to be something lacking in the boy's sense of his own "me-ness", in that neither his presence nor his conversation conveyed self-assertion or self-expression: "He walks as if he is in a shadow...He would say, 'He wants'—never 'I want'."

Autistic individuals' relative incapacity for intersubjective contact with others, what I have just referred to as a meeting of hearts and minds, together with their probably deficient sense of self, are issues to which I shall often return. For now, I want to emphasise what this may mean for the autistic individual's *experience* of other people. Perhaps the most succinct and striking account is that provided by an intelligent young autistic adult interviewed by Donald Cohen (1980: p. 388). This man described how the first years of his life were devoid of people:

> I really didn't know there were people until I was seven years old. I then suddenly realised that there were people. But not like you do. I still have to remind myself that there are people...I never could have a friend. I really don't know what to do with other people, really.

This passage serves to link the earlier account of what a mother called her son's absent "sense of relationship to persons", with the autistic individual's delay in recognising that there are "persons". Even when such realisation dawns, there remains a difficulty in knowing how to relate to people *as* people. There appears to be delay and restriction in the autistic person's acquisition of knowledge about the very nature of persons as a special class of "things" with their own thoughts, beliefs, feelings, and subjective orientations towards the world.

To conclude this preliminary first look at the picture of autism, I need to emphasise how there are additional, regularly occurring features of the disorder that are more "cognitive" in quality. I say "more" cognitive, and I place the word "cognitive" in quotation marks, for two principal reasons: first, because I would not consider that the impairments I have already described are non-cognitive, it is just that they encompass realms of human psychology that are sometimes contrasted with the cognitive domain; second, because the term "cognitive" means quite different things when applied to adult-type psychological function and when applied to infant-level processes and capacities. Be that as it may, autistic children and adults think and speak in ways that are distinctly abnormal, and perhaps abnormal in a manner that is characteristically autistic. They are markedly delayed in developing creative symbolic play, an ability that normally flowers around the middle of a normal child's second year of life. When representational play does emerge, it is often stereotyped and relatively impoverished in content. Their language is usually delayed to a degree that is out of keeping with their non-verbal cognitive capacities such as visuospatial (jigsaw) pattern recognition. Their social use of language is especially unusual, in that they often fail to adjust what they say to the context in which they say it, and are insensitive to the interests, needs, and knowledge of their listeners. Their thinking is often "concrete" and inflexible, unattuned to contextual subtleties, insensitive to metaphor, and often awkward and one-track in style.

Perhaps this is enough of an inventory to illustrate how any theoretical account of autism will have to explain the co-occurrence of characteristic abnormalities in several seemingly disparate areas of psychological function. I shall oversimplify by drawing an initial, crude distinction between the social and intellectual domains. This is a distinction I create in order to dissolve, or at least reconstitute, at a later stage. For now, I wish to use it as a starting-point for introducing certain themes that will thread their way through my essay.

THE INTERPERSONAL DOMAIN

What does it mean for a human being to have truly interpersonal relations? How is knowledge of the nature of persons with their own mental life acquired? The central thrust of my argument is that knowledge and understanding of persons, or to put this differently, a conceptual grasp of the nature of minds, is acquired through an individual's experience of affectively patterned, intersubjectively co-ordinated relations *with* other people. A young child comes to know about people's psychological states through having subjective experiences that are shared with, opposed to, or otherwise articulated with the experiences (and not merely the "behaviour") of others. I think that intuitively, this makes far more sense than any other proposal concerning the basis for our knowledge of Other Minds; but beyond this, I draw upon a range of philosophical writings, notably by Ludwig Wittgenstein (1958, 1980), Peter Strawson (1962), and especially David Hamlyn (1974, 1978). I shall leave more detailed argument for subsequent chapters, but I want to convey the gist of this line of thought from "genetic epistemology". I shall do so by citing a clinical illustration.

About fifteen years ago, when I was a junior psychiatrist on the general wards of the Maudsley Hospital, London, and before I had embarked on psychological investigations of autism, I was involved in caring for a 20-year-old man who was subsequently given the diagnosis of Asperger's syndrome, a condition with a typical developmental history closely allied to that of autism (Frith, 1991; Wing, 1981a). He was someone with impressive cognitive abilities in certain domains, and had achieved "A" level standard (the English equivalent of American high advanced-placement test scores) in English and German. On the other hand, this man was highly unusual in his bodily co-ordination, for instance walking with the most awkward, almost bizarre, gait. It was especially striking how he seemed unable to achieve any fluency in his interpersonal relations. For example, he would sit unblinking through the hour of our weekly ward group, staring ahead silently. I cannot recall any sense of "affective contact" with him.

Now this individual had a number of preoccupations, but foremost amongst these was his inability to grasp what a "friend" is. He would ask again and again: "Are you a friend?", "Is he a friend?", and so on. The ward staff made every effort to teach him the meaning of the word "friend", they even found someone to act as a "befriender" to accompany him on outings to the local shopping centre. All this was to no avail—he seemed unable to fathom what a "friend" is.

These curious circumstances prompt us to reflect on the question: What is so special, and in this case so elusive, about the concept of "friend"? After all, this patient had little difficulty with other concepts that would have been far more problematic for young normal children. As children, most of us can be taught the meaning of the word "friend" because we experience something of what it is like to engage with others in ways that are fitting between friends. We know what it is to have friends, to be a friend, to enjoy doing with friends those things that are the stuff of friendship. One cannot *really* know what a friend is, simply by "observing" as one who stands outside and watches behaviour. One needs to participate with others in a "form of life" (Wittgenstein, 1958) in which one experiences the kinds of interpersonal relatedness and relationship that constitute friendship.

I think that this patient with Asperger's syndrome was severely constrained in the extent to which he could share things with other people, in what one might broadly describe as an emotional way. To an important degree, he seemed to stand outside and observe—and the kind of non-participatory observing of which he was capable seemed insufficient to afford him an understanding of friendship.

I consider that there are important points of similarity between the concept of "friend" and the concept of "persons". As Hamlyn (1974) argues, we cannot have a proper conception of a possible object of knowledge unless we understand what relations can and cannot exist between the object and ourselves. In order to know what persons are, we need to experience and understand the kinds of relations that can exist between ourselves and others. Amongst other things, truly personal relations involve reciprocally co-ordinated exchanges of feeling, as well as having the potential for a variety of forms of sharing. An individual would not have an adequate conception of a person, if he or she believed that one can *only* experience or treat people as things.

All this might seem a long way from the issue of what underpins a child's understanding of minds. I hope to show that, on the contrary, we are close to the heart of the matter. To begin with, minds are properties of embodied people. To ascribe mindfulness is, except in the marginal case of animals, to ascribe "personhood". More than this, it is from a child's experience of persons that he or she ultimately derives concepts of "mind". The claim here is that very young children begin with innately constituted propensities and capacities to relate to and experience other people in special ways and, from this starting point, follow a social-developmental pathway to the time at which they acquire concepts about people's feelings, intentions, thoughts, beliefs, and so on. The whole process pivots around the child's experience of personal relatedness, and more specifically, around the qualities of such experience that make knowledge of persons with minds possible.

I think it is very probable that early childhood autism presents us with the negative image of such a developmental progression. In so far as autistic children lack something essential to what is biologically given to effect intersubjective co-ordination with other people, they are deprived of what it takes to acquire knowledge of persons and to understand minds. To return to the words of Cohen's (1980) autistic patient:

> I really didn't know there were other people until I was seven years old...I never could have a friend. I really don't know what to do with other people, really.

SELF AND OTHER

The account I have been giving thus far could be reframed from the vantage-point of "self" development. One point of intersection is obvious: to know oneself is to know oneself as a person amongst others. I have my thoughts, feelings, beliefs, and so on, and you have yours; *I* want to do this, so don't you do it; that item is *mine*, not yours; *I* have these attributes, they matter to me as being descriptive of "me"; and so on. From a less self-centred perspective, we also know what it means to experience and express a sense of community with others, a sense of "we". In order to acquire a developed concept of self, children need to appreciate the nature of persons and to recognise the existence of other selves with whom they have much in common, but from whom they are distinct.

The story of the development of self is a highly intricate one, however. A preliminary issue is whether there might be more than one developmental line along which the very young child acquires increasingly sophisticated self-awareness. In particular, there seems to be an important distinction between the qualities and structures of what Martin Buber (1958) calls I–Thou and I–It relatedness. As we shall see, the patterning of infants' observable exchanges with other people appears to be qualitatively different from those manifest in relation to things. This raises the question of whether infants may have different forms of experience in their social and non-social transactions, and correspondingly different senses of self within the different contexts. Alternatively and perhaps more plausibly, there might be some structure to an infant's sense of self that is applicable to all contexts, but this is augmented by additional potentialities for "selfhood" that are realised primarily within inter-personal settings.

The second major issue concerns the stages through which successively more elaborated senses of self are developed. Major goals are the achievement of self-reflective awareness and the appraisal and assertion of oneself in relation to other selves conceived as such. What are the hurdles to be crossed here, and what conditions foster or hamper developmental progress?

A third issue has to do with the interrelationships among young children's sense of self, their intuitive or more intellectual understanding of minds, and their capacities to symbolise and to conceptualise. How far are each of these important developmental domains dependent upon, or otherwise co-ordinated with, the others?

The phenomenon of autism may help us to think about these issues, if not to solve them. Autistic children do appear to have *specific* problems with I–Thou relatedness (Hobson, 1983a, 1989a), and with the develop-ment of an "interpersonal self" (Hobson, 1990a; Neisser, 1988). We have already seen that such disorder may have a direct bearing on deficits in interpersonal understanding. I shall now suggest a connection with the origins of the capacity to symbolise.

THE CAPACITY TO SYMBOLISE

As Charles Morris (1938) emphasised, a sign refers to something for someone. Strictly speaking, we should think not so much of the sign as "referring", but rather of the someone who attributes or recognises a referring relation between the sign and whatever it signifies. Signs may then be subdivided into symbols and signals. Susanne Langer (1957: pp. 60–61) stressed the contrast thus:

> A term which is used symbolically and not signally does *not* evoke action appropriate to the presence of its object...Symbols are not proxy for their objects, but are *vehicles for the conception of objects (Langer's italics)*.

To have a conception of an object is to have a particular way of thinking about it. One may conceive of an object in a number of different ways, a fact exemplified by the possibility of applying an infinite number of co-referential linguistic terms to the same thing. One function of symbols is to lift out particular aspects of meaning; or from a complementary perspective, particular meanings can be "carried" by symbols that are embodied in one or another physical form.

Perhaps it is easiest to consider all this in the context of simple symbolic play. A boy who pretends that a matchbox "is" a car has distilled out whatever meanings of "car-ness" he requries for play, and attributes these to his very un-car-like symbolic vehicle (please forgive the pun). He maintains a dual attitude in continuing to recognise the real properties of the matchbox, but at the same time disregards such properties and instead pretend-takes the matchbox as instantiating car-properties (Alan Leslie, 1987, provides a detailed analysis of this process, albeit in different terms). One way of describing such play would be to say that the child has come to appreciate an important distinction between "thought" and "thing". He can apply thoughts about cars to things that are not at all like cars; he can confer aspects of his psychological attitude towards cars on to something quite different. He makes a psychological connection between symbol and referent, in this case between the matchbox and a car, whilst at the same time respecting their differences.

A critical question for the developmental psychologist is how an infant comes to achieve the capacity to symbolise in this way. I shall be arguing that there is an important *social*-developmental contribution here. More specifically, I shall highlight the potential significance of an infant's capacity to perceive other people's outer-directed psychological attitudes towards a visually specified world. Suppose that even in infancy, a child comes to recognise that a given object or event may be the focus of attention for another person. Suppose that more than this, the child perceives how the other person has an emotional attitude towards the object, and registers something of the contrast between that attitude and the infant's own feelings toward the object in question. Here we have a situation in which there is a triangulation among two "psychological attitudes" and a single "thing" related-to. It is a situation in which the infant is in a position to apprehend the difference between what a thing means to the infant herself, and what it means to someone else.

At this point, the perceptually specified world is becoming a multiply-referenced world. A single object or event may have several meanings-for-persons. So, too, a person may be seen to be a creature who not only has psychological attitudes, but also one who through these attitudes can and does confer meanings on objects and events in the world. Once the child comes to recognise and then exercise his or her *own* potential to attribute person-dependent rather than object-specified meanings, at this point he or she acquires the capacity to symbolise. The child can take an object to mean this, that or the other, whilst continuing to respect its objective properties; he or she can use a symbolic prop to carry particular conceptions of the world (the conception "car", for example) abstracted from other meanings or characteristics (such as size, mobility, and so on) that the referent may have. If this account is correct, then an infant's capacity to relate to another person's psychological relatedness to the world may have developmental significance for the child's subsequent ability to modify his or her own psychological attitudes and attributions in creative symbolic play.

In fact, a principal stimulus to this line of theorising (first outlined in two papers of 1989a and 1990b in which I drew upon and took issue with the seminal ideas of Alan Leslie, 1987) was the coincidence between autistic children's deficits in social relatedness and understanding on the one hand, and their limited creative symbolic play on the other. The central notion is that autistic children's primary social-relational impairments place severe developmental constraints on their potential to evolve creative symbolic play. As we shall see, there may be aspects of the psychology of congenitally blind children that also bear upon this thesis. It is a thesis which weaves together interpersonal-affective and intellectual domains of psychological development, and one for which considerations from developmental psychopathology may prove decisively important.

I shall now return the focus to autism. Perhaps it is worthwhile to consider what it would mean to explain this perplexing condition.

EXPLAINING AUTISM

Aetiology and pathogenesis

It is not a simple matter to define what an adequate theory of autism should look like. It seems a simple matter to pose the question: "What causes autism?", but in fact there are numerous ways in which an answer might be framed. Each of these would address but a fragment of the theoretical problem. This essay will have a restricted focus on a certain domain of study, the psychological; moreover, it will be concerned with a particular aspect and *level* of psychological explanation, and give little space to many facets of autism that must be found an appropriate place within a more comprehensive theoretical account. In order to place matters in context, therefore, I shall make some rather sweeping observations about the nature of explanation as applied to a clinical condition such as autism, and mark the points at which competing and/or complementary accounts articulate with what I have to say.

The first matter is to draw a distinction between aetiology, what most people would consider the underlying "cause" of the condition, and pathogenesis, the ways in which abnormality is expressed and disorder develops and evolves. There is a considerable weight of evidence that physical factors which disrupt brain function play an important aetiological role in the causation of autism. In order to acknowledge the importance of this body of research, as well as to excuse my decision to devote the remainder of this essay to other preoccupations, I shall cite some of the evidence forthwith. From a clinical perspective, neurological signs such as motor abnormalities and late-onset epilepsy are highly suggestive of primary dysfunction of the nervous system (Damasio & Maurer,1978; Rutter, 1970), and autism is associated with all degrees of mental retardation, with perinatal complications and with other more specific conditions such as phenylketonuria and tuberose sclerosis (Wing, 1988a). Then there is substantial evidence for a genetic predisposition in at least a proportion of cases (Bolton & Rutter, 1990). For example, Susan Folstein and Michael Rutter (1977) conducted a groundbreaking study of 21 twin pairs in which at least one co-twin had a diagnosis of autism. None of the 10 dizygotic (non-identical) pairs had two autistic twins, but in four out of 11 monozygotic (identical) pairs, both twins were autistic. Moreover, there was evidence for a significant degree of cognitive disability in the large majority of those who were monozygotic twins to autistic individuals, but in only one out of ten who were dizygotic twins. Or again, the prevalence of autism in the siblings of autistic individuals is low (about 3% of sibs have the diagnosis), but this is over fifty times the prevalence observed in the normal population—and once again, cognitive disabilities are more common even among siblings who do not have autism *per se* (August,

Stewart, & Tsai, 1981). Something relevant for the condition of autism may be inherited, although quite what that is remains unclear. Although recent evidence concerning autism-specific abnormalities in brain structure and in neurophysiological function is tentative (for lively contributions, see Dawson, 1989), it is probable that neuroscientific research will also yield findings that further illustrate biologically based contributions to the aetiology of autism.

Having said this, we need to be clear about the limits of aetiological explanation. To begin with, it is yet to be established that any given pattern of inheritance, or any given distribution of neuroanatomical abnormality or neurological dysfunction, is applicable to all autistic people. Therefore it remains to explain how seeming heterogeneity in the aetiology of autism can be reconciled with relative homogeneity in the clinical presentation of the disorder.

Second, we need to understand not only what is inherited or acquired in, say, neurological and/or neurofunctional terms, but also what are the essential psychological impairment or impairments that occur as a result. In other words, how are the effects of physical disorder expressed on a psychological plane? Does our general knowledge of brain–behaviour correlates provide us with a way of explaining the clinical and psychological characteristics of autistic individuals, by mapping their disabilities and abilities according to the specialised functions subserved by particular brain regions that might be selectively damaged in autism? One suggestion is that neuropsychological abnormalities reflecting disorder in the frontal lobes and/or the limbic system (the primitive functional core of the brain that includes circuits which connect the frontal and temporal lobes with more primitive subcortical structures) might be implicated in a majority of cases (Ozonoff, Pennington, & Rogers, 1991a). This might indeed be so, and could be of aetiological significance for autistic individuals' abnormalities in social relatedness as well as certain of their difficulties in devising and executing plans of action (e.g. Hughes & Russell, 1993). However, it remains doubtful whether any such account *on its own* will be sufficiently specific and wide-ranging to encompass the qualitatively distinct and seemingly disparate cognitive/conative/affective deficits and abilities of autistic people. Thus far, attempts to find a neurologically-specified pattern of psychological dysfunction that is specific and universal to autistic individuals, and to map such dysfunction on to the profile of abilities and disabilities that characterise the disorder, have been very partial and less than convincing.

Perhaps we should not be too optimistic about discovering a straightforward link between neurological lesions and the "autistic" pattern of psychological dysfunction—in which case, we shall need to introduce some further conceptual ingredients into our theoretical mix. In order to explain how we might do this, I shall move on to the specifically psychological plane of explanation, and return to extra-psychological considerations as needs be.

Psychological Explanation

The first matter is to clarify the stratified nature of psychological explanation, whether this applies to normal or abnormal development. Our present task is to make sense of a bewildering array of diverse disabilities characteristic of autism, whilst at the same time allowing for the psychological abilities that are sometimes (not always) spared or even exceptionally developed in autistic individuals. One way in which we might achieve this aim, is to define a small number of psychological deficits that "cause" the array of apparently disconnected clinical phenomena. What has emerged in the last few years as a prime candidate for such a causative psychological deficit is in the area of what I have called the autistic individual's limited "concept of persons" (Hobson, 1982a) and what Simon Baron-Cohen, Alan Leslie, and Uta Frith (1985) have termed the child's impaired "theory of mind". My own starting point was autistic individuals' limited concept of the nature of persons as having subjective experiences and psychological orientations to the world, whereas Baron-Cohen and his colleagues began with a focus on autistic children's limited understanding of "beliefs". The two perspectives converge in suggesting that what may be common to most if not all individuals with autism, is a certain specific limitation in understanding the nature of people's mental states. As a number of other researchers have also argued (e.g. Mundy, Sigman, & Kasari, 1993; Rogers & Pennington, 1991; Tager-Flusberg, 1993), such a conceptual deficit might lead to and/or be associated with a cluster of additional impairments not only in social understanding, but also in the realms of language and more generalised cognitive function.

But to return to the question of levels of psychological explanation: just because deficient concepts of mind might be basic to a number of secondary psychological features of autism, this does not mean that here is *the* basic level of psychological explanation. A further meaning of "basic level" is the point at which one reaches the bedrock of psychological primitives which do not themselves have psychological explanation, but which need to be explained in non-psychological frames of reference such as in neurological or physiological terms. It is an open question whether certain cognitive mechanisms that are closely allied to concepts of mind are or are not innate. Alan Leslie (1987) supposes that the capacity for "metarepresentation", which is said to subserve one person's ability to mentally represent other people's mental representations, is normally innate but missing in autistic people. I suggest that rather than *this* being innate, there is a social–developmental path that leads to a normal child's ability to conceptualise the nature of mind, one that has gone awry in children who are autistic. In other words, I believe that Leslie's theory is pitched at a level of explanation which is basic for *certain* of autistic children's deficits—this is precisely the level for which I invoked the idea of the autistic child's limited concept of persons with minds—but that such an account needs further, yet more basic explanation in psychological terms. To put it in a nutshell, I think that autistic children's deficient or aberrant capacity for intersubjective engagement with others is what causes their limitation in understanding minds.

The Interpersonal Dimension

Now suppose it is true that failings in intersubjective engagement are the *sine qua non* for autism. Might we not pursue still more basic explanations, even within the psychological domain, and see whether we can uncover causes for this impairment, for instance in autistic individuals' difficulties in sustaining attention (e.g. Dawson & Lewy, 1989), or in the timing of their interpersonal exchanges (Wimpory, 1986)? My response here is: Yes and No. "Yes", in the sense that there might very well be lower-order psychological deficits that explain the abnormal patterning of autistic children's interpersonal behaviour and experience (e.g. Wing & Wing, 1971). On the other hand, as we have already seen, there might be a range of *diverse* deficits, which singly or in combination effect a sufficient disruption at this intersubjective level. If this were so, then not one of these deficits need be present in all cases of autism, and some might "cause" the disorder only when they operate in concert with other pathogenic factors (a point I shall illustrate later, when considering the case of congenitally blind children). A cause that is basic to a given set of effects may be analysed into subcomponent parts, any single one of which would not give rise to the same effects, and no particular combination of which is pathognomonic of the disorder. My "No" response partly arises from these latter arguments, in that failures in intersubjective engagement, however these might be caused and however variable in form, would still constitute the final common pathway to autism. The lack of engagement would remain the essential, universal feature of the disorder. More important still, it is my claim that the autistic child's limited experience of intersubjective engagement *per se*, not "attention difficulties", "abnormalties in interpersonal timing", nor any other description of their impairment, is what severely constrains their ability to develop an understanding of the nature of persons and *thereby* to evolve a range of supervenient cognitive, linguistic, and social capacities. In this sense, abnormalities in the intersubjective domain would constitute an irreducible bedrock in the explanation of autism.

On the other hand (again), the subcomponent deficits that may operate in any given case of autism are likely to find direct expression in their own, individual manifestations. Such manifestations may or may not be specific to the interpersonal domain; they may be very general. Therefore not all the features associated with autism need be explained in terms of impairment at the intersubjective level. I shall come to stress how we need to define the scope and limits of *each* level and mode of explanation with reference to each of the clinical features of autism, considered one by one.

I need to remark on some further complications that arise if we choose to adjust our focus on to the intersubjective domain. It is already apparent that if a number of features of autism are spin-off effects of contributory but inconsistent lower-order psychological deficits, then one might expect to find a degree of heterogeneity amongst autistic individuals. The matter becomes more complicated still when one considers how the above-mentioned final common pathway to (for example) a deficient understanding of minds might be defined by what happens or fails to happen *between* the autistic individual and other people. The notion of *inter*subjective contact is one that applies between and across individuals. It encompasses the various means by which one person's subjective experiences are both linked with and differentiated from the experiences of others, starting at the level of non-verbal communication but evolving through increasingly sophisticated levels of interpersonal exchange, especially as mediated by language. What this means is that autism may need to be understood with reference to the "system" of child-in-relation-to-other. As I mentioned in passing, there might be a variety of forms of "impairment in intersubjectivity". The proposal is that what is common to autism is a sufficiently profound disruption in those forms of patterned interpersonal interchange that affect sharing, conflict, or other modes of co-ordinated experience between the child and others. Such psychological co-orientation between people, entailing not only mutual engagement but also mental co-ordination between one person and another *vis-à-vis* an external shared world, is what seems to be critically deficient in autistic individuals.

This perspective does not relinquish our earlier concerns with what is common to people with autism, but at the same time it allows for even more markedly heterogenous psychopathology (and neuropathology) in the individual autistic child by locating the disorder in the qualities of relatedness that exist between the child and others. I am *not* suggesting that autism arises simply through a failure of environmental, and more specifically interpersonal, provision. I believe that abnormalities intrinsic to these children are always operative in constraining the children's capacities for personal relatedness, and that in this sense the condition is *not* psychogenic. To put it plainly, I think it is likely that autism involves either pathology in subcortical brain structures that are the primitive neurological core required for interpersonal bodily/mental co-ordination, or extensive pathology across a number of structures necessary for perceptual–affective, cognitive and motivational propensities and abilities integral to intersubjective communication. Autism is a rare and profound disorder. It would appear that the personal category of experience and understanding is a remarkably robust characteristic of human psychology. We need to respect the degree to which non-autistic people are endowed with very deep-rooted and resilient capacities for personal relatedness, and to acknowledge the awesome handicaps of those who seem to lack something fundamental in this respect.

THE PERSPECTIVE OF DEVELOPMENTAL PSYCHOPATHOLOGY

This, then, is an outline sketch of my proposed account. I shall spend the remainder of the book filling in the sketch. Already some readers may feel impatient to know what "disruption in intersubjective co-ordination" really means, and be sceptical whether abnormalities in non-verbal communication could give rise to the syndrome we call "autism". At face value, it seems far-fetched to propose that what Kanner (1943) called "inborn autistic disturbances of affective contact" might cause a major part of these individuals' characteristic cognitive, linguistic, and communicative disabilities. Yet this is the proposal I wish to explore, and also to qualify, in the succeeding chapters.

Perhaps I should acknowledge that although there is good evidence for parts of my account, there is also much within it that is contentious. Despite this, I shall not devote much space to measuring the theory against its competitors. Instead I shall pursue my aim of exploring the logical as well as psychological grounds for supposing that an account of this kind is necessary for explaining the levels and qualities of emotional and cognitive disability that are characteristic of autism. I believe it is also needed to encompass what we ourselves feel when relating to autistic individuals— the deficient or tenuous sense of intersubjective contact itself.

In attempting to address these matters, I shall adopt the stance of developmental psychopathology. Already my argument has criss-crossed between normal and abnormal development. In this way I have introduced the final ingredient that is often lacking in "medical model" accounts of psychopathology—that "causes" and "levels of explanation" need to be identified across time and across sequences of development, as well as within any current timeframe. We shall not arrive at a satisfying explanation of autism unless we consider how abnormalities in early-appearing psychological propensities and capacities may delay, distort, or prevent the emergence of more sophisticated abilities that are founded upon them. This in turn requires that we have a theory of normal development adequate to serve as a yardstick against which to evaluate the evolution of childhood psychopathology. Yet the degree to which a theory of normal development renders autism comprehensible may serve as one criterion for its adequacy. Hence the need for developmental psychopathology, an approach that prompts us to frame our thinking about abnormal development with reference to normal development, and to re-evaluate developmental theory in order to encompass psychopathological phenomena. This dialectic is one that promises to enrich our understanding of normal child development, not autism alone. It may also reveal something about what it means to engage in truly interpersonal relations, and how far such relations are pivotal for cognitive and linguistic as well as social development.

CHAPTER TWO

The Picture of Autism

In an early subsection of Chapter 1, I provided a brief snapshot of autism. Now I wish to reflect on the broader clinical picture. Throughout this book I shall be citing published case descriptions of autistic individuals, in the belief that these convey a more vivid and in some ways more accurate picture of autism than do lists of abstracted clinical features. Yet it is also true that each case presents its own idiosyncrasies, and there is a danger that we may be waylaid by detail and lose the wood for the trees. Besides this, of course, I may bias the reader's perspective by judicious selection and editing of the material presented. In order to lessen these risks, I shall complement case descriptions with a formal overview of the clinical features that seem to characterise the great majority of autistic individuals.

THE EARLIEST YEARS

Almost always, but not quite invariably, autism begins within the first three years of life. As Michael Rutter and Eric Schopler (1987) discuss, specifically autistic features vary appreciably in the age at which they are detectable, and the disorder may have an onset in infancy yet not be recognised until some time later. As a result, the evidence for developmental impairment or distortion that is often present from very early on in the children's lives may be rather non-specific in kind. The occasional autism-like disorders that occur after the age of three are rare and are usually due to acquired brain disease or late-onset genetic disorders (e.g. Corbett, Harris, Taylor, & Trimble,1977).

Considerable theoretical importance may be attached to the question of whether the onset of "autism" is typically within or beyond the first year of life. As Lorna Wing (1981b) observes, however, the age of onset in childhood conditions is notoriously difficult to establish. Retrospective parental reports suggest that many but by no means all autistic children have had significant delays in the development of motor abilities, speech, and communication during their first and second years (e.g. Dahlgren & Gillberg, 1989; Ornitz, Guthrie, & Farley, 1987). One difficulty in interpreting these findings is that one needs to distinguish delays that are manifestations of general intellectual retardation, from delays or "deviance" from normal development that are specifically autistic in quality. This is why comparisons with reports from parents of non-autistic retarded children are so valuable. Wing (1969) requested parents of autistic, normal, intellectually impaired (Down's syndrome), language-disordered, and partially blind and partially deaf children, aged from four to 16 years at the time of the study, to complete a schedule of questions designed to elicit a history of abnormalities characteristic of early childhood autism. Wing concentrated on the scores for those clinical features ascribed to the children when they were aged between two and five years. On a number of counts, there were marked contrasts between the autistic children and those who were normal or who had Down's syndrome. The autistic children were abnormal in their visual attentiveness to objects and people, in their relative failure to use or understand gestures such as pointing, in their movements which were often odd, in their manner of relating to people, in the ways they showed emotional responses to situations, in exhibiting socially embarrassing behaviour, and in their lack of play. The autistic children contrasted somewhat less on certain of these measures when compared with children who had a receptive disorder of language, and less still when compared with partially blind and partially deaf children—but overall, they were clearly impaired on a range of perceptual and social-relational abilities from early in life. In a more recent study, Sven Dahlgren and Christopher Gillberg (1989) asked mothers of a population sample of autistic children and closely matched non-autistic retarded and normal children aged between seven and 22 years, to complete a 130-item questionnaire on the child's behaviour in the first two years of life. Amongst the features that discriminated the autistic from the two control groups were the children's isolation, their lack of play, their strange reactions to sound, their failure to attract attention to their own activity, their lack of smiling at times when one might expect it, and their empty gaze (see Gillberg et al., 1990, for clinical assessments as well as maternal reports on autistic children presenting under three years of age; Klin, Volkmar, & Sparrow, 1992, for evidence of social impairment in young autistic children; and Stone & Lemanek, 1990, for parental reports of current functioning in three-to six-year-olds).

A recently published study by Simon Baron-Cohen, Jane Allen, and Christopher Gillberg (1992) adds a further dimension to these observations. Family doctors or health visitors were asked to complete a brief questionnaire in relation to a sample of 18-month-olds who had older siblings with autism, and who were therefore at risk of inheriting the disorder, and a control sample of normal infants. The key questions were whether the children took an interest in other children, whether they enjoyed playing peek-a-boo or hide-and-seek, ever engaged in pretend play, used an index finger to point as an expression of interest in something, or ever brought objects to show to a parent. The only children who failed on more than one of these items were four children out of the 41 in the high-risk group (none of whom showed gross motor or intellectual delay). These were the only four children to receive a diagnosis of autism by 30 months of age. At least in some autistic children, therefore, characteristic social and cognitive impairments are manifest in the second year of life.

Thus we find reports of autism-specific abnormalities in the domains of social-affective relatedness, self-consciousness and play, even in very young autistic children. Given the importance of appreciating the profoundly abnormal qualities of autistic children's interpersonal relatedness and imaginative activity, and the theoretical and clinical significance of their dramatically impoverished experience as well as understanding of other people, I shall provide more detailed illustrations by returning to two classic accounts of young autistic children. The first is a description by the psychoanalyst Melanie Klein (1930) which was written over a decade before Kanner (1943) first identified the syndrome of autism, but one which almost certainly portrays a Kanner-type child. Here is a vivid portrayal of the way in which an autistic child's lack of co-ordination with other people is at once bodily and mental. The following is Klein's description of a four-year-old boy named Dick (Klein, 1930: pp. 221–223):

... as regards the poverty of his vocabulary and of his intellectual attainments, (he) was on the level of a child of about fifteen or eighteen months. Adaptation to reality and emotional relations to his environment were almost entirely lacking. This child, Dick, was largely devoid of affects, and he was indifferent to the presence or absence of mother or nurse. From the very beginning he had only rarely displayed anxiety...he had almost no interests, did not play, and had no contact with his environment. For the most part he simply strung sounds together in a meaningless way, and constantly repeated certain noises. When he did speak he generally used his meagre vocabulary incorrectly. But it was not only that he was unable to make himself intelligible: he had no wish to do so...sometimes he would repeat the words correctly, but would go on repeating them in an incessant, mechanical way...Dick's opposition and obedience lacked both affect and understanding...he displayed very considerable insensibility to pain and felt nothing of the desire, so universal with little children, to be comforted and petted...He had let his nurse go without manifesting any emotion, and had followed me into the room with complete indifference. There he ran to and fro in an aimless, purposeless way, and several times he also ran round me, just as if I were a piece of furniture, but he also showed no interest in any of the objects in the room. His movements as he ran to and fro seemed to be without co-ordination. The expression of his eyes and face was fixed, far-away and lacking in interest...With her [his own nurse], as with everyone else, Dick had failed to establish emotional contact.

It is noteworthy that Klein compares the autistic child's manner of relating to persons as one that might be appropriate toward a "piece of furniture". That is indeed what it can feel like to be in the presence of a young child with severe autism—one feels *oneself* to be a piece of furniture. It is not usually so weird an experience to relate to older autistic individuals, for such individuals may approach one and make some effort to converse by asking and answering questions, often in a stereotyped manner—but it is still a rather unearthly experience. If one considers a normal human being to be the uniquely appropriate "measuring instrument" for the appraisal of intersubjectivity (and there is no other that can register autistic children's lack of affective contact with persons), then one might wonder whether the "feel" of such a profoundly abnormal quality of interpersonal relatedness is pathognomonic of autistic social relatedness. I should stress that there is variability in the quality of one's own emotional contact and engagement with autistic individuals, and of course it is contentious whether there is anything autism-specific in this regard—but notwithstanding the many reservations and qualifications that should attend my saying so, I do agree with Kanner (1943), and think there is.

My second example is abstracted from another of Kanner's (1943) evocative clinical descriptions:

Case 2: Frederick was seen at the age of six years. His mother stated that she had never known him to cry in demanding attention. He was not interested in hide-and-seek, nor very good with co-operative play. Until the previous year, he had mostly ignored other people. He looked curiously at small children and would then go off all alone. He acted as if people weren't there at all, even with his grandparents. To a certain extent, his mother said, he liked to stick to the same thing. On one of the bookshelves at home there were three pieces in a certain arrangement. Whenever this was changed, he always rearranged it in the old pattern. By the age of six, he could count up into the hundreds and read numbers, but he was not interested in numbers as they applied to objects. He had great difficulty in knowing the proper use of personal pronouns. On receiving a gift, he would say of himself: "You say 'Thank you'".

Here is Kanner's (1943: p. 224) account of the child's behaviour when attending the clinic for the first time at the age of six years:

He was led into the psychiatrist's office by a nurse, who left the room immediately afterward. His facial expression was tense, somewhat apprehensive, and gave the impression of intelligence. He wandered aimlessly about for a few moments, showing no sign of awareness of the three adults present. He then sat down on the couch, ejaculating unintelligible sounds, and then abruptly lay down, wearing throughout a dreamy-like smile. When he responded to questions or commands at all, he did so by repeating them echolalia fashion. The most striking feature in his behavior was the difference in his reactions to objects and to people. Objects absorbed him easily and he showed good attention and perseverance in playing with them. He seemed to regard people as unwelcome intruders to whom he paid as little attention as they would permit. When forced to respond, he did so briefly and returned to his absorption in things. When a hand was held out before him so that he could not possibly ignore it, he played with it briefly as if it were a detached object. He blew out a match with an expression of satisfaction with the achievement, but did not look up to the person who had lit the match.

The first thing to note is how this autistic child could be attentive towards and even absorbed with inanimate objects, yet he seemed oblivious to the presence of persons with whom he could engage and communicate. Obviously he registered the physical presence of people, as when he moved a person's hand. Yet it was towards the hand as a detached object, not towards the person whose hand it was, that Frederick acted. By no means are all autistic children quite so impersonal in their social behaviour, but those who are seem to demonstrate a profound lack of interpersonal *relatedness*, not merely a limitation in their thinking about or understanding of other people. Frederick's attention was not drawn towards other people, though he could look curiously at small children, and there was little to suggest that he perceived other people as special (although of course he might have been actively ignoring or denying such specialness). Nor did he wish to engage others with himself—his mother had never known him to cry in demanding attention—and there was that quality of unconnectedness, the lack of reciprocity with others in his bodily gestures, his emotional expressiveness and his language. He did not look up to see the other person's reactions to his own achievement in blowing out the match; he might almost have been alone. Frederick's seeming unawareness of "persons" was paralleled by an apparent unselfconsciousness, and it is little wonder that he was not interested in hide-and-seek. He also had difficulties in understanding personal pronouns, and rather than using the pronoun "I" or addressing another person with a "Thank you", he seemed to echo what he might have heard others saying when they had given something to him in the past. He also showed a preference for ordered, familiar arrangements of things.

THE CARDINAL FEATURES OF AUTISM

It is time to set individual case-descriptions of autistic children in a broader context. We need to stand back in order to appraise the varieties and associated features of the syndrome. For the present I shall treat autism as a condition "in the child"—which in an important sense, it is—and only later return to the complementary thesis that autism is an interpersonal disorder.

The first large-scale epidemiological study of autism was conducted by Victor Lotter (1966, 1967), who established that the prevalence of Kanner-type autism in the county of Middlesex was 4.5 per 10,000 children. However, the most detailed and revealing study of this kind is the one carried out by Lorna Wing and Judith Gould (1979) in the former London borough of Camberwell. A number of summaries of this work as well as a follow-up report have been published (Wing, 1981b, 1988a,b). These investigators screened 35,000 children under the age of 15 years for the presence of at least one of the following items, regardless of level of intelligence: (1) absence or impairment of social interaction, especially with peers; (2) absence or impairment of the development of verbal and non-verbal language; and (3) repetitive, stereotyped activities of any kind. The one additional group to be included was that of ambulant severely retarded children, whatever their pattern of behaviour and impairments. These criteria resulted in the selection of 132 children. Professional workers or parents involved with the children were interviewed with a structured schedule to assess the children's behavioural skills, and the children themselves were observed in the classroom or at home.

The total 132 children were subdivided into two groups according to the quality of their social interaction. The 58 children whose social interaction was appropriate for their mental age were called the "sociable, severely retarded" group, and the 74 with abnormal social interactions were called the "socially impaired" group. Seventeen of this latter group had the full syndrome of Kanner-type autism as defined by social aloofness and indifference, especially to peers, and elaborate repetitive routines—yielding a prevalence rate of 4.9 per 10,000—but the overall prevalence of impairments in reciprocal social interaction was 21.2 per 10,000 of the population. Even within this larger group, all the children with social impairments had repetitive stereotyped behaviour and almost all had an absence or abnormalities of language and symbolic activities. This has led Lorna Wing to talk about the "autistic continuum" of cases who manifest the "triad" of impairments in social interaction, communication, and imagination, usually associated with a repetitive, stereotyped pattern of activities. Here is impressive evidence that there really is a syndrome of autism which we need to explain.

From the wealth of data provided by the Wing and Gould (1979) study, I wish to highlight a point about the association between autism and mental retardation, and then to spend time on a second issue about the qualities of social impairment observed in autistic spectrum children. Concerning the first of these matters, I simply note that mental retardation (IQ below 70) was closely associated with the triad of social impairments: approximately half of the children with IQs below 50 presented with this clinical picture. Even amongst children with the full, typical picture of autism, over 90% had IQs between 20 and 69. Such an association between autism and mental retardation has been reported by many other investigators (e.g. Kolvin, Humphrey, & McNay, 1971; Lockyer & Rutter, 1969). Indeed, Wing (1988a) has stressed that there is an especially marked association between IQ and the severity of the manifestation of social impairment, the children most aloof and indifferent to others being those who were also the most severely retarded. On the other hand, as Rutter and Schopler (1987) point out, Wing's approach tends to emphasise impairment rather than specific types of "deviance" from normal, and so it is not surprising that the picture of typical autism is rare amongst the profoundly retarded. Whether one adopts a broad or narrow perspective, however, one needs to consider the source and significance of this association between mental retardation and autism-like impairments in interpersonal relatedness.

The second matter concerns the way that Wing and Gould (1979) classified the qualities of social interaction which they observed. They grouped such behaviour under four headings, as follows:

1. "Social aloofness" covered very severe impairment of social interaction. Some of these children were aloof and indifferent in all situations. Others would make approaches to obtain things they wanted, but returned to aloofness once the need was gratified. Some liked simple

physical contact with adults such as cuddling, tickling, or games of chasing, but had no interest in the purely social aspects of the contact. The social indifference was especially marked towards other children, rather than adults.

2. "Passive interaction" described the behaviour of children who did not make social contact spontaneously but who amiably accepted approaches and did not resist if other people dragged them into games, although their engagement remained superficial.

3. "Active, but odd interaction" characterised children who did make spontaneous social approaches, mostly to adults, but in an odd, one-sided fashion. Their behaviour was inappropriate because it was undertaken mainly to indulge some repetitive, idiosyncratic preoccupation. They had little interest in or feeling for the needs and ideas of others. They did not modify their speech or behaviour to adapt to others but continued to pursue their own interests.

4. "Appropriate interaction" was manifested by non-autistic individuals whose social interactions were appropriate for their mental age. They enjoyed social contact for its own sake, both with adults and with other children. It is important to note that here were included a few children whose mental ages were very low, in some cases under 12 months, but who nevertheless used eye contact, facial expression, and gesture to indicate interest and to try to join in conversation as best they could, anticipating and engaging in social exchanges.

More recently, Lorna Wing has added a further category to the socially impaired groupings. She points out that in those who have most made progress, the problem that remains may be quite subtle:

> ...best described as a poverty of grasp of the most subtle rules of social interaction and a lack of perceptiveness towards others. People with this type of impairment give the impression that they have acquired a superficial knowledge of social behavior through intellectual learning rather than through intuition (Wing, 1988b: p. 93).

One of my purposes in citing these descriptions at length, is to place individual case descriptions within the context of a clinical picture that varies not only across autistic children, but also within the lifespan of particular individuals. It is inevitable and perhaps necessary that in trying to understand a complex condition such as autism, we tend to oversimplify and even caricature the phemonema we are trying to explain. The fact is that whichever feature or features of autism one chooses to focus upon, the picture is neither all-or-nothing nor even qualitatively consistent across autistic individuals. This said, there *is* quite a lot that is special to autism, both in the quality and concurrence of clinical features. For example, autistic children's difficulties in interpersonal relationships and play are both quantitatively and qualitatively more severe than one might expect from intellectual retardation alone (Volkmar et al., 1987). We have to tolerate the tension of trying to reconcile our respect for the individuality of each autistic person with his or her particular capacities or difficulties, and our conviction that it makes sense to identify "something" as autism. The big question, of course, is what that something is.

It is emphatically not the case that autistic individuals treat people exactly like things, a fact borne out by the above clinical accounts as well as by experimental studies to be reported later. Yet it is very significant that many of the terms employed in formal as well as in more free-ranging accounts of autism have reference not so much to "behaviour" as narrowly construed, but rather to the meaning of such behaviour in personal and/or interpersonal terms. For example, the American classification of psychiatric disorders, DSM-III-R (American Psychiatric Association, 1987), records how the autistic individual has a marked lack of awareness of the existence or feelings of others; he or she shows little or abnormal seeking of comfort at times of distress; imitation of others, if present at all, tends to be mechanical; the child does not actively participate in simple games with others; there is impairment in the ability to make peer friendships; and there are severe problems with communication. Similar expressions about the children's lack of interpersonal engagement are abundant in the descriptions of practically everyone who has insight into the nature of autism. This is precisely the kind of language that we need to characterise the ways in which "autism" seems to differ from our own emotional life and socially meaningful relationships. Although for the sake of convenience I shall give separate consideration to "interpersonal relatedness" and "interpersonal understanding" in autism, what cements the two is something to do with what interpersonal transactions *mean* for the autistic child, how they are experienced. It is a central thesis of this essay that interpersonal relatedness is felt and experienced as well as being demonstrated; the observable deficits in reciprocal social interaction are at the same time limitations in the autistic child's experience of mutuality and complementarity, of psychological connectedness with and differentiation from other people. This is, of course, a controversial claim— yet even within DSM-III-R, there is tacit acknowledgement of the centrality for autism of deficits in the intersubjective (with emphases on both "inter" and "subjective") realms of experience and relatedness.

The second feature of note is that in the diagnostic scheme of DSM-III-R, the only direct reference to relation*ships* is that which concerns peer friendships, although relationships have relevance too for comfort-seeking, copying others, and so on. In fact, the strictly defined diagnostic criteria of

DSM-III-R are preceded by a more discursive preamble in which the "qualitative impairment in reciprocal social interaction" is said to be:

> characterized by failure to develop interpersonal relationships and by lack of responsiveness to, or interest in, people...Adults may be treated as interchangeable, or the child may cling mechanically to a specific person. The attachment of some toddlers to their parent(s) may be bizarre, e.g., a child may seem to recognize his mother primarily on the basis of smell (American Psychiatric Association, 1987: p. 34).

My point here is simply to observe an equivocation that reflects our current uncertainties about the nature and standing of autistic individuals' frequently unusual forms of personal relationship.

BEYOND CHILDHOOD

What kind of adults do autistic children become? Twenty-eight years after he had first described autism in 1943, Leo Kanner (1971) reported on his attempts to trace the 11 children who had featured in his original paper. Two of the cases had been lost to follow-up; one had died; five had become institutionalised, with some self-help skills but in most cases only very limited interpersonal contacts; and three had achieved some kind of social adjustment, albeit with restrictions on the range and depth of their personal relationships. For example, Kanner wrote that his Case 5, Donald, was one of the "success stories". At the age of 36 years, Donald had not only sustained regular employment as a bank teller, but he had also joined local golf and investment clubs, owned his own car and enjoyed relative independence. On the other hand, he was still living with his parents at home, showed no interest in the opposite sex, and was said to display a marked lack of initiative. His mother was prompted to write: "I wish I knew what his inner feelings really are". For Elaine (Kanner's Case 11), things did not turn out so well. At the age of 39 years, she was still in hospital, where she was said to take care of her personal needs and be fairly neat and clean. A hospital report recorded:

> Her speech is slow and occasionally unintelligible and she is manneristic. She is in only fair contact and fairly well oriented. She cannot participate in a conversation, however, except for the immediate needs. If things do not go her way, she becomes acutely disturbed, yelling, hitting her chest with her fist, and her head against the wall. In her lucid periods, however, she is cooperative, pleasant, childish, and affectionate (Kanner, 1971: p.140).

Once again, therefore, one can see how there is considerable diversity in what becomes of autistic children. Michael Rutter (1970) reported a follow-up of 64 individuals who had been seen at the Maudsley Hospital between 1950 and 1958, and who were now between 15 and 29 years old. Approximately half the children were in long-stay mental subnormality or mental hospitals, and rather fewer than 20% (although 42% of those with an IQ of over 70) were in employment. Only one individual was said to be completely normal with a skilled job, living in his own flat and leading a normal social life. In half of the Maudsley patients, interpersonal relationships had tended to improve as the children got older. A few children became somewhat outgoing in personality, although "remaining shallow in affect and lacking in empathy", but more usually the children were reserved, without social know-how and seemingly unaware of the feelings of others. Of the 64 children, only two had close friends of their own and only one had heterosexual friendships. About half the cases were without speech when adolescent, and those who talked did so in a monotonous flat delivery, with a pedantic mode of expression that lacked the normal to-and-fro of conversation. A number of the children had developed fits. The outcome was especially poor for children with IQs below 50 and those with a severe language disorder. This pattern of results is fairly representative of other follow-up studies (e.g. Lotter, 1978; Rumsey, Rapoport, & Sceery, 1985).

I would highlight two contrasting points that emerge from all this. The first is that intellectually able (high IQ) autistic children may develop in quite surprising ways. For example, as Cathy Lord (1984) points out, particular autistic individuals may begin as "aloof" but later become "passive" or even "active but odd" in their social manner. There are sensitive case histories (e.g. by Gajzago & Prior, 1974; Park, 1986) that document how even classic Kanner-type young children may become communicative and co-operative with peers, relating with affection to family members and even outsiders. In a follow-up report of nine individuals who had been diagnosed as autistic in childhood but who had achieved relative social integration as adults, Kanner, Rodriguez, and Ashenden (1972) remarked on how they were unusual amongst autistic adolescents in that they

> ... became uneasily aware of their peculiarities and began to make a conscious effort to do something about them. This effort increased as they grew older. They "knew", for instance, that youngsters were expected to have friends. Realizing their inability to form a genuine buddy-buddy relationship, they—one is almost tempted to say, ingeniously—made use of the gains made by their obsessive preoccupations to open a door for contact (Kanner et al., 1972: pp. 29–30).

As Rutter (1970), Rumsey et al. (1985) and others have also observed, failure to make friends can be a source of distress and unhappiness to such autistic people—it is not that all autistic people lack the interest or motivation to engage in friendships.

This leads to my second point of emphasis—the persisting problems with interpersonal relatedness experienced by almost all those who have at some time justified the diagnosis of autism. To return to the account of Kanner et al. (1972: p. 30): "Again and again we note a felt need to grope for ways to compensate for the lack of inherent sociability". Autistic people's lack of social perceptiveness and understanding is often accompanied, as in the 14 high-functioning autistic men studied by Rumsey, Andreasen, and Rapoport (1986), by relatively unchanging facial expressiveness, decreased spontaneous movements, a paucity of expressive gestures, a lack of affective responsiveness, a dearth of vocal inflection, and a more general affective flattening.

In order to reaffirm the link between this and subsequent chapters on social awareness and social understanding in autistic individuals, I shall cite some final observations by Elizabeth Newson (1984), who in collaboration with Mary Dawson and Peggy Everard conducted a study of the natural histories of 93 people of normal or near-normal intelligence. Newson et al. (1984) describe how most autistic children do eventually become more socially appreciative, in that they begin to be rewarded by social contact and even by body contact, taking pleasure in the expression of affection and in the social approval of the people they know best—but still they have difficulties with social empathy. Almost none of the young people studied had quite normal social awareness. At best they engaged in repetitive conversation but continued to be insensitive towards the reactions of others.

It is clear that in order to deal with the nature of normal and autistic modes of interpersonal relatedness, we need to consider the qualities of social perception and social experience that both underpin and reflect what may be observed in a person's "social behaviour". These provide topics for subsequent chapters. To serve as a bridge to that discussion, I shall conclude the present chapter with some indication of what life might be like for those who are autistic.

AUTISM "FROM THE INSIDE"

I now shift the focus from what autistic children are like, to what it is like to be autistic. I shall not attempt to do justice to this vitally important subject. One reason is that I do not consider I have had the kind of first-hand experience (whether as parent, teacher, clinician, or psychotherapist) to derive a proper view of the matter. Besides this, I believe there are complex individual differences among autistic individuals in their experiences of, and ways of coping with, both the personal and non-personal world. All I shall do, therefore, is to offer some illustrative fragments of what intelligent autistic people have communicated at interview or in their autobiographical writings. In other words, I shall confine myself to the most explicit forms of self-description given by a very small number of unusually able and articulate autistic individuals. Even to the extent that these accounts are to be taken at face value—and in an excellent review of this matter, Francesca Happé (1991) points out the need for circumspection in interpreting such descriptions—they may be as revealing for what they leave out as for what they include, and might hardly apply at all to more retarded autistic children. Indeed, I hope the following will bring home how theories of autism (including my own) are challenged by the social as well as intellectual sophistication of some exceptional autistic people.

The first autistic person, Gerry, was a case diagnosed by Kanner at the age of four and interviewed 27 years later at the age of 31 by Jules Bemporad (1979). In his late childhood and early adolescence, Gerry demonstrated a marked social naïveté and lack of propriety, despite average performance on IQ tests. For example, he completely disregarded his appearance; he had to be reminded to change his clothes, comb his hair, and so on. From about the age of eleven, Gerry gradually came to perceive that he was different from other youngsters. He now expressed the desire to be with other children but his behaviour was so inappropriate that he was either rejected or ignored. On one occasion when he was 14, the family took a trip to a Mexican border town. Gerry suddenly disappeared. The family searched frantically for him all day, and finally found him at their motel, ten miles away. He had walked all the way back because he disliked the smell of the market where they had been shopping. He did not understand that his family might be concerned about his disappearance and so had not told anyone he was leaving. He simply could not appreciate how other people felt.

When interviewed at 31 years of age, Gerry had no ability to make small talk. He blamed his current isolated condition on the evils of modern society. He seemed unable to deal adequately with what he perceived to be the unpredictability of other people. He simply could not empathise with others, and could not predict what they would do. This left him confused and frightened. He reported essentially no daydreams and did not recall nocturnal dreams. He described sexual feelings in an oblique way but no sexual fantasies.

When asked about his memories of childhood, Gerry described confusion and terror. He recalled living in a frightening world which presented painful stimuli which he was unable to master. Noises were unbearably loud, smells overpowering, nothing seemed constant; everything was unpredictable and strange. Animate beings were a particular problem. He could not predict nor understand other children's behaviour. He recalled liking to spin objects, but could not account for his need for sameness beyond stating that was how things should be. He did not mention any relationship to family members when reconstructing his childhood; they seemed of little importance. Of his adolescence, he conveyed how he had no idea how to go about making interpersonal contact. He said that he realised that he was a burden to his family, but he attributed this to his stuttering.

The second autistic person, Temple Grandin (1984, 1992), has a PhD and international standing as a designer of livestock equipment. Grandin emphasises her lifetime sensory and perceptual problems, her childhood difficulties with speaking, and her predominantly visual mode of thinking:

> My senses were oversensitive to loud noise and touch. Loud noise hurt my ears and I withdrew from touch to avoid overwhelming sensation. I built a squeezing machine which helped me to calm my nerves and to tolerate touching…All my thinking is visual, like videos played in my imagination. Even abstract concepts such as getting along with other people are visualized through the use of door imagery (Grandin, 1992: p. 105).

Grandin compares her hearing with having a hearing aid stuck on "super loud", and she remarks on her inability to synchronise her clapping with that of others or with music. Even in adulthood, she "had an odd lack of awareness of my oddities of speech and mannerisms until I looked at videotapes" (Grandin, 1992: p. 113). She finds difficulty in recognising faces, and in holding one concept in mind while performing another intellectual operation. She prefers factual, non-fictional reading materials over novels with complicated interpersonal relationships. As Happé (1991) perceptively notes, Grandin's accounts are notable for their lack of emphasis on her own emotional or family life, and for their portrayal of autism as an abnormality of perceptual processing and cognitive style. It is as if she is relatively unengaged with her own lack of engagement with others.

The latter statement is certainly not true of David Miedzianik, one of the most thoughtful and linguistically gifted of autistic writers, whose 1986 autobiography is full of direct and indirect references to his loneliness and social misery. There is also something in the rather repetitive and disjointed style of his writing that conveys a great deal about the quality of his solitude. I shall end this chapter with some of his reflections on trying to relate to girls, with which Miedzianik (1986: pp. 101–103) concludes the autobiography:

I find it hard to talk to girls, I never seem to know the right things to say to them. I personally don't think it makes much difference what someone like me tells them. I am in a bad set-up, so no matter what I say won't make them take much interest in me. Perhaps if I could have a bit of a lucky break with the writing I might find it easier to find a lovely girl to like me. I feel that ashamed, having to admit to girls that I am doing nothing. I usually try to kid them on that I am doing well as a writer but they don't fall for that one very easy.

...Recently I have met a few girls because I seem to be a bit more popular now. I think the writing has helped me get on with the girls better. By the way, the summer weather has been terrible this year and I think my flu is coming back a bit now. I keep feeling all sweaty just the same as before I got flu the winter of 1985. The weather hasn't been good this year and I think if you are in low spirits you pick colds and flu up quicker.

I think that's all I will write. Someone says I should have written about the moods I have, but I think I have described fairly well why I think a lot that's happened to me is enough to make anyone moody. Yes, I think anyone normal would find it hard to lead the kind of existence I have. I think if some girl would take a real interest in me I would just bother with her and no other girl, but I spend my time talking to a lot of girls, hoping I can find one that will take a real interest. Well, I think that really is the last I will write.

CHAPTER THREE

Interpersonal Relatedness I: The Normal Infant

I have opened this book by writing about the clinical presentation of people with autism. In so doing, I hope to have illustrated how natural it is to think of the disorder as one that entails a profound disturbance in interpersonal relatedness. Perhaps this seems so obvious, that it hardly needs comment. Yet there are many psychologists and psychiatrists who would have misgivings about the appropriateness of conceptualising the social impairment of autism in terms of a problem with "relatedness", and many more who would question the prominence I shall be giving to this aspect of the syndrome in explaining autistic children's handicaps. What does interpersonal relatedness mean, anyway? I have already said that in order to characterise what is abnormal about a condition such as autism, we need an adequate account of what goes on in normal development. It is for this reason that I now turn to the normal case, and attempt to capture some ways in which "personal relatedness" is foundational for early development. I shall be concerned with infancy and just beyond, up to the age of about two years, for the reason that it is from the very beginning of life that we need to trace the development of increasingly sophisticated forms of interpersonal relations.

Perhaps I should begin with a note of caution. There is a danger that in surveying some detailed observations of the first two years of life, my point about personal relatedness may become obscured. After all, it is perfectly appropriate to evaluate the course of infant development within different frames of reference, for example by tracing changes in an infant's cognitive or affective capacities, without saying very much about an essentially or irreducibly personal dimension to what is happening. All I can do at this stage, is to state that there are grounds from philosophical as well as psychological reasoning for maintaining a focus on the interpersonal domain. Let me cite just one philosopher here. In discussing what he calls the Field of the Personal, John Macmurray (1961: p. 61) writes:

> ... the unit of personal existence is not the individual, but two persons in personal relation; and...we are persons not by individual right, but in virtue of our relation to one another. The personal is constituted by personal relatedness. The unit of the personal is not the "I", but the "You and I".

It is in keeping with this view that Macmurray identifies the baby's essential natural endowment as the impulse to communicate with another human being.

The purpose of the present chapter, then, is to explore this kind of thesis from the vantage-point of developmental psychology. To begin with, I shall gather together a handful of descriptions that illustrate how children under one year old behave when they are psychologically engaged with other people. I shall supplement these accounts with a few additional reflections on infants' capacities for social perception. Then I shall turn to consider some developments that take place during the second year of life, with special reference to children's new-found capacities for self-reflective awareness. It is against this backdrop that I wish to set the phenomenon of autism in the chapters that follow. Although I shall introduce theoretical perspectives when these help to unify the account, I intend to suspend a lengthier discussion of theory until later.

I need to add one final introductory remark. A serious omission from my account is any consideration of the many issues raised by psychoanalytic approaches to early development. Being unequal to the task of integrating psychoanalytic and non-analytic observations, I have chosen to restrict the scope of this discussion rather than overcondense (and perhaps trivialise) psychoanalytic insights into the developing mind.

EARLY PERSONAL RELATEDNESS

Over the last three decades, increasing observational and experimental evidence has suggested that even very young infants engage in forms of personal relatedness that differ from their manner of relating to things. An early report by Peter Wolff (1969) suggested that within the first two weeks of life, infants' crying was arrested more effectively by a human voice than by a rattle or other mechanical sound. Then before the first two months were over, the infants seemed likely to cease mild crying and initiate a period of sustained, alert interest if a person appeared in their visual field, whilst even if previously content, they were likely to cry if a person left. Berry Brazelton and his colleagues (Brazelton, Koslowski, & Main, 1974) filled out this picture by filming infants from four weeks old under two conditions; first, as they related to an object (a small fuzzy monkey suspended on a string) which was brought towards the infant's "reach space" and then withdrawn again; and second, as the infants interacted with their mothers in relaxed face-to-face contact. The authors reflected on their observations as follows:

> We felt that we could look at any segment of the infant's body and detect whether he was watching an object or interacting with his mother—so different was his attention, vocalizing, smiling, and motor behavior with the inanimate stimulus as opposed to the mother (Brazelton et al., 1974: p. 53).

The detailed descriptions provided by Brazelton et al. (1974) are difficult to summarise adequately. The infants tended to stare fixedly at the object, with small jerks of the face and limbs, and to have their attention hooked on the object; as it entered their reach space, the infants' mouths opened as if they were anticipating mouthing the object, and from six weeks of age, they would make jerky hand movements towards it. "This state of intense, rapt attention built up gradually to a peak which was disrupted suddenly by the infant's turning away from the object, becoming active, and flailing his extremities" (Brazelton et al., 1974: p. 54). Only at about 16 weeks were such abrupt transitions from attentiveness to withdrawal replaced by less jagged patterns of responding. When the infants were interacting with their mothers, on the other hand, the cycles of attention and withdrawal were quite different. There seemed to be patterns of interpersonally regulated "affective attention", with smoother and shorter spans of attentiveness and looking away. For example, the infants' eyes and face would brighten as they looked towards their mother, and their extremities extended towards her; as she responded, the infant's face alerted further and there were fleeting smiles, grimaces, and vocalisations, as well as smooth movements of the hands and feet. There was often an increase in bodily activity leading to vocalisation, and smiling increased when the mother smiled in unison. There might be a brief peak of excitement, followed by a gradual waning of this state, accompanied by looking away that effected a temporary withdrawal from the stimulating encounter. Sensitive mothers seemed to modify their own active participation to correspond with these cyclical changes.

Developmentalists such as Colwyn Trevarthen and Daniel Stern (e.g. Stern, 1985; Trevarthen, 1979) have long been energetic in drawing attention to the finely tuned patterns of co-ordinated face-to-face interchange that occur between care-givers and their infants in the early months of a baby's life. In fact the most dramatic demonstrations of such interpersonal meshing have emerged as a result of systematic interventions to disrupt the flow of this dyadic to-and-fro. Following up early reports of infants' responses to still-faced mothers (Carpenter, Tecce, Stechler, & Friedman, 1970; Tronick, Als, Adamson, Wise, & Brazelton, 1978), Jeffrey Cohn and Edward Tronick (1983) instructed mothers of three-month-old infants to interact with depressed expressions during three-minute periods of face-to-face interaction. The effect was that the infants became negative and showed protest and wariness, continuing in this way for a short while after the mothers returned to a style of normal interaction. Another example comes from the work of Lynne Murray and Colwyn Trevarthen (1985), who sat individual two- and three-month-old infants before a television monitor which showed the mother's "live" face, looking towards the infant. The mother herself was situated in another room, but she too could relate to a TV monitor showing her baby facing her, close-up. Through such an arrangement, mother and baby were able to engage with each other via television in a surprisingly natural and fluent way. A "perturbation" was achieved by employing a videotape feedback system to introduce a delay of 30 seconds in the time when the mother's responses were relayed to the baby over the TV link. This meant that from each participant's point of view, what should have been a co-ordinated to-and-fro became almost totally desynchronised. The effect was considerable infant distress, with the infants turning away from and darting brief looks back towards the mother's image—a qualitatively different set of reactions than occurred when the mother merely looked away or even displayed a blank-faced posture.

Rather similar, if less dramatic, findings have emerged from studies of more natural situations orchestrated by Jeanette Haviland and Mary Lelwica (1987). These workers asked the mothers of 10-week-old infants to enact a range of affective states in their facial and vocal expressions during face-to-face exchanges with their babies. The infants reacted to each affective state of their mother, with affective states of their own. These were manifest not only in facial and other bodily gestures, but also in patterns of gaze that were not presented by the mothers. In response to the mother's first presentation of joy, for example, the infants increased their own manifestations of joy and interest, and their decrease in mouthing during this condition contrasted with increased mouthing when the mother posed sadness. When the mother first appeared angry, on the other hand, infants showed increased anger accompanied by a decrease in movements.

In each of the studies described, therefore, we can see how young infants showed organised expressions of affect and attention when the form and timing of their mothers' natural style of engagement were disrupted. The person-with-person configurations of mutual gaze and of facial, vocal, and gestural interchange seem to involve not merely the co-ordination of behaviour between infant and mother, but also some kind of psychological linkage which when established—or when broken—has emotional consequences for both participants. There is a sense in which the infant (or some "mechanism" within the infant) seems to *expect* appropriate forms of dynamic, bodily expressive response from another person.

I shall now move on a few months to around the middle of the first year of life. A number of authors (e.g. Bakeman & Adamson, 1982; Schaffer, 1984, 1989; Trevarthen & Hubley, 1978) have commented on the way in which infants of this age tend to become relatively more preoccupied with the non-social objects around them, and to require quite vigorous and organised input from an adult if they are to sustain prolonged phases of dyadic interaction. One of the most effective ways of achieving such interaction is to engage the infant in ritualised games such as peek-a-boo, many of which involve some joint focus on an object or set of events, a shared "topic". Jerome Bruner (1983) has highlighted the ways in which games of these kinds provide routinised "formats" for the structuring of interpersonal transactions. The essence of the format is that the response of each member is dependent upon a prior response of the other, so that there are demarcated roles that may eventually become reversible.

Then in the period beginning around eight months of age, there emerges a set of novel infant propensities and activities. The infant not only acquires new ways of relating to the care-giver as a person, but so too she becomes able to co-ordinate interpersonal with object-directed actions and attitudes. Over the next three months, there appears a cluster of new accomplishments (Bretherton, McNew, & Beeghly-Smith, 1981; Trevarthen & Hubley, 1978). The list includes the infant's capacity to follow the eye-gaze or point of another person, to request help and respond to simple verbal requests by others, to indicate or show objects to others (often looking to the other person's eyes, to check whether he or she is attending), to initiate as well as accept invitations to games such as peek-a-boo, to shake the head to express refusal, to imitate conventional gestures (e.g. hugging) and actions with objects, to utter greetings ("Hi!") and name-like words, and to pretend to carry out adult activities such as telephoning or mopping the floor.

This is indeed an impressive catalogue of abilities. We shall need to return and consider them one by one, evaluating what they might signify for the infant's understanding of persons and developing awareness of self. For now, however, I shall simply note with Inge Bretherton and her colleagues (Bretherton et al., 1981), that at this point an infant appears to recognise how other people are both like self and distinct from self psychologically. Through the manifest intent to communicate, for instance in showing objects and monitoring the other person's bodily expressive responses, the infant shows some level of awareness that "showing" may be necessary and potentially sufficient to achieve a special kind of interpersonal co-ordination and (probably) a sense of sharing with another person. By obeying and refusing, by offering greetings and farewells, by requesting things and initiating games, the infant reveals a capacity to relate in various ways to another person's wishes and intentions. By imitating conventional actions and gestures, the infant demonstrates an ability to identify with and assume the actions of another person, an ability that requires an appreciation of both commonalities and distinctions between self and other. As Bretherton et al. (1981) suggest, the recognition that self and other are objectively and subjectively simular but distinct is already implicit in such early forms of intentional communication.

There is a further aspect of the social relations of infants towards the end of the first year of life, to which I shall pay close attention when it comes to review the theoretical implications of these phenomena. This concerns the infant's capacity to perceive and respond to another person's affective orientation towards things and events in the environment, what has been called "social referencing" (Campos & Stenberg, 1981; Feinman, 1982; Feinman & Lewis, 1983; Klinnert, Campos, Sorce, Emde, & Svejda, 1983; Walden & Ogan, 1988). The study by James Sorce and colleagues (Sorce, Emde, Campos, & Klinnert, 1985) will serve as an illustration here. Infants aged 12 months were placed on the shallow side of a "visual cliff", which takes the form of an apparent sudden drop beneath a transparent surface. The infant's mother and an attractive toy were positioned across the deep side. The results concerned those infants who, on noticing the drop-off, looked spontaneously to the mother's face. When the mother posed a happy face, 14 out of the 19 infants crossed to the deep side; when the mother posed a fearful expression, none of the infants ventured across. When the mothers posed an angry expression, only two out of 18 infants proceeded across the cliff, and 14 actively retreated by moving back to the shallow side. In this and in other comparable circumstances, infants around one year of age seem to have the capacity to seek out their mother's affective expression, relate this to a current situation, and react accordingly with feeling and action. The infants appear to recognise that another person's expression has meaning with reference to an environment common to themselves and the other person.

There is convincing evidence to suggest that the phenomena of social referencing are not simply a reflection of how an infant's general mood state may be altered by an adult's affective expressions (Feinman, Roberts, Hsieh, Sawyer, & Swanson, 1992). Rather, there is an impact on the infant's appraisal of the specific object or event to which the adult's expressed state "refers". For example, Robin Hornick, Nancy Risenhoover, and Megan

Gunnar (1987) tested the reactions of 12-month-old infants to a series of three toys, towards each of which the mother displayed a different attitude in facial, vocal, and gestural expression—either positive, negative (disgust), or neutral. Maternal displays influenced responses only to the toys that were the targets of the attitudes. For example, the children played less with the toy towards which the mother showed disgust, but there was no significant effect on play with other toys in the vicinity, nor were changes in the infants' general mood state discernible. Moreover, once all three toys had been presented and reacted-to, a second trial was conducted in which the mothers showed neutral affect. Once again, the children avoided and played less with the toys towards which their mothers had previously shown disgust. The authors concluded that the infants seemed to understand that the messages were specific to those particular toys. Tedra Walden and Tamra Ogan (1988) reported similar findings, in that infants of 10–13 months spent more time touching a toy towards which a parent had expressed positive feelings, than a toy in relation to which the parent had communicated a fearful attitude ("What a scary toy!"). As Inge Bretherton (1992) argues persuasively, there is also strong convergent evidence from studies of communication and language development that even before infancy is over, very young children seek and are able to understand another person's interpretation of a situation.

I shall mention one additional set of developments occurring in the final third of the first year. This is rather different from the changes described so far, in that it concerns the quality of a child's relationships rather than his or her modes of relatedness. Of course there is no absolute distinction between relationships and relatedness. They are overlapping concepts at rather different levels of description. Nevertheless, there are aspects of relationships such as the child's need for affection and comfort from another person, or the child's distress upon separation from and delight at reunion with a care-giver, that have not featured in my discussion of qualities of relatedness. It would be a signal failure to omit reference to the growth of the child's capacities for love and hate, yearning and rejecting, mourning and forgiveness, jealousy and envy, and so much else besides that make relationships what they are. I shall not be dwelling on such important matters in this essay, even though they will need to be addressed if we are to understand autism. Rather, I shall confine myself to a rather superficial treatment of the issues, and merely mark their significance for future research. With regard to normal development, therefore, I simply note the new quality of focussed attachments that children manifest from around 8 months. They seek proximity to and comfort from their care-giver(s), they show distress on separation and (often) pleasure in reunion, and they use the care-givers as a "secure base" from which to explore and find reassurance when anxious (Bowlby, 1969). At the same time, strangers come to be treated more warily (Schaffer, 1966). Of course, not all infant–care-giver pairs are the same in these respects, and important individual differences have been documented in separation and reunion reactions (Ainsworth & Wittig, 1969; Sroufe, 1986). Nevertheless, there are marked changes in what close relationships *mean* to infants at the end of the first year, and almost certainly, corresponding changes in what have been called the "internal working models" by which the child psychologically represents him- or herself and others in relationship to one another (Bowlby, 1969; Bretherton, 1985).

CAPACITIES FOR SOCIAL PERCEPTION

Many of an infant's capacities for social relatedness have some form of perceptual anchorage. It would be wrong to reduce the above account to one in which perception as narrowly defined has a dominant role. On the contrary, I would emphasise how intimately perception is linked to action and feeling, and is itself to be considered as a relational psychological function. For example, for a normal child to perceive a smile *as* a smile is for the child to be drawn into a quality of relatedness to the smiling person (however conceived), such that the child is inclined to smile or otherwise to feel and behave in accordance with what is perceived. The important point here is that the perception is *not* a two-stage process of which the first stage is the perception of meaningless behavioural or other bodily forms (e.g. "upturned mouth"), and the second is an intellectually-based attribution of psychological meaning. Rather, the perception is of the meaning itself, and what that meaning is depends on the child's propensities to action and feeling that the perceptual input calls forth. To perceive a smile is to be inclined to feel certain things, for example—it *is* that kind of perception. The argument is a general one, not restricted to the perception of emotional expressions. Therefore I want to highlight certain early-developing capacities for social perception that are important for promoting personal relatedness and for establishing the developmental pathways that lead to interpersonal understanding.

It is more or less self-evident that if an infant as young as two months can engage in the kinds of interpersonal exchanges I outlined earlier, then that infant must have an appropriately tuned perceptual system as well as a set of organised motor–affective response tendencies. The infant needs a sensitivity to the temporal patterns and "activation contours" of personal events (Stern, 1985), and innately determined propensities to give organised, bodily expressive actions and gestures in response (e.g. Hiatt, Campos, & Emde, 1979; Malatesta, 1981). An especially striking illustration of very early interpersonal co-ordination is provided by studies of imitation by newborn babies (e.g. Field et al., 1983; Field, Woodson,

Greenberg, & Cohen, 1982; Meltzoff, 1990; Meltzoff & Moore, 1977). For example, when infants under two days old were presented with a model who posed fixed happy, sad, and surprised facial expressions, they tended to show widened eyes and wide mouth opening in response to the model's surprised face, lip widening to the happy face, and tightened mouth with protruding lips accompanied by a furrowed brow to the sad expression. Or to take a different kind of observation, there is evidence that in the first few days of life, infants become distressed at the sound of another infant's cry but not at equally loud non-human sounds (Sagi & Hoffman, 1976; Simner, 1971). It is important not to presume that there is continuity in the "mechanisms" that effect social exchanges in infants and in older children, but these observations constitute impressive evidence for precocious channels of interpersonal co-ordination.

There is indeed a great deal of experimental as well as observational evidence to suggest that even young infants are predisposed to show selective attentiveness to a variety of objects and events with human-like qualities (for example, from the studies reviewed in Field & Fox, 1985; Lamb & Sherrod, 1981), and to recognise specific individuals as familiar according to their physical appearance, vocal characteristics, and smell (e.g. Field, 1985; Zucker, 1985). Although one must be cautious not to assume too much about the meaning of such perceptual input for very small babies, it remains the case that when discriminable input leads to differential responsiveness in the infant, some degree of "meaningfulness" is being perceived.

The task of establishing the meaning(s) that infants perceive is a complex one, for both theoretical and methodological reasons. Consider what is involved in recognising emotions, for example (Klinnert et al., 1983; Nelson, 1987; Oster, 1981; Walker-Andrews, 1988). There are several levels of meaning that are relevant here. To begin with, one might wish to demonstrate that infants can abstract the invariant features of given emotional expressions across individuals who might differ in, say, age, sex, or identity. On the next level, the infant might be able to appreciate which expressions are associated with each other (e.g. how a fearful face is likely to accompany a fearful vocalisation), or which expressions are accompanied by which kind of action (e.g. a fearful face being linked with an inclination to flee). Then there is the question of whether the infant manifests differential affective responsiveness to expressions of emotion in others, or whether the infant adjusts her behaviour appropriately in contexts of social referencing, as described earlier. Beyond this is the stage when the child understands that expressions are indeed expressive of the subjective emotional life of persons, so that the child might seek to comfort a mother in distress, to placate an angry individual, and so on. In due course, this and further levels of understanding (about mixed or unconscious emotions, for instance) would be expressible in the child's own language.

These considerations have direct implications for the ways one might wish to study "emotion recognition" in infants and young children, whether they are normal or abnormal. For example, evidence from the relatively lifelike and naturalistic studies described earlier points to very early capacities for emotional sensitivity and responsiveness, but more controlled experiments on infants' abilities to recognise the emotional characteristics of photographed faces, a decidedly artificial and impoverished form of "social stimuli", date the emergence of such abilities to the second half of the first year (e.g. Caron, Caron, & Myers, 1982; La Barbera, Izard, Vietze, & Parisi, 1976; Young-Browne, Rosenfeld, & Horowitz, 1977). On the other hand, experiments of these kinds do have a value in demonstrating more precisely what infants can do (rather than what they can't do) even in such unusual conditions, from relatively early on in life. Here is an example. Arlene Walker (1982) presented infants of five and seven months with two filmed facial expressions side-by-side, accompanied by a single vocal expression characteristic of the feeling expressed in only one of the faces. For instance, there were two moving facial images of a woman speaking continuously, one with a happy face and the other with a sad face, and the infants heard a vocalisation broadcast from a point between the two faces. The infants increased their looking time to the facial expression corresponding with the emotion expressed by the voice, even if the face and voice were out of synchrony. However, such selective attentiveness was not recorded when the faces were presented upside-down. Walker concluded that the infants perceived the faces and voices to have a common meaning. Thus capacities for perceptual sensitivity and emotional responsiveness towards the emotional expressions of others appear in at least partial form during the early months of life. No wonder—it is hardly news that relations between infants and adults are highly intricate, emotional affairs for those involved.

It may also be appropriate to consider the phenomena of social referencing as the manifestation of a special class of social–perceptual abilities. I think it would be premature to suppose that at nine or ten months of age, the infant has a *concept* of other people with minds. What we observe is that the infant perceives and reacts to the affective attitude expressed in another person's facial, vocal, and other bodily gestures. This attitude-as-perceived has both an emotional "value", and a perceptible outer-directedness towards events, objects, and people in the world. I shall be laying much emphasis on the developmental significance of the infant's capacity to perceive another person's attitude to *particular* objects and events. The reason is that this might provide the basis for the infant to grasp how objects and events have meanings-for-others which may differ from meanings-for-self. I have already considered the processes by which infants apprehend emotional meanings. The important thing to add is that there are separate mechanisms by which infants perceive that another person's subjective orientation is "targeted". In fact there are probably a set of rather different mechanisms that operate here, since the directedness of attitude may be discerned through the other's direction of eye-gaze, bodily orientation, focus of action, and so on (e.g. Butterworth & Jarrett, 1991). My point is that for an infant to perceive another person's attitude with the functional significance of an attitude, she may not need to conceptualise what an attitude is. What she requires are capacities to register emotional meanings *and* to respond to those meanings as having reference to the world "out there". We might give an account of such capacities on the level of social perception—providing, that is, we have an appropriate view of what perception entails.

To conclude this section on social perception, I need to mention a final instance in which there might prove to be more or less hard-wired perceptual–relational propensities that have special importance for the differentiation of social relations. Ethologists and proponents of the ecological approach to perception have emphasised the evolutionarily determined perceptual bases for recognising such meaningful human attributes as babyishness and gender (e.g. Hess, 1970; McArthur & Baron, 1983; Runeson & Frykholm, 1986; Shaw & Pittenger, 1977). There is developmental evidence to support the plausibility of such approaches. For example, infants of six or seven months are able to discriminate age-related and sex-related features of human faces in photographs (Fagan, 1972, 1976; Fagan & Singer, 1979), and they can categorise male and female voices (Miller, 1983). Indeed by the end of the first year, infants seem able to differentiate the sexes according to cues of body movement alone, as represented by moving dots of light attached to a walking person's trunk and limbs and recorded on videotape (Aitken, 1977; Kujawski, 1985). Once again, it is significant that these perceptual discriminations are accompanied by differences in relatedness towards people in the different categories. For example, infants as young as seven months display attentiveness and positive affect to an unfamiliar child who approaches, but they are likely to avert their gaze, move away, and show distress when a strange adult comes near (Brooks & Lewis, 1976). We are reminded that personal relatedness is not of a piece—it has its own set of rather distinct categories as well as modes of expression.

THE DEVELOPMENT OF SELF

It would be possible to recapitulate much of what has gone before from the point of view of the infant's developing senses of self—and indeed I have tried to do just that in other writings (Hobson, 1990a). Perhaps it is obvious that a story about the infant's evolving forms of relatedness towards and understanding of other persons maps on to an account of the development of self. The differences are primarily ones of emphasis and scope. For example, an account of self-development needs to address the primitive forms of non-reflective awareness that exist in the first nine months of life, including some sense of coherence, agency, affectivity, and continuity (Stern, 1985) as well as some experience of appropriating and repudiating things (Cooley, 1902; Freud, 1925). Such an account would include a more detailed consideration of the infant's relationship with the non-social world of objects than I have permitted myself so far. Having said this, each step towards a more sophisticated awareness or notion of self entails a shift in the quality of an infant's personal relatedness, and each new stage in the social sphere may be seen to promote or reflect increasing self-awareness. Perhaps the most dramatic illustration comes with a change that occurs during the second year of life, when there is a qualitative alteration in the child's consciousness of herself and others as "selves". I shall resume my account of normal development by highlighting certain of these changes.

Consider a phenomenon that is especially pertinent for my own emphasis on the processes of intersubjective linkage and differentiation amongst individuals—that of empathy. Martin Hoffman (1975, 1984) has outlined a number of distinct modes of empathic arousal, from those that are relatively automatic, such as the direct or conditioned elicitation of an infant's feelings by expressions of feeling in others, to more sophisticated forms of responsiveness through language-mediated association and role-taking. Formal studies of one-year-olds' reactions towards other people in distress, and towards their parents showing affection or anger towards each other (Cummings, Zahn-Waxler, & Radke-Yarrow, 1981; Zahn-Waxler, Radke-Yarrow, & King, 1979), confirm anecdotal evidence that children of this age may show distress, sympathy, and anger towards others in such contexts. The detailed descriptions of particular events often reveal a great deal about the kind of developments in self- and other-understanding that are taking place, and Hoffman (1984) cites some excellent examples.

One description concerns an 11-month-old girl who saw another child fall and cry. At first she stared at the hurt child, looking as though she was about to cry herself, but then she put her thumb in her mouth and buried her head in her mother's lap, which is what she would do if she hurt herself. Another concerns a boy who, at a similar age, would respond to his own distress by sucking his thumb with one hand and pulling his ear with the other. He would also do this when he saw someone else in distress. At 12 months, however, something new happened. On seeing a sad look on his father's face, he himself looked sad and then sucked his own thumb while pulling on his father's ear!

Incidents involving somewhat older children provide evidence for greater differentiation in the child's sense of self *vis-à-vis* other selves. A

15-month-old boy called Michael was fighting with a friend over a toy, when the friend started to cry. Michael appeared disturbed and let go, but the friend continued to cry. Michael paused, then offered his teddy-bear to the friend. When this did not work, Michael paused, went to fetch his friend's security blanket from the next room, and gave it to him. At this point, the friend stopped crying. Although as Hoffman points out, there are alternative explanations for this sequence of events, it does appear that Michael worked out how his friend might be comforted by something that was of personal significance, just as he himself would be comforted by his own teddy-bear. Observations of these kinds are not confined to sympathetic distress. Marcy, a girl of 20 months, wanted a toy that her sister was playing with. When she asked for it, her sister refused. Marcy paused, as if reflecting on what to do, and then went straight to her sister's rocking horse—a favourite toy that her sister never allowed anyone to touch—climbed on it, and began yelling "Nice horsey! Nice horsey!", whilst keeping her eye on her sister all the time. Her sister put down the toy Marcy wanted and came running angrily, whereupon Marcy immediately climbed down from the horse, ran directly to the toy, and grabbed it.

Strongly implicit in this series of descriptions, is a concurrent set of developments manifest within social contexts: first, development in the awareness of other people not only as centres of consciousness with whom sharing is possible, but also as *individuals* who can feel distress or desire, who can be comforted or provoked, and for whom objects can have personal significance; second, development in the child's sense of herself as an individual; and third, development in the capacities to reflect on the characteristics and psychological states of individual "selves", and to take action appropriately. It is important to note the close interrelationships among these developing capacities.

Really, one would like independent sources of evidence about the emergent forms of "person-understanding". Especially valuable here is a child's spontaneous expressions of self-awareness in language, although of course there are likely to be specifically linguistic constraints on the time when appropriate forms of language are acquired. An early and striking manifestation of self-awareness is the two-year-old's ability to comprehend and use personal pronouns such as "I" and "you", "mine" and "yours", and so on. Peter and Jill de Villiers (1974) point out that "I" and "you" are words that can only be understood by non-egocentric individuals who recognise the context of the relationship between the speaker and the addressee, and who have grasped reciprocal roles in discourse (Bruner, 1975a). On the other hand, children might begin with partial understandings. Rosalind Charney (1980) reported evidence that children first learn the pronouns most relevant to themselves as participants in dialogue. At an early stage, personal pronouns refer to one person only—the child—but only so long as he or she occupies a particular speech role. Thus to begin with, Charney's one- and two-year-old subjects comprehended "your" when they were addressed, but did not produce "your" correctly to refer to others; they used "my" in the speaker role, generally a "my" embedded in action and lacking independent meaning, but they did not understand the term in all contexts in which it was used by others (also Loveland, 1984). Although this early pattern of pronoun comprehension and use was not fully mature, the children seemed to have grasped that when other people used "I" and "my" in contexts of action-with-speaking and perhaps feeling-with-speaking, then these were actions and attitudes with which they themselves could identify (Kaye, 1982). If this is correct, then it implies that the children were not only aware of the distinction between self and other, but were also aware of a commonality that meant that self and other could assume a similar orientation or action, and along with this the appropriate personal pronoun, on different occasions (Sharpless, 1985). In fact, Shula Chiat (1981, 1982) illustrates how a given child may instantiate adult and non-adult meanings of personal pronouns in one and the same period of development.

Also revealing is Charney's (1980) observation that nearly all instances of the earliest, person-in-speech-role uses of "my" were produced while a child was acting on the object—searching for, grabbing, acting upon, or claiming it, usually when the object was *not* the child's—as opposed to indicating more permanent ownership. Similarly, in the case of children for whom the pronouns did not yet function as independent linguistic units, "I" and "me" were used while searching for, requesting, affecting, claiming, or noticing an object, but not while describing the child's own body or its movements. During this early period, then, children might employ their own *names* to refer to their body movements (e.g. sit), their states (e.g. sick), permanent relations of possession (e.g. clothing), and photographs of themselves, but they mainly reserved personal pronouns for settings in which they were participating agents. Only later did the pronouns become referring expressions. Thus at least some of a child's earliest uses of first-person pronouns seemed to occur in contexts of action in relation to (implicit) others, recognised as such. This is in keeping with Cooley's (1902: p. 160) suggestion that the child's early "first-personal pronoun is a sign of...the phenomenon of aggressive appropriation, practised by himself, witnessed in others...". The evidence is suggestive that in the normal case, an understanding of "I" entails some understanding of "you".

It is also relevant to note Jerome Kagan's (1982) observations on what he called "self-descriptive utterances" during young children's play with mother at home. These utterances included the use of personal pronouns or names with a predicate, such as "my book" or "Mary eat", but also utterances referring to action when the child was engaged in that action, such as "climb" or "up" when the child was climbing. According to Kagan, self-descriptive utterances were absent around 18 months but increased dramatically between 19 and 24 months, and by 27 months they included sophisticated statements such as "I do it myself", or "I can't do it". As Kagan (1982) remarks, the relatively high prevalence of these kinds of utterance around the end of the second year might reflect (amongst other things) how children have become motivated to comment on their own behaviour, now that they have acquired a new level of awareness of what they are doing.

As I have implied, however, such linguistic expressions might not be the first manifestations of self-consciousness to appear. Further research reported by Kagan (1982) is relevant here. Children from the age of 13 months were settled at play with toys, when their mother and an experimenter joined in. The experimenter modelled three acts that were appropriate for the child's level of maturity—for instance, demonstrating three brief scenarios with dolls for children just under two years old—and then said: "Now it's your turn to play". Although there was no explicit instruction for the children to replicate the actions, and although "non-modelling" interventions had little effect, the responses of children from the middle of the second year (and especially around the second birthday) included reactions of distress such as clinging to the mother, inhibition of play and crying. On the other hand, when some minutes later the children's distress had abated and they had left the mother's side to play again, they would frequently display an exact or fragmented version of one of the model's prior actions, and smile. Kagan interprets these observations in terms of the child's new-found sense of obligation to implement the acts of the model, and their awareness of their difficulty in meeting the standards required in doing so. Kagan provides additional evidence that from the middle of the second year, children display a concern for normative standards that are probably dictated by adult approval or disapproval, for example in their responses to flawed objects and in their language ("broken", "dirty", "can't", "hard to"). Or again, in what appears to be the more private domain of attaining a goal through effort, such as by completing a puzzle, "smiles of mastery" were rare at 17 months but increased after this time and peaked at 25 months of age. About the time that children acquire normative standards that are linked with adult approval and disapproval, therefore, there also appear "mastery standards" that seem to be less directly associated with parental judgements, but which nevertheless appear to reflect the attainment of a goal-for-self.

As Charlotte Bühler (1937) commented many years ago, a certain degree of self-evaluation is inherent in the independent planning of the young child who begins to hold fast to his or her goals. Bühler's own account of early social development sets these kinds of observation in the wider context of self-other relationships, as follows:

The following experiment is very illustrative. The adult forbids the child to touch a toy that is within the child's reach. He then turns away or leaves the room for a moment. All the 1–2-year-olds understand the prohibition as cancelled at the moment that contact with the adult is broken, and play with the toy. If the adult returns suddenly, 60 per cent of the children of 1;4 [1 year; 4 months] and 100 per cent of those of 1;6 show the greatest embarrassment, blush, and turn to the adult with a frightened expression. From 1;9 on they attempt to make good what has happened by returning the toy quickly to its place. From two years on they attempt to motivate the disobedience, for example, by claiming the toy as their own. After the age of two the child expresses will, insistence on its own rights, and possessive impulses in its relations with adults (Bühler, 1937: pp. 66–67).

Bühler also cites the studies of Florence Goodenough (1931) as showing how "obstinacy attacks" are especially prevalent in the middle of the second year—the terrible two's. The point I would stress is that the child's understanding of others *vis-à-vis* him- or herself encompasses the fact that people are sources of opposition and competition as well as co-operation. Other people are recognised to have their own motives to acquire, possess, or persuade, they have feelings which bear a relation to the environment as experienced by and as meaningful to the people themselves. The child's initial understanding of the nature of persons as a special class of things with the property one might call a "subjective orientation", has now become integrated into a conceptual grasp of people as "selves" who have their own ways of according significance to the world of people and things. The child has come to appreciate the force of the world-according-to-the-other, as well as to fulfil (at times) his or her own potential to resist this.

Amongst many other characteristics of this period, I shall mention two. The first concerns symbolic play. It is from around the middle of the second year of life that children substitute a toy for the self and others in pretend sequences. For example, the child might feed or scold a doll, or give a doll the role of agent in the feeding or scolding scenario. The psychological stance or role of self and other have become abstracted from the individual(s) whose stance or role they were or might have been, and can be conferred on (representative) others. Once again, "selfhood" is now a property attributed to other people or to symbolic vehicles that represent people.

The second characteristic concerns children's reactions to their own reflection in a mirror. There is now an extensive literature on mirror self-recognition in primates as well as human children (as reviewed by Anderson, 1984, and Gallup, 1982, for example), but the most thorough set of studies relevant to the present discussion is that conducted by Michael Lewis and Jeanne Brooks-Gunn (1979). These authors extended their research with mirrors to encompass children's reactions to videotapes and photographs of themselves or others. The classic test of mirror self-recognition (derived from Gallup, 1968) is to examine an individual's reaction to his or her own reflection, when a mark has been placed on the person's nose without the person knowing. Lewis and Brooks-Gunn summarise their own and others' findings by stating that mark-directed behaviour was never exhibited by infants younger than 15 months of age but became increasingly common thereafter, with approximately three-quarters of 18–20 month-olds showing mark recognition. In addition, Lewis and Brooks-Gunn observed silly or coy behaviour in very few infants under 15 months of age but much more commonly around 18 months, a finding that corresponds with Amsterdam's (1972) reports of the onset of self-conscious behaviour such as self-admiration and embarrassment. At this time there was also a kind of mirror-self imitation (so-called), as the children would make faces and stick their tongue out, or watch their face disappear and reappear at the side of a mirror.

It is of note that in the studies of Lewis and Brooks-Gunn (1979), even infants of 9–12 months reacted with pleasure to their own mirror-image, often looking at, kissing, and hitting it. Moreover, these groups of very young children increased their body-directed behaviour after being marked with rouge, even though they did not touch the mark itself. They also reacted differently to their contingent (mirror-like) and non-contingent (earlier-recorded) images on videotape, and were able to use a mirror to turn towards an approaching stranger. However, it was only from around 15–18 months that there was unequivocal self-recognition according to facial features independent of the cues provided by contingent movement of the image, as manifest in the children's ability to point to their own (named) picture from a collection of others, and somewhat later, to give their own picture the correct name.

It is important to realise how complex a set of phenomena we are dealing with. Obviously, mark-directed mirror behaviour requires that an individual appreciates the properties of reflecting surfaces (Loveland, 1986), and there is evidence from mentally retarded children (Mans, Cichetti, & Sroufe, 1978) and animals (Gallup, 1982) to indicate that given appropriate experience of mirrors, a certain level of cognitive ability may be most important for developing this special form of visually guided reaching. Obviously, too, an individual has to recognise some change in facial appearance if he or she is to react to that change by touching the altered spot. The questions then arise, why and how does the individual relate to the change? In what way does it matter that it is *oneself's* appearance that has changed? This is an issue that has been raised with reference to the primate research in this area: does a relatively un-focussed increase in mark-directed behaviour actually reflect body-consciousness rather than self-consciousness? The question is difficult to ask in a precise way, for the obvious reason that one's awareness of one's body as one's own is part and parcel of recognising oneself. Nevertheless, the kind of self-consciousness that characterises coyness, embarrassment, and self-admiration involves something more. Here one not only recognises that oneself-as-embodied is the potential object of other people's evaluative attitudes, but one also demonstrates how such attitudes *matter*. The individual sees and feels him- or herself in relation to what might be seen and felt from another person's point of view. Probably we are all aware that we are seldom alone when we look at ourselves in a mirror or a picture, even when we are alone.

OVERVIEW

What has emerged from this selective review of the development of personal relatedness and self-other transactions and understandings in the first two or three years of life?

The first set of observations concerned the quality of dyadic, person-to-person exchanges that occur between infants and their care-givers in the early (if not the very earliest) months of life. Here my emphasis has been on the patterning of the relatedness between infant and adult. The observed interpersonal co-ordination is not merely "behavioural", although certainly it involves a mutual interplay in both the forms and timing of bodily expressive actions and expressions. What is just as impressive, is how the interchange is one of psychological engagement or emotional participation between infant and care-giver. This is not to claim that the young infant experiences other people as people with minds, and as people towards whom communication is directed with intention. No, the point is simply that the infant does, as it were, find herself relating differently to people and things. We can observe how in fact, infants' own actions and bodily-expressed psychological states are often dovetailed with or otherwise responsive to the actions and bodily-expressed psychological states of their partners. The infants' responses to "perturbations" in maternal responsiveness are especially dramatic illustrations of this fact. It is therefore no surprise to find experimental evidence for infants' growing capacities for social perceptiveness and responsiveness even towards abstracted features of people, around the middle of the first year of life.

It is necessary to introduce a caveat here. Reasonably enough, I hope, I have tried to exemplify what is special about an infant's manner of relating to persons by describing just that—infant–adult relatedness. However, the infant's potential for personal relatedness may not be applied solely to what we as adults recognise to be persons. Indeed as writers such as Hamlyn (1974) and Macmurray (1961) point out, infants may face a difficult task in discriminating what is impersonal. Although we would expect that for a fully-fledged and sustained sequence of interpersonal exchanges, an infant should require a real person with whom to relate, the infant's own capacity for *potentially* intersubjective engagement might be tapped by less-than-personal objects or events. When a young infant smiles at a drawn circle with dot-like "eyes" waved before him, how are we to say whether or not the circle is a proto-person from the infant's point of view? It is certainly true that infants are not consistent in discriminating people from things (Frye, Rawling, Moore, & Myers, 1983), but this does not settle whether there are special forms of relatedness that become increasingly (but never absolutely) restricted to people. The findings from studies such as those of Murray and Trevarthen (1985; also Sylvester-Bradley, 1985) might be interpreted as indicating that there are indeed distinctive modes of early infant behaviour and experience that are social in quality, but that at times these might be manifest in non-social contexts.

My account moved on to consider how the somewhat separate forms of infant–care-giver and infant–object relations become co-ordinated into what has been called triadic infant–object–care-giver relations in the last quarter of the infant's first year (Adamson & Bakeman, 1982; Trevarthen & Hubley, 1978). This juncture corresponds with a new level of self- and other-awareness, and with what Daniel Stern (1985) calls the emergence of an intersubjective self. I noted a range of new accomplishments that mark this transition, including the capacity for social referencing, actions that appear to fulfil the infant's intention to share experiences of objects by showing or pointing out objects to the care-giver, new forms of imitation and empathy, and so on. Then around the middle of the second year, a flowering of creative symbolic play appears to coincide with manifestations of more sophisticated self-consciousness and social role-taking. Soon the child's rapidly expanding vocabulary provides evidence for explicit understanding of self and other.

I shall break off the story at this point, and return to pick up the threads in Chapter 5. I hope I have fulfilled my intention to capture something of what I mean by the normal infant's capacities for personal relatedness. It is against the background of infants' developing modes of interpersonal co-ordination that now I wish to reappraise the picture of autism.

CHAPTER FOUR

Interpersonal Relatedness II: The Case of Autism

The purpose of this chapter is to consider some of the ways in which systematic research has furthered our understanding of autistic children's abnormalities in personal relatedness. I shall not be repeating what I have already noted about reports of abnormalities in autistic *infants*. Rather, I want to consider studies of autistic children who are well past infancy, but in whom it is possible to investigate a level of psychological functioning that would correspond with infant-style relatedness in normal individuals. Here will be included varieties of non-verbal communication from emotion perception and expression, through to joint attention, social referencing, and imitation, together with patterns of attachment and expressions of self-reflective awareness. Obviously there might be a number of ways in which abnormality could arise in these children—one should not presume that what is abnormal at the age of five years was also abnormal at the age of one year—but it is only when compared with the abilities and propensities of normal infants that the disabilities of children with autism are seen in an appropriate light.

I shall develop an account that roughly corresponds with the course of the previous chapter. I begin with infant-level modes of relatedness and relationship, and then shift the focus on to matters of social perception and finally on to the development of self. I shall defer the treatment of more explicit forms of interpersonal understanding, including the distinction between self and other as expressed in personal pronoun usage, until the next chapter.

INTERPERSONAL RELATEDNESS AND RELATIONSHIPS

As in so many other areas of research into autism, Neil O'Connor and Beate Hermelin (Hermelin & O'Connor, 1985; O'Connor & Hermelin, 1963) were among the first to apply the experimental method to investigate the social deficits of autistic children. For example, they reported that severely retarded autistic children as well as control subjects turned towards, looked at, or approached a seated person more than inanimate stimuli such as pictures or toys. On the other hand, the autistic children made such "orientation responses" more rarely and more briefly than non-autistic subjects of similar intellectual ability, and their behaviour alternated frequently between approach and retreat. There was clearly something unusual in the organisation of the children's attentiveness and behaviour towards people, not merely an absence of relatedness.

The following studies illustrate how research workers have extended and refined this early work, in an attempt to specify more precisely what is present as well as what is absent or abnormal in the social relations of autistic children and adolescents. I shall begin with systematic observations of autistic children's behaviour in natural settings. These reveal how, even in middle childhood and beyond, autistic individuals' relations with other people appear to lack the reciprocity and mutual engagement shown by normal infants even before their first birthday.

We can start with some observations on the business of becoming engaged.

Making and Breaking Contact

One classic body of research is that conducted by Cathy Lord and her colleagues, who have investigated the development of peer relations in children with autism (Lord, 1984; Lord & Garfin, 1986; Lord & Hopkins, 1986). We have already seen how autistic individuals' social interactions may improve over time, and how their impairments are often most marked when they relate to other children and adolescents rather than adults. There are probably a number of sources of difficulty here, including the failure of peers to approach and respond to a seemingly uncommunicative or strange autistic child, the autistic child's own limited motivation or capacity to engage in verbal or non-verbal reciprocal exchanges with others, and his or her lack of imaginative play. In Cathy Lord's studies (summarised in Lord, 1984), six autistic children who were aged around 10 years and who had a non-verbal IQ of around 40 were observed with same-aged non-autistic children who were asked to "help the autistic child learn to play" in a setting where toys were freely available. Prior to this intervention, the autistic children were studied as they interacted with each other in small groups, and although they spent about one-quarter of a 15-minute observation time oriented towards each other, they rarely initiated or responded to social approaches. Indeed, no autistic child made more than four initiations or more than four responses in 15 minutes. When non-handicapped peers were first introduced, only one autistic child made any initiations, and overall the autistic children responded to fewer than 25% of the peers' attempts to get them to play. Active avoidance consisted of maintaining distance and self-stimulating, and five out of the six autistic children showed no co-operative play at all. Over the succeeding daily 15-minute play sessions, however, the autistic children became more oriented towards and responsive to the non-handicapped children. They even sustained exchanges that went beyond a single response to peer initiations, which most commonly involved the offer of an object with a gesture of approach. On the other hand, initiations by the autistic children themselves were still rare, and most of these comprised offers of materials without speech. In this and a subsequent study with higher functioning individuals, the autistic children continued to have difficulty in co-ordinating aspects of social behaviour such as looking at someone before handing them something, they seldom used language, they were still primarily passive, and they continued to use objects in very limited ways. It seemed particularly important that the autistic children were enabled to know what their partners wanted them to do, and more active and structured approaches by another person seemed to help (also Clark & Rutter, 1981). Indeed, playmates had to work very hard to keep social interactions going. As Lord (1984: p. 220) comments, the autistic children "failed to use, or did not use effectively, very basic social and affective behaviors that are typically observed in normally developing 7- to 9-month-old infants".

In collaboration with Joyce Magill (Lord & Magill, 1989), Cathy Lord also studied autistic and control children for their spontaneous greetings upon meeting a familiar adult. The autistic children were less likely to use multiple actions in their greetings, they required more prompting, and they were less likely to smile. Although at first there was no clear group difference in subjects' direction of gaze, when the sample size was subsequently increased, significant differences in eye contact were recorded. My colleague Tony Lee and I have recently completed a somewhat similar study in which we videotaped autistic and closely matched non-autistic adolescents, as a familiar adult introduced each of them to a stranger who allowed a two-second pause before saying "Hello". After collaborating with the stranger in a task, the subjects' spontaneous and then prompted farewells were recorded. The findings were that two-thirds of the non-autistic subjects but only one-third of the autistic subjects made a spontaneous greeting; nearly one-half of the non-autistic subjects but only three autistic subjects (out of 24) initiated a farewell; and whereas nearly all of the non-autistic subjects made eye contact in the greeting situation, either before or after a prompt, almost half of the autistic group failed to do so. Such studies provide unsubtle but impressive demonstrations that, even when age and intellectual ability are taken into account, adolescents with autism are less likely to initiate or terminate interpersonal "engagement" in natural (and partly conventional) ways which involve verbal but also non-verbal channels of communication.

One task is to discern the functions of those kinds of interpersonal exchange that appear to come naturally to autistic children, and those that seem to be relatively impoverished. The word "functions" is rather coarse for what I mean, in that it seems to imply that people always do things for some ulterior purpose. In fact, of course, most human beings find certain social activities rewarding in and of themselves. In particular, we sometimes share experiences for the pleasure of sharing experiences. The point is that we need to identify the character of those forms of interpersonal and thing-related transactions that seem to have meaning for autistic children, and those for which there appears to be little significance. "Sharing experiences" is an especially important case in point.

Sharing Experiences and Sharing Things

In 1978, Frank Curcio reported a study of 12 mute autistic children who were aged between four and 12 years. A principal aim of the work was to assess the children's profiles of sensorimotor development, but in addition Curcio wanted to investigate the forms of non-verbal communication that autistic children display. He was especially interested in the distinction drawn by Elizabeth Bates and her colleagues (Bates, Camaioni, & Volterra, 1975), between "proto-imperatives" on the one hand, and "proto-declaratives" on the other. Proto-imperatives are acts or gestures that reflect an infant's efforts to "use" another person to obtain a desired object or event. Protodeclaratives such as showing and pointing to something are intended simply to draw another person's attention to, and perhaps to share the experience of or even comment on, the something in question ("Look at that!"). Curcio's approach was to request teaching staff to complete a questionnaire recording specific occasions on which the autistic children used a sound or a gesture to achieve a social or non-social aim. He supplemented this source of information by conducting one-hour observations of each child in the classroom, and he also introduced a specific test to prompt the children to seek assistance to obtain an object.

What emerged was that all the children used some form of proto-imperative gestures by which they induced adults to help them attain a goal. In so doing, however, only half initiated eye contact, and five of the 12 used the teacher's hand as a tool by guiding it towards the container which they wanted opened. More striking still, not one autistic child was reported or observed to show objects to an adult in a spontaneous way. The second kind of potentially protodeclarative act, that of pointing, was observed in only five of the 12 subjects, and even in these cases it was used not to communicate something about an object's properties or existence, but instead served a need-fulfilling function. What makes this observation so impressive, is that in the normal case an infant develops proto-imperative and protodeclarative attention-sharing gestures at roughly the same time towards the end of the first year of life.

Thus it seemed there might be something specific in autistic children's lack of protodeclarative gestures. Then, in an intensive study of young autistic and normal children who were in the prelinguistic and early stages of language development, Amy Wetherby and Carol Prutting (1984) provided corroborative evidence. Four autistic and four normal children were videotaped in play and in a "structured communication condition" including eight situations that were designed to prompt communicative exchanges with the investigator. For example, the investigator ostentatiously ate desirable food without offering any to the child, she activated and de-activated a wind-up toy, and she looked at a book that belonged to the child. In such circumstances, each of the four autistic subjects was able to regulate the adult's behaviour to achieve an environmental end such as getting food, but none attracted and directed the adult's attention to him- or herself or to an object, as an end in and of itself. Thus all four autistic children displayed a high frequency of acts in which they requested objects or actions or showed protest, but unlike the language-matched normal children, none showed off, commented on or labelled things, or acknowledged the adult who was interacting with them.

These two seminal studies anticipated a significant body of research conducted in the mid-1980s by Kate Loveland and Susan Landry in the University of Texas, and by Marian Sigman, Peter Mundy, and colleagues in the University of California at Los Angeles, on the topic of "joint attention" in autism. Loveland and Landry (1986; Landry & Loveland, 1988, 1989) compared a group of autistic children aged between five and 13 years with another group of children with developmental language delay who had similar abilities in aspects of their linguistic and non-verbal cognitive functioning. In certain of their studies they also tested normally developing two-year-olds. Each child was videotaped playing with one of the investigators in a playroom stocked with toys. Interspersed among free play periods during which a child's efforts to initiate interactions could be recorded, there were two sets of more structured conditions. In the first set, the adult stage-managed interactions that required the child either to produce or comprehend personal pronouns (e.g. "Who's got the...?") or the demonstratives "this/that" or "here/there"; or she required the child to respond to attention-directing gestures such as pointing, showing, gaze shifting, and tapping an object; or she combined attention-directing gestures with language (e.g. a point plus "What's that?"). The second set of conditions was intended to elicit attention-directing "requesting" behaviour from the children, and included situations in which the investigator set desirable food or attractive objects beyond the child's reach. The principal findings were that autistic children were less able than other children to respond correctly to language or gestures used to direct their attention, and they themselves were significantly less likely to use pointing or showing gestures. It was especially in the spontaneous situation that autistic subjects' very rare usage of pointing and showing, as well as their infrequent use of the terms "this/that" or "here/there", contrasted with the higher prevalence of such gestures and utterances in both language-delayed and normal children. Moreover, the children's use of "joint attention" gestures was positively associated with language abilities within the group of autistic as well as control subjects, suggesting a developmental relationship between these two domains of functioning.

The research of Marian Sigman, Peter Mundy, and their colleagues (Mundy, Sigman, & Kasari, 1990; Mundy, Sigman, Ungerer, & Sherman, 1986, 1987; Sigman, Mundy, Sherman, & Ungerer, 1986) neatly complements these findings. These investigators tested younger autistic children, mostly aged between three and six years, and non-autistic mentally retarded children who were closely similar in general intellectual ability as well as in chronological age. This meant that "general mental retardation" was not responsible for any group differences in subjects' propensities and abilities to indicate things to others. Second, the researchers employed a rather different approach to testing by using an abridged form of the Early Social-Communication Scales (ESCS; Seibert, Hogan, & Mundy, 1982). In this procedure, the child and experimenter sat facing each other across a small table. A set of toys including a hat, a comb, a book, a ball, a car, five small wind-up mechanical toys and five hand-operated toys were in view but out of the child's reach. Colourful posters were hung on the walls of the room. The experimenter presented or activated the toys one at a time, and every so often pointed to and looked at the wall posters. He or she also engaged the child in physical social games such as tickling, and in turn-taking activities such as rolling a car back and forth, or taking turns in using a comb or hat. Verbal interactions were kept to a minimum.

The 25-minute sessions were videotaped and the tapes were rated for the following categories of non-verbal communication by trained observers: (1) "social behaviour", which referred to the child's capacity to elicit attention or physical contact and to engage in turn-taking with the experimenter; (2) "joint attention" behaviour, which involved the use of gestures intended to direct attention to an object or event, and thereby to establish a common focus of attention between the child and the experimenter; and (3) "requesting" behaviour, that is, actions and gestures used to request aid in obtaining objects and events. The joint attention category included not only pointing and showing, but also a pattern of alternating looks between a toy and the experimenter's face, and looking to the focus of the experimenter's own pointing. In keeping with the findings already reported, it was the paucity of joint attention and indicating behaviour that most clearly discriminated the autistic from control subjects. For example, the autistic children showed eye contact after they had been tickled, and they quite often made eye contact when a toy was moved out of reach—but they very rarely engaged in "referential looking" between an active mechanised toy and the experimenter. Even when studied interacting with their usual care-givers, in relation to whom they directed as many looks and vocalisations as did the other children, autistic subjects rarely pointed to or showed objects simply for the sake of sharing experiences. Only six out of 18 autistic children ever pointed to objects or showed them to their care-givers in this way, whereas 17 out of the 18 children in each of the other groups used an indicating gesture at least once. The autistic children also engaged with their care-givers in mutual eye-contact for shorter periods of time, and more frequently walked away from the interactions, than did the mentally retarded subjects.

Another major focus of interest in these studies has been the relation between the subjects' joint attention skills and their language abilities. In keeping with the findings of Landry and Loveland (1988), Mundy et al. (1987) reported that within a sample of autistic children, individual subjects' abilities to comprehend and use protodeclarative gestures were correlated with measures of their language ability and symbolic play. To explore this matter further, Mundy et al. (1990) studied a group of 15 autistic children with a mean age of about four years, together with groups of non-autistic mentally retarded children matched for mental age and language age respectively, over the period of a year. They found that, in contrast with the situation for control subjects, the autistic children's language development was predicted not by measures of initial language score or IQ, but rather by the initial measures of gestural non-verbal "joint attention skills". This body of work suggests that one constraint on autistic children's developing capacities for language and symbolic play might be a relative disability in co-ordinating their own and others' attention towards objects and events in the world.

There is one further study that adds an extra dimension to these observations. Simon Baron-Cohen (1989a) tested a group of relatively able autistic children aged from six to 16 years, together with control groups of normal and Down's syndrome children, for the ways they interpreted different kinds of pointing by another person. There were two conditions, in one of which (the proto-imperative condition) the experimenter pointed to toys positioned in a semicircle close to the child but at some distance from the experimenter, and in the other of which (the protodeclarative condition) he pointed to locations such as out of the window or in his briefcase, such that the experimenter but not the child could see what was there. In each case the experimenter asked a question of the form: "I am going to use my finger to say something. What am I saying?" Seventy per cent or more of the subjects in each diagnostic group were correct in interpreting proto-imperative points (which when necessary, were done in a rather insistent way), mostly responding to the gestures as requests for the objects pointed-to by passing them to the experimenter. Yet whilst the majority of the non-autistic subjects responded to the protodeclarative gestures by looking along the line of the point, or asking "What is it?", only 2 out of 20 autistic children reacted in this way, and most did nothing at all.

What the above studies so clearly demonstrate and illuminate, is how there are certain kinds of social impairment that are relatively specific to autistic individuals. These impairments are not attributable to low levels of general cognitive or linguistic ability, nor are they general to all forms of social interchange. Amongst the results were indications of autistic children's lively responsiveness to games of physical contact such as being tickled, their capacities to make eye contact and sometimes to combine this with gestures in requesting situations (even though pointing may prove to be less common here), and their interest in prompting and sustaining social routines involving turn-taking. All this is important for any theory (such as that proposed by Marian Sigman and Peter Mundy, as well as my own) which suggests that there is something centrally important about autistic children's lack of engagement with other people. Clearly, such accounts cannot be claiming that autistic children are handicapped in all kinds of behavioural "engagement" between themselves and others. Rather, the idea is that there is a quality of interpersonal psychological engagement, a subjective linkage to but differentiation from the subjective life of other people, that autistic people experience only very partially. In order to be at all convincing, this notion should explain why it is that protodeclarative but not proto-imperative gestures are notable for their relative absence in autistic children, why the children fail to respond to others' bids for joint visual attention, and why it is that only certain patterns of eye contact such as prolonged "referential looking" and mutual gazing seem to be missing in their personal relatedness. I shall return to these matters in due course.

Affective Co-ordination

One way in which an individual's subjective experiences are linked in with those of others, is through processes of empathy or "fellow-feeling". To make a bald statement of this kind is to beg many questions, not least whether primitive forms of empathy are foundational for more elaborate kinds of intersubjective contact and understanding (as I shall argue), or whether the capacity to feel with and for other people is somehow derivative from "cognitive" role-taking capacities. Whatever the resolution of this issue, there can be little doubt that the question of empathy is relevant for our theories of autism, and that studies of autism may contribute to our thinking about the nature of empathy and the sources of psychological sharing. What, then, has experimental research been able to add to clinical descriptions of autistic children's impairments in affective contact with others?

Interpersonal Co-ordination of Affect. Perhaps the most appropriate way to embark on this topic is to return to the place where we left off in the previous section of this chapter, with the joint attention studies conducted at UCLA. Kasari, Sigman, Mundy, and Yirmiya (1990) employed their videotapes of semistructured child–experimenter interactions to assess how matched autistic and non-autistic retarded three-to-six year-olds, and mental-age-matched normal children with a mean age of two years, expressed affect towards the experimenter in the contexts of joint attention and requesting. Allowance was made for the low levels of joint attention amongst the autistic children. Subjects' facial expressions were coded second by second for a total of eight minutes, using a standardised coding instrument (the Maximally Discriminative Movement Coding System designed by Izard, 1979). Although the autistic children showed uniformly low levels of positive affect towards the adult, they diverged most markedly in their decreased level of positive feeling during situations of joint attention. These were the situations in which the normal children smiled most of all. As the authors indicate, this result seems to point to autistic children's lack of affective sharing in circumstances when normal children are especially prone to show pleasure in attaining an adult's interest in their own focus of attention.

This evidence of autism-specific abnormality in face-to-face affective co-ordination is supported by two further studies. In the first, Margaret Snow, Margaret Hertzig, and Ted Shapiro (1987) videotaped ten autistic children aged between two-and-a-half and four years, and ten age- and intelligence-matched developmentally delayed children, as they interacted with the mother, a child psychiatrist, and a nursery school teacher who were told to behave "just as they normally would" in a comfortable room stocked with toys. Twenty 15-second intervals of child interaction with each partner were coded using a checklist of emotionally expressive actions such as smiles and laughter. The results were that whereas almost all the positive affect of the non-autistic children was expressed towards the other person, the autistic children's less frequent displays of affect were as likely to occur at seemingly random, self-absorbed moments as in the context of social interaction. On the other hand, occasions of partner-related smiling and laughing were observed even amongst the autistic children, who showed some selectivity in smiling less to the psychiatrist than to the more familiar adults.

In the second study, which was conducted by Geraldine Dawson and her colleagues (Dawson, Hill, Spencer, Galpert, & Watson, 1990), 16 autistic children aged two to six years and 16 normal children matched for receptive language were videotaped interacting with their mothers in three different contexts: free play, a more structured situation in which the mother asked the child to help her to put away some toys, and a face-to-face situation over snack time. It is important to note that this kind of comparison with non-retarded children leaves some uncertainty whether differences in the autistic children's behaviour might reflect mental retardation rather than autism *per se*. In the event, however, the findings were interesting not only for the group differences that emerged, but also for the fact that there were no significant differences in the autistic children's frequency or duration of gaze at the mother's face, nor differences in the frequency or duration of smiles in the face-to-face interaction over a snack. However, autistic children were much less likely than normal children to combine their smiles with eye contact in a single act that seemed to convey an intent to communicate feelings. Not only this, but whilst ten out of 14 normal children with codable data smiled in response to their mother's smile, only three out of 15 autistic subjects ever did so. It was also observed that the mothers of the autistic subjects were less likely to smile in response to their children's smiles, which after all were rarely combined with sustained eye contact. Obviously there are a number of possible explanations for this pattern of results, but they raise the question of how much sharing or co-ordination of affective states between the mothers and their autistic children was taking place.

A recent set of studies from the UCLA group has included direct examination of the interpersonal co-ordination of affect between young autistic children and other people in circumstances where familiar or unfamiliar adults have simulated distress, fear, and discomfort (Sigman, Kasari, Kwon, & Yirmiya, 1992). Subjects were 30 young autistic children with a mean age of under four years, and closely matched non-autistic retarded and normal children. The technique was to code these children's behaviour when an adult pretended to hurt herself by hitting her finger with a hammer, simulated fear towards a remote-controlled robot, and pretended to be ill by lying down on a couch for a minute, feigning discomfort. In each of these situations, the autistic children were unusual in rarely looking at or relating to the adult. When an adult pretended to be hurt, for example, the autistic children often appeared unconcerned and continued to play with toys. When an adult showed fear towards the robot, autistic children were not only less attentive towards the adult (with over half this group but hardly any control subjects failing completely to look at the adult), but they were also less hesitant in playing with the robot subsequently than were non-autistic mentally retarded control subjects. Here we find evidence emerging that autistic children are relatively "unengaged" not only in one-to-one interpersonal-affective transactions, but also with another person's emotional attitudes towards objects and events in the world.

The studies cited so far have been quasi-naturalistic investigations of person-to-person affective exchanges. Those that follow are rather different in emphasis and style in-so-far as they concentrate respectively on autistic children's expressions and perception of emotion. Having said this, I should like to repeat something I stressed in an earlier chapter, about the indissoluble connections among affectively patterned interpersonal relatedness, affective responsiveness and the perception of emotional expressions. To perceive (say) a smile as a smile is to be drawn into a certain kind of relatedness to the person who smiles—typically, one that involves being inclined to smile oneself. Nor is this simply a matter of "smiles", in that smiles (or scowls, or expressions of sadness, or looks of terror) are both perceived to be, and are experienced in oneself to be, but one aspect of an emotional state that has other biologically given concomitants in bodily gestures and actions. If it were habitually the case that children "smiled" but then ran away, we should question the sense in which children's smiles were "smiles". One implication is that to perceive emotional expressions may entail at least the potential for appropriate forms of emotional responsiveness, and a profound impairment in responsiveness may amount to a profound impairment in the very perception of "emotion". Moreover, the capacity for patterned *intra*personal co-ordination of affective expressions and inclinations to action—and with these, the capacity for normal configurations of emotional experience—might contribute to and even be a precondition for *inter*personal co-ordination of feeling and action. It is possible that a given individual might suffer a selective inability to recognise rather than respond to others' expressions of feeling, an "affective agnosia", but until such a case is argued I shall assume that studies of autistic individuals' affective responsiveness and perceptiveness are but two sides of the same coin. It will also become clear that the division between these and the studies already discussed is an arbitrary one.

Emotional Expressiveness.   Let me begin with a classic study by Derek Ricks (1975, 1979). Ricks tape-recorded six three- and four-year-old non-verbal autistic children, six non-verbal non-autistic retarded children of the same age, and six normal infants aged between eight and 11 months, in four situations. The first was a request situation, when the children were hungry and their favourite meal was prepared and shown to them; the second was an occasion of frustration, when the meal was withheld for a few moments; the third was one of greeting, when the children saw their mothers on waking in the morning, or when she returned to the room after an absence; and in the fourth, involving pleased surprise, the child was presented with a novel and interesting stimulus, the blowing up of a balloon or the lighting of a sparkler firework. The recordings of the children's vocalisations in each of these situations were edited, and played back to the mothers of the children. For example, an autistic child's mother would be presented with two sets of recordings. In the first was heard four children—the mother's own child, two other autistic children, and a non-autistic retarded child—making in succession the four vocal signals from the situations designed to elicit request, frustration, greeting, and surprise, respectively. Here the mother's task was to identify in which context each vocalisation had been recorded, to identify her own child, and to identify the non-autistic child. The second set of recordings comprised the request vocalisations of all six autistic children, and the task was for the mother to identify her own child.

The results were as follows. When this kind of procedure was conducted with recordings of normal infants' vocalisations, mothers could easily identify the message of each signal of every infant, but found some difficulty in identifying which signals came from their own child. When the tapes of the autistic and non-autistic retarded subjects were presented to the autistic children's mothers, these mothers too could recognise the contexts from which their own autistic child's vocalisations had been derived, and they could also identify the signals of the one non-autistic child on tape (often explaining that the child "sounded normal"). What they were unable to do, was to recognise the contexts associated with the vocalisations of autistic children other than their own. Each such child's signals seemed to be idiosyncratic. Correspondingly, and in contrast with the parents of normal children, they could readily and unerringly identify their own child from the various vocalisations. Ricks concluded that whereas normal infants seem to have an unlearned set of emotionally communicative vocalisations, autistic children either do not develop these signals or, having reached the age of three to five, and in contrast to non-autistic retarded children of the same age, they no longer use them. On the other hand, they do produce idiosyncratic signals which appear to express something like states of wanting something, being frustrated in not getting it, and so on. It is not the case that their expressions are totally unorganised or lacking in meaning.

The question of the spontaneous organisation of affective expressions was also addressed in a study of the facial expressions of the young autistic and control children who took part in the UCLA joint-attention studies (Yirmiya, Kasari, Sigman, & Mundy, 1989). Segments of the videotapes of the semistructured child–experimenter interactions that involved the presentation of activated toys, a song-and-tickle social game, a turn-taking activity, and a balloon-blowing episode were selected. The children's facial expressions were coded second-by-second, using the anatomically based scheme of Izard (1979). The principal findings were that the autistic children were more flat or neutral in affective expressions than were mentally retarded children, but more important than this, they displayed a variety of unique and ambiguous expressions that were not displayed by any of the other children. Although the authors described these in terms of negative and incongruous blends of expression, for example of fear-with-anger or anger-with-joy, it is uncertain whether what might normally serve as reliable indices of fear, anger, and so on had the same meanings here. The evidence suggests that for autistic children, the intrapersonal co-ordination of facial expressions might not be normal, with obvious implications for the patterning of the children's personal and interpersonal affective experiences.

These observations are complemented by the work of investigators who have asked autistic individuals to pose emotionally expressive faces and voices. Thus in an experiment conducted by Tim Langdell (1981), judges rated children's attempts to make happy and sad faces as more inappropriate than those of non-autistic retarded children. A more elaborate study has recently been conducted by Hope Macdonald, Michael Rutter, and colleagues (Macdonald, Rutter, Howlin, Rios, LeCouteur, Evered, & Folstein, 1989). In this case raters judged that high-functioning autistic subjects' posed facial and vocal expressions were more "odd" than those of control subjects, and the (photographed) faces were also less easily classified with respect to the emotions expressed. In deliberate as well as spontaneous expressions of emotion, therefore, the evidence points to qualitative as well as quantitative abnormalities in individuals with autism.

One additional study of emotionally expressive gestures takes a rather different form. Tony Attwood, Uta Frith, and Beate Hermelin (1988) observed autistic and Down's syndrome adolescents interacting with their peers for a total of 20 30-second periods in the playground and at the dinner table. All 15 Down's subjects interacted socially during the period of observation, but only 11 of the 18 autistic children did so. Although the mean number of gestures per interaction did not distinguish the groups, there were differences in the kinds of gesture employed. Both groups used simple pointing gestures and instrumental gestures to prompt behaviour, such as those to indicate "come here" or "be quiet"; but whereas 10 out of 15 individuals with Down's syndrome used at least one expressive gesture such as giving a hug of consolation, making a thumbs-up sign, or covering the face in embarrassment, not one such gesture was seen in the autistic group. This was despite there being plenty of occasions on which a gesture of consolation, embarrassment, or apology would have been appropriate.

Emotion Perception.   There is now a substantial body of experimental research to suggest that not only are autistic children abnormal in the ways they express emotion, but there are also autism-specific deficits in emotion perception and understanding. The controversy that surrounds this area of work is well-justified, for there are complex methodological considerations which make it difficult to be confident whether apparently clear-cut evidence for such deficits is or is not offset by other more equivocal findings. The most persuasive evidence for autism-specific deficits has come from studies that have compared sizeable groups of closely matched autistic and non-autistic retarded subjects on tests that compare performance in judging emotion-related and emotion-unrelated materials such as photographs, drawings, or videotape and audiotape recordings of people and non-personal objects. The most serious sources of contention are that often the group differences in the profiles of performance on index and control tasks have been quantitatively small, and that when emotion recognition abilities are adjudged solely with reference to subjects' levels of language ability, the differences sometimes (not always) entirely disappear. It has also been said that evidence for similar deficits in non-autistic retarded individuals render it doubtful whether the problems are special to autism, but it is difficult to see how this view can be sustained when many of the studies have employed such retarded individuals as control subjects. I do not think it would be helpful to embark on a lengthy discussion of the methodological issues, nor to attempt a review of the full range of published studies. For the interested reader, as indeed for the acute critic who recognises the underlying complexity to "mental age" matching between autistic and non-autistic subjects, I have attempted to do this elsewhere (Hobson, 1991a). What I shall do instead, is to summarise a handful of experimental studies that have yielded results which are at least highly suggestive.

The first experiment I shall describe is one that my colleague Jane Weeks and I designed to test the hypothesis that autistic children are abnormal in their relative lack of attentiveness to facial expressions of emotion (Weeks & Hobson, 1987). As we have seen already, autistic children often appear to be relatively unengaged with and unaffected by other people's expressions of feeling, and we wanted to explore this in an admittedly stylised but standardised way that might reveal how there is something special to autism here, and moreover something that is not explicable solely in terms of impaired cognitive abilities, as narrowly understood. We selected 15 autistic and 15 non-autistic retarded subjects who were pairwise matched for chronological age, sex, and verbal ability. In view of the proposal that autistic children's seeming difficulties on emotion recognition tasks might simply be a function of their language impairment, it is worth emphasising that our subjects were closely similar in their verbal abilities as assessed by three subtests of a widely-used intelligence test, the WISC-R. Subjects were given a task of sorting photographs of people to "go with" one or other of a pair of target photographs showing the head and shoulders of individuals who contrasted in three, two or one of the following respects: sex, age, facial expression of emotion, and the type of hat they were wearing. The features that were varied were kept simple: either a happy or a non-happy (rather glum) face, either a male or a female, either a floppy hat or a woollen hat. The instructions were that the child should notice one way in which the two pictures were different, and sort the 16 photographs of new people accordingly. These 16 photographs comprised a mixture of people with systematic combinations of age, sex, facial expression, hat, and so on, such that we could tell which feature was the one selected as the criterion for sorting. We deemed that sorting was consistent if a child sorted 13 out of 16 cards by a particular feature, and as it turned out the child's strategy was almost always clear.

In order to establish a hierarchy of salience of the features under study, we adopted the following method. Suppose that a child initially sorted by hat. The next pair of standards would be of individuals wearing the same hat, but still different in emotional expression and sex. The same 16 sorting-cards were shuffled, and subjects sorted them afresh. If the child then sorted by sex, the standards would be changed so that they now wore the same hat and were of the same sex. Finally, only one experimenter-designated feature remained as a basis for sorting.

The results were that two-thirds of the subjects of each diagnostic group began by sorting the photographs according to sex, or more accurately, by some feature that corresponded with sex (which with the materials we were using, might have been hair length). There was therefore no question that the autistic children could discriminate the photographs and sort accordingly. However, whilst ten of the 15 non-autistic children sorted by emotional expression before they sorted by hats, only three of the 15 autistic children did so, and nine autistic children sorted by hats in preference to facial expression (the remaining three autistic subjects sorting by neither hat nor facial expression). This finding was statistically significant, given our prediction that autistic children would overlook or otherwise neglect the facial expressions in favour of hats. The point is further emphasised by the following finding. Equal numbers of autistic and control subjects spontaneously sorted by sex at some point during the task, and an equal number sorted by hat; but whereas all 15 of the non-autistic children sorted by facial expression sooner or later, only six out of 15 autistic children did so. For the remaining nine autistic children, the contrast in facial expression did not seem to register. Even when give explicit instructions to sort by facial expression, five out of 15 autistic subjects failed to sort consistently.

Only after we had completed this experiment did we discover that William Jennings had conducted a rather similar unpublished study which had yielded results that were comparable to our own (Jennings, 1973). In Jennings' study, autistic children paired photographs on the basis of emotion about one-quarter as often as control subjects, and there was other evidence to suggest that this was not due to an inability to discriminate between the expressions (by whatever perceptual strategy). Therefore the results of these experiments seem to dovetail with real-life indication that autistic children are not "arrested" by expressions of emotion, to the degree that non-autistic children are.

I shall now turn to two experiments which were designed to test whether autistic children have difficulty in recognising the emotional meaning that is common to facial expressions which differ in other respects. Just now I hinted that autistic children might apply abnormal perceptual strategies in making judgements about relatively artificial task materials. If it is possible for the children to discriminate and classify what we consider to be "emotion-related" features of expressions in a "non-emotion-related" way, then they may perform misleadingly well in (say) expression-matching tasks, even if they are impaired in registering the subjective emotional meanings of real-life expressions. This has two implications for the experimental design of expression-matching tasks. First, one needs to devise task materials that render it difficult to achieve matching *unless* one perceives emotional meaning. The less the emotion-matched materials conform with other criteria for perceptual similarity, the better. Second, one should try to devise control tasks that reveal autistic and non-autistic subjects' relative abilities to make subtle perceptual judgements that correspond with non-emotional meanings. In this way it may become possible to appraise how far both autistic and non-autistic subjects' abilities and/or disabilities are specific to the emotion domain. I hope the following experiments will illustrate what I mean.

My colleagues Janet Ouston and Tony Lee and myself wanted to test whether autistic subjects who were matched for verbal ability might be impaired in discriminating happy, unhappy, angry, and afraid faces in photographs (Hobson, Ouston, & Lee, 1988a). We employed four standard photographs arranged in a semicircle, which differed either in the emotions expressed in each face, or in the identities of the individuals portrayed. Subjects were given new photographs in sets of four. In the emotions task, the photographs showed the same expressions as the standards, but on the faces of new individuals. The subjects' task was to match the emotions despite the different faces that were expressing the feelings. In the "identities" control task, the standard photographs showed the four different individuals who appeared in the pictures to be sorted, but they differed from the latter (which featured the various emotional expressions) by being neutral in emotional tone. In this case, therefore, subjects had to match identities across changes in emotional expression.

This was not all. In order to explore the possibility that autistic children might perform well by applying some form of non-emotional perceptual analysis, we repeated the two forms of task with modifications: first, the faces on the cards to be sorted had blanked-out mouths, and second, they had blanked-out mouths and foreheads. Our intention was to retain the "feel" of the emotions even in these latter materials (to establish an advantage for emotion-sensitive subjects) whilst at the same time to reduce the availability of non-emotion-related cues (to thwart alternative strategies for sorting).

The first result was that the autistic and non-autistic subjects were equally proficient in sorting full faces of different people according to the same emotions, and equally proficient in sorting full faces of people with different emotions according to their individual identities. This might seem to be strong evidence against highly specific emotion recognition deficits in autism, at least with respect to facial expressions. Yet whereas on the identities task, the performance of the two groups showed a similar steady decline as the photographs became increasingly blanked-out, on the emotions task the performance of autistic subjects worsened more abruptly than that of control subjects as cues to emotion were progressively reduced. It seemed that autistic subjects were relatively unable to use the "feel" in the faces to guide performance. Not only this, but correlations between individual subjects' scores on the identity and emotion tasks were higher for autistic that for non-autistic subjects, again suggesting that the autistic subjects might have been sorting the expressive faces by non-emotional perceptual strategies.

In fact, there was a final condition. Here the standard photographs and the full-faces for sorting were each presented upside-down. Still the task was to match emotions across identities, and identities across emotions, but the upside-down presentation was intended to disrupt the normal processes of face recognition. Not surprisingly, the performance of control subjects slumped. Much more surprisingly, although in keeping with the findings from Langdell's (1978) study of autistic children's ability to identify upside-down photographs of peers, the autistic children's performance became significantly superior to the control group on matching both identities and emotions! This startling result not only confirms the importance of the "alternative strategy" hypothesis, but it also casts doubt on the validity of "identity recognition" as a control task. For one is left quite uncertain whether autistic children recognise identities as well as emotions in an abnormal and perhaps only partially comprehending way.

The second face-matching experiment I mention briefly. This illustrates how even when subjects are matched for verbal ability, and even in the absence of non-emotion-related control tasks, a well-designed task of an appropriate level of difficulty may yield evidence of autism-specific deficits in emotion recognition. Sally Ozonoff, Bruce Pennington, and Sally Rogers (1991a) tested a group of high-functioning autistic individuals and a heterogeneous control sample, who were matched for age and verbal IQ, on a battery of tests including one of emotion perception. A photograph of a face displaying an emotional expression served as the target, and subjects were asked to choose one out of four photographs that "felt the same way". Correct choices varied from the target in the identity of the model and the intensity of the expressed affect. There were 34 items, half of which contained distractor photographs that shared similar perceptual features with correct choices; for example, a face expressing fear was used as a distractor for the target emotion of surprise, since both emotions share the feature of an open mouth. Nine emotions were depicted, four "simple emotions" (happiness, sadness, anger, and fear) and five "complex emotions" (surprise, shame, disgust, interest, and contempt). The autistic group performed significantly less well than the control group in matching both simple and complex emotions, and made a higher number of errors on items with an obvious perceptual foil. The authors interpreted this result as suggesting that the autistic subjects were using a different, more perceptually driven matching strategy than controls—which of course would be in keeping with the drift of the present argument. If this were so, however, it would surely indicate that autistic subjects' scores on the task might provide a misleading overestimate of their underlying, genuinely emotion-related perceptual abilities; in which case one wonders if the scores should have been included in the discriminant analyses which the authors employed to track down the primary or universal abnormalities of the syndrome. The argument here is a general one, of course, and concerns the systematically overconservative nature of these kinds of abstracted tests of emotion perception.

To argue in this way is not to propose that the experiments described here are without value—indeed they have already served a purpose in drawing attention to the plausibility of primary emotion-related deficits in autism. The point is rather that the principal contribution of such studies is to establish whether there are significant group differences, not to provide a quantitative estimate of the severity of any underlying deficits. As I have already noted, the likelihood of detecting group differences at all is strongly influenced by the degree to which one can assess subjects' abilities to perceive and/or understand the emotional meanings of the materials presented. This brings me to a further set of studies in which my colleagues and myself tried to render meaning-independent perceptual strategies relatively ineffective by testing for cross-modal, face-to-voice emotional matching.

For the experiment in question, autistic and non-autistic retarded children and adolescents were pairwise matched according to age and verbal ability. They were presented with six photographed standardised facial expressions of emotion (Ekman & Friesen, 1975), and were asked to select which was the one to "go with" each of six successive emotionally expressive vocalisations (both verbal and non-verbal) recorded on audiotape. The principal challenge in designing this experiment was to devise a range of appropriately difficult control tasks in which sets of six photographs of related objects or events could be matched with corresponding audiotaped sounds. If possible, the objects or events should be comparable to emotional expressions in undergoing changes in visual appearance which included a significant dynamic component, and the changes in meaning should be reversible and signify changes in state. Otherwise, the uncontrolled non-emotion-specific variable might be responsible for differences in group performance. The nearest we managed to fulfilling this counsel of perfection involved a task using photographs and recorded sounds of six reversible states of a single substance, water—a stream, a waterfall, a lake, a shower, a fountain, and the sea—and another that featured the sounds and photographs of a person engaged in different kinds of "walking"—running downstairs, walking on shingle, walking on a pavement, walking on rubble, running on a pavement, and walking on snow. The remaining sets of materials comprised photographs and sounds of six kinds of bird, electrical appliance, vehicle, and garden tool, respectively. The rationale was that if these tasks were approximately equal in difficulty to the emotion recognition tasks, and if autistic subjects were as proficient as control subjects in matching such non-emotional sounds and photographs but performed less well in co-ordinating the voices and faces of emotional expressions, then there would be evidence of at least some specificity to their difficulties in the social–affective domain.

The results revealed that there was indeed a different profile of performance in the two groups, with the autistic subjects achieving relatively poor scores on the emotion tasks vis-à-vis the non-emotion tasks.

For example, in 16 out of 21 pairs of matched autistic and non-autistic subjects, those with autism did relatively less well in the emotion tasks (and had higher "non-emotion minus emotion" scores) than did their matched non-autistic control subjects. This finding was supported by results from a further study of subjects' free-response labelling of a subset of the photographs and sounds, in that once again the autistic subjects were poorer than control subjects at naming the emotions as depicted in faces and voices, relative to their abilities in naming the non-emotional objects depicted in photographs and sounds (Hobson, Ouston, & Lee, 1989).

It will be clear that there is no hard-and-fast distinction between tests of children's abilities to perceive emotion, and tasks that assess their understanding of emotion or emotion-related concepts. This is not to deny that there are important differences between perception and knowledge, but it does reflect at a methodological level the more profound theoretical contention that certain forms of understanding have a grounding in more direct perceptual–affective processes. Before I turn to evidence concerning autistic children's more explicit understandings of psychological states, including those to do with feelings, I want to mention certain other aspects of the potential for interpersonal connectedness that have received systematic investigation.

IMITATION

Imitation is a feature of social life that has particular importance for the study of autism. One reason is that, like the affective exchanges to which I have given prominence, imitative exchanges between people may establish correspondences in attitude as well as action across individuals. A complication here is that the term "imitation" covers a set of very different kinds of interpersonally co-ordinated behaviour and experience. If one considers the normal case, for example, one might begin with the evidence for neonatal imitation, including imitation of affective expressions, and for infants' responsiveness to their care-givers' frequent imitations of themselves (Field et al., 1982, 1983; Meltzoff & Moore, 1977, 1983). Such capacities might be taken to exemplify biologically prepared mechanisms for establishing psychological commonality or mutuality across individuals. Not only as infants but also as adults, we can find ourselves echoing the gestures of other people. On the other hand, the more elaborate kinds of imitation observed in normal infants from the end of the first year of life may presuppose a capacity to recognise and "identify with" other people who are perceived to have attitudes and to engage in actions. If this is the case, imitative capacities may serve as an index of growth in interpersonal understanding, over and above their role in promoting further development. I shall return to this topic in a later chapter, but I signpost the issues at this stage in order to point out how our present state of knowledge about the imitative capacities of autistic individuals is tantalising in its incompleteness.

The first thing to note is the general agreement that autistic children demonstrate abnormal delay and limitation in their imitation of others (e.g. DSM-III-R, American Psychiatric Association, 1987; Dahlgren & Gillberg, 1989). For example, retrospective parental histories gathered by Lorna Wing (1969) suggested that a majority of autistic children between the ages of two and five years have difficulties in copying movements or actions, for instance showing left–right or up–down disorientation. Subsequent systematic studies have revealed something of the scope of this abnormality. One of the first experimental investigations was that conducted by Marian De Myer and her colleagues (De Myer, Alpern, Barton, De Myer, Churchill, Hingtgen, Bryson, Pontius, & Kimberlin, 1972). These workers compared autistic and non-autistic retarded children on tests of body imitation that ranged from peek-a-boo and nose-touching to finger–thumb opposition and standing on one foot, as well as on tests of motor-object imitation such as stringing beads and spontaneous object use such as putting on clothing. Three- to seven-year-old autistic children of low IQ were found to be especially poor in body imitation and somewhat impaired in motor-object imitation, but they were relatively able when it came to spontaneous object use. Thus the problem appeared to be one that was not so much in the execution of movements, but rather to do with recognising the correspondence between the body movements or actions of the experimenter and those they could execute themselves.

In fact, autistic children seem to face difficulties on a number of levels. For instance, there is evidence indicating that young autistic children are less adept on the Uzgiris–Hunt Gestural Imitation Scale, which tests for imitation of actions ranging from banging a hammer or stirring a spoon in a cup to wrinkling the nose, than they are in other sensorimotor skills (Curcio, 1978; Dawson & Adams, 1984; Sigman & Ungerer, 1984) . They are also poor in imitating vocalisations. In one study, the better imitators amongst autistic four- to six-year-olds were also the ones who were socially and verbally responsive (Dawson & Adams, 1984). Masataka Ohta (1987) tested older, higher functioning autistic children (aged six to 14 years, with a non-verbal IQ of over 70) for their ability to copy finger and hand movements and "T signs" made with open-palm hands. Imitations that were partially rather than fully correct were much more common in autistic than control subjects. At yet another level we have the observations of J. Hammes and Tim Langdell (1981), who reported that relatively low-ability autistic children were less able than matched non-autistic children to engage in pantomime and to copy pretend actions such as pouring tea from an empty pot into an imaginary cup—a disability that clearly relates to more general problems in symbolic functioning. So, too, Candace Riguet and colleagues (Riguet, Taylor, Benaroya, & Klein, 1981) found they could elicit a higher level of play in autistic children by modelling symbolic acts, but this technique was no better than a literal demonstration and the resultant play was more limited in form than the imitative play of control subjects with similar verbal abilities.

So much for autistic children's difficulties in imitation—undoubtedly present, rather wide-ranging, and as yet, not very well specified. What makes the picture so interesting, as is often the case with autistic children, is the presence of apparently discrepant *abilities* in the imitation domain. One obvious example is the echolalia so typical of autism, when the child seems to "echo back" other people's utterances, either wholly or in part. Are echolalic children imitating a person talking, or are they registering and responding merely to words, or perhaps even echoing meaningless sounds? The answer is complex, for echolalia may serve a number of functions, some of a specific communicative kind (Paul, 1987; Prizant & Duchan, 1981) —yet even in its least meaningful manifestations, echolalia attests to a child's potential to match utterance to auditory input. Why, then, is the potential for "copying" not realised? The mystery deepens with the evidence that when autistic children with low imitative ability are themselves imitated by an experimenter, the children's social responsiveness and eye contact are likely to improve (Dawson & Adams, 1984; Tiegerman & Primavera, 1981). So autistic children seem to register imitation of their own actions by someone else. Not only this, but Ricks (1979) found that three- to five-year-old autistic children differed from retarded and young normal children in mimicking almost exclusively their own vocalisations recorded on audiotape, whilst seeming to ignore the vocalisations of adults, other autistic children, or even a normal child imitating the autistic child's own previous vocalisations.

I have already stated my view that these abnormalities in imitation arise from disorder on a number of levels. I should like to re-emphasise the distinction between two broad classes of imitative propensity and ability. The first concerns relatively automatic mechanisms by which normal infants (and older children and adults) perceive and assume the actions and attitudes of others. Here the imitation *leads to* interpersonal correspondences in action and attitude, but does not itself acquire a prior awareness on the infant's part that they are attempting to copy another person, conceptualised as such. The second class of imitation entails that the infant both identifies the goal-directed actions and/or attitudes of the other person, and identifies *with* the person in a deliberate attempt to copy the other. It is probably with respect to both forms of imitation, that autistic individuals are abnormal. They are seldom engaged with others in such a way as to "find themselves" identifying with others, and very rarely do they strive to adopt the stance of someone else.

ATTACHMENT

I have stressed how, when reviewing autistic children's abnormalities in the interpersonal domain, we need to avoid overstatement. A case in point concerns the children's attachment to other significant people. There are now several published studies that indicate how young autistic children *do* respond to separation from and reunion with their care-givers, at least in the short-term (Rogers, Ozonoff, & Maslin-Cole, 1991; Shapiro, Sherman, Calamari, & Koch, 1987; Sigman & Mundy, 1989; Sigman & Ungerer, 1984a). The context in which this has been examined is one based on the "strange situation" devised by Mary Ainsworth and her colleagues (Ainsworth, Blehar, Waters, & Wall, 1978), in which children are observed playing in the presence of a care-giver and a stranger, and their reactions to brief separations from and reunion with these individuals are studied. It transpires that many (not all) two- to five-year-old autistic children are like matched non-autistic retarded children in showing somewhat variable reactions to the departure of the care-giver, sometimes showing behavioural and/or mood changes such as fretting, and in responding to reunion by spending more time alongside the care-giver than the stranger. When allowance is made for their sometimes idiosyncratic behaviour, a substantial number of autistic children are rated as "securely attached" (Rogers et al., 1991; Shapiro et al., 1987). The children's relationship with their care-giver is clearly different from that with the stranger.

Such findings are certainly important, but they should not be overinterpreted. The "strange situation" is one powerful but rather circumscribed index of a child's attachment to someone else. It has proved to be immensely valuable for the study of individual differences in non-autistic children, but with markedly atypical children the general implications of the focussed observations are more difficult to assess. It is clear that a care-giver does matter in *some* way to autistic children, and this is reflected in unsubtle but telling signs of distress and affiliation on brief separation and reunion. What is less clear is how the care-giver comes to have this significance for autistic children, and how far the quality and longer-term implications of such "attachments" conform with those of non-autistic children (also Rogers et al., 1991). As we have seen, there are important respects in which autistic children do *not* relate to their parents normally. They often do not turn to their parents for comfort, they do not seem interested in sharing things and experiences, and they seldom seem to show a normal quality of caring towards these significant other people. There is still a long way to go before the nature of the autistic children's mental representations of themselves in relation to others, what John Bowlby (1973) has called "internal working models" and what psychoanalysts refer to as "internal object relationships", are understood (Hobson, 1990c).

SELF-DEVELOPMENT

It is not yet possible to provide an adequate account of early "self"-development in autistic children, although I have tried to make a start in this direction (Hobson, 1990a). The clinical vignettes of earlier chapters provide a rich source of insight into the children's relative lack of self-consciousness as well as their seeming obliviousness towards other people as "selves" with their own interests, inclinations, motives, sensibilities, and so on. In addition, I have already linked autistic children's dearth of imitation with their lessened propensity to identify with the attitudes of other people.

One of the most refined clinical-cum-theoretical accounts is that presented by Gerhard Bosch (1970) in a book entitled *Infantile autism* and subtitled (in translation): *A clinical and phenomenological-anthropological investigation taking language as the guide.* This fore-warns of the density of Bosch's writing, steeped as it is in the tradition of Husserl's phenomenological philosophy. In attempting to delineate "the particular mode of existence of an autistic child" (Bosch, 1970: p. 3), Bosch illustrates how the child often seems to lack a sense of possessiveness as well as self-consciousness and shame, to be delayed in "acting" on others by demanding or ordering, and to be missing something of "the 'self-involvement', the acting with, and the identification with the acting person" (p. 81). Bosch interprets the autistic child's delay in using "I" and "you" with reference to such "paths to the 'I' in language" (p. 64). He also suggests that "counter-attack or defense is impossible because the child has no experience of attacking or defensive relationship with others" (p. 99). Perhaps most prescient of all, he emphasises that "delay occurs in the constituting of the other person as someone in whose place I can put myself...[and]...in the constituting of a common sphere of existence, in which things do not simply refer to me but also to others" (p. 89).

I trust these brief quotations will suffice to convey the gist of some incisive and important clinical observations, which in my view have been sadly neglected. Many of the ideas await experimental investigation (which we have plans to pursue). Bosch pays special attention to self-development as reflected in personal pronoun usage, and this will provide a topic for the next chapter. Here I shall restrict myself to summarising relevant results from mirror-recognition studies of self-consciousness, to describing a recent investigation of pride, and then adding a few remarks about other dimensions of selfhood.

Young autistic children who are not severely cognitively impaired do remove rouge from their faces when they perceive themselves in a mirror (Dawson & McKissick, 1984; Neuman & Hill, 1978; Spiker & Ricks, 1984). What most autistics do *not* show, are the signs of coyness so typical of young normal and non-autistic retarded children. Thus autistic children can make use of their own reflections to register what it means to have their own body marked, and they are likely to act accordingly in trying to remove the mark from their faces. What is far less certain, is whether such behaviour is motivated by a concern with the way the child "looks" to other people, and with the evaluative attitudes that others may entertain in seeing them marked in an unusual manner. They perceive a body in the mirror, and recognise that this is the body towards which they can act in a self-directed way; but they may not conceive of themselves as "selves" in the minds of others (Hobson, 1990a).

This suggestion receives some support from a recent study conducted by Connie Kasari, Marian Sigman, and colleagues (Kasari, Sigman, Baumgartner, & Stipek, 1993) with their young autistic and non-autistic retarded subjects (mean age 42 months) and mental age-matched normal children (mean age 23 months). Each subject completed a puzzle, and the experimenter and parent reacted neutrally; then the child completed a second puzzle, and after three seconds, both adults gave praise. Although autistic children were like mentally retarded and normal children in being inclined to smile when they succeeded with the puzzles, autistic children were less likely to draw attention to what they had done or to look up to an adult, and less likely to show pleasure in being praised. Indeed a number of the autistic children were unusual in looking away from the adult after completing the puzzle or being praised. There seemed to be something missing or abnormal in the children's feelings towards the approval and attention they might gain from (and the experiences they might share with) the adults present.

There is a great deal more to be studied about autistic individuals' awareness and concepts of self. For example, little is understood of the ways autistic people conceptualise their own characteristics, including biological characteristics such as age and gender. Some years ago I too conducted some studies that have potential relevance for this topic. I was exploring the idea that a normal child's knowledge of what age differences and sex categories *mean* might partly depend upon biologically based propensities to perceive and relate to old and young individuals, and to males and females, in different ways. For example, I know what it is to be a man—from the inside, as it were, not merely in terms of being able to list male characteristics—in part because of my biological predisposition to relate to women and to men in ways that are special to women and to men. Or again, I know what a baby is, partly because of my innate tendencies to relate to babies with baby-appropriate attitudes. Although this might seem an implausible line of thinking (except perhaps to ethologists, e.g. Hess, 1970), it is relevant that even human infants seem to have perceptual and relational propensities that are reflected in early discrimination between males and females, and adults and children (e.g. Brooks & Lewis, 1976; Fagan, 1972, 1976; Miller, 1983). My hypothesis was that lacking this basic form of differentiation in perceptually anchored interpersonal relatedness, autistic individuals might for this reason find it difficult to appreciate the nature of age and sex in themselves and others.

I will not describe my studies in detail, mainly because I believe they have methodological limitations, and amount to pilot studies. The principal findings were that compared with normal and non-autistic retarded control subjects who were matched for non-verbal mental age, autistic subjects had difficulty in choosing drawings and then photographs of the faces of a man, a woman, a boy and a girl for such individuals depicted on videotape in characteristic gestures, vocalisations, and contexts (Hobson, 1987). In a further study (Hobson, 1983b), autistic children were less likely to sort photographs of people and animals according to age- and sex-related characteristics. If these results are borne out in further studies with more adequate control tasks than I employed, then one might wonder whether corresponding perceptual-relational abnormalities could augment autistic individuals' problems in identifying with others, and result in serious difficulties with sexual identity and orientation. Here is but one of many complex issues in the field of self-development that needs investigation.

CONCLUSION

In this chapter, I have covered a hotch-potch of issues that are gathered together under the umbrella of "personal relatedness" in autism. Whether in their capacities for relating to peers and adults; for understanding or producing behaviour to share experiences with other people; for reacting to others' distress or fear and for engaging in social referencing; for perceiving, expressing, and co-ordinating feelings in relation to others; for imitating another person's actions or attitudes; for becoming "attached" to other people; or for achieving basic forms of self- and other-awareness, autistic children appear to show signs of marked abnormalities at what would correspond to infant-level functioning in a normal individual. At the beginning of the chapter, I acknowledged that evidence derived from studies of autistic children well past infancy needs to be treated with circumspection, if it is to be used to support the idea that infant-level processes are disordered in autism. Having said this, there are also indications that at least in many autistic children, abnormalities in personal relatedness are early in onset and profound in degree.

When I step back and review these studies alongside the clinical observations of autistic individuals of all ages, I find myself convinced that abnormalities in perceptual-relational non-verbal communication and interpersonal-affective co-ordination are basic to most if not all cases of autism. Although there might be justification for tracing the cognitive dimensions of such disorder, I think it is misleading to characterise these as "cognitive" deficits and abnormalities. After all, the concept of "cognition" exists partly by virtue of the semantic contrasts with "conation" and "affect" (O'Neil, 1968), and yet matters of volition and feeling are integral to the abnormalities we have been considering. I believe the way forward is to conceptualise autistic children's fundamental disorder to be disruption in the usual, interpersonally co-ordinated patterns of intersubjective *relatedness*.

What remains evident, is that autistic individuals have cognitive deficits. I shall be arguing that an important class of such deficits that are characteristic of autism arise as developmental sequelae to the abnormalities in personal relatedness. Perhaps the most obvious candidates have to do with autistic individuals' concepts about other people and the self, especially concepts about people's minds. It is with these issues that the next chapter is concerned.

CHAPTER FIVE

The Growth of Interpersonal Understanding

In this chapter, I shall juxtapose a condensed review of research on the interpersonal understanding of normal two- to five-year-olds, with an equally abbreviated but hopefully representative account of parallel research that has been conducted with autistic individuals. My intention is to trace how autistic children's impoverished experience of personal relatedness has developmental implications for their limited grasp of concepts concerning the nature of people with minds. The psychological concepts in question are those that normal children acquire around their fourth birthday, such as concepts of belief and false belief, but they also include a number of less sophisticated mental state concepts and early manifestations of self–other understanding.

"EXPLICIT" INTERPERSONAL UNDERSTANDING IN NORMAL DEVELOPMENT

The transition between the first two years and later phases of childhood corresponds roughly with a momentous watershed in development—the acquisition of language. Up to now, I have attempted to follow the early development of interpersonal understanding by observing how a normal infant's social behaviour becomes increasingly elaborate and in some ways more adult-like over the first two years of life. With the advent of language, we have a new means to explore how much or how little the child understands about the nature of persons and of "selves". We can study the content of the child's spontaneous language, we can observe the contexts within which and purposes for which language is used, and we can ask the child questions or pose language-dependent problems to solve. Although it would be foolhardy to forsake naturalistic as well as experimental investigations in our enthusiasm for asking children questions—and the work of Judy Dunn (1988) serves to remind us of how we need to keep the multifarious goings-on of family life firmly in our sights if we are not to lose perspective—it is certainly the case that language affords unique insight into the mind of the speaking child. Therefore I shall now consider what we may discover by attending to the things that young children say.

Naturalistic Studies of Early Language

One place to start is with some observations on children's spontaneous speech. For example, when do children comprehend and use words that refer to people's mental states? This is not an easy question to answer. For instance, as Marilyn Shatz and her colleagues emphasise (Shatz, Wellman, & Silber, 1983), mental state terms are used for a variety of conversational functions (e.g. "you know" as a pause-filler), and even in other contexts it is difficult to establish whether children fully grasp the meanings of particular lexical items. One is on firmer ground when a child appears to contrast, say, belief with knowledge, or pretend with reality-oriented action. On the other hand, there is a danger of becoming over-conservative in appraising young children's understanding: when Shatz et al. (1983) claim that "attempts at mental reference begin to appear in some children's speech in the second half of the third year" (p. 301), they base this view on analyses of some carefully vetted speech involving words such as "remember", "think", "know", and "dream". It would be rash to conclude that younger children use such terms without any comprehension of their psychological meaning, and more especially, that terms applying to other mental states acquire psychological meanings only after this stage. Even on purely logical grounds, as Wittgenstein (1958) so forcefully indicated, the ways in which words "refer" to mental states may be more complex and various than such an account allows, for example when they replace natural expressions of feeling.

What, then, of younger children's usage of other mental state terms? Inge Bretherton, Sandra McNew, and Marjorie Beeghly-Smith (1981; also Bretherton & Beeghly, 1982) asked 32 mothers to say when their young children first produced internal-state labels, and whether she or he used them first to refer to herself/himself, to others, or to pictures. The mothers were first interviewed when their infants were ten and a half months old, then at 13 months and finally at 20 months old. The mothers were requested to supply a concrete example of each word use. These workers adopted a more liberal (but equally justifiable) stance than did Shatz and her colleagues, and included labels that describe affective expressions such as "kiss" or "cry" as well as more specifically psychological labels (such as "love", "happy", "mad", or "scared"), on the grounds that such words have strong connotations of emotional state. A relatively large proportion of 20-month-olds applied words of the former category to themselves and to others (as well as the "moral" terms "good" and "nice"), and a small but not negligible number used psychological labels such as sad, mad, scared, and hungry. When presented with pictures of emotionally expressive faces of children, twelve subjects spontaneously referred to pictures of sad children as "he cry", "crying", "baby cry", "uh-oh cry", sometimes with wiping of tears, imitation of crying noises, and kissing the baby picture. Through a review of the literature, Bretherton et al. (1981) also traced a number of examples in which children who had recently turned two years old seemed to be reasoning about the causes or resolution of mental states, such as two children of 25 months who said, "I'm sad I popped it" about a balloon, and "Those ladies scare me." A further study by Judy Dunn, Inge Bretherton, and Penny Munn (1987) which involved home recordings of conversations between mothers and their young children, confirmed that by 24 months of age, children were taking an active part in talking about feeling states such as those of sadness, distress, happiness, affection, and tiredness.

The above observations do not imply that children of this age understand all there is to know about mental states, nor that they understand very much about propositional states such as knowing or believing or thinking that such-and-such is the case. What they offer is a corrective to accounts that might imply too radical a disjunction between the child's understanding of behaviour and their understanding of mind. To achieve a balanced view we need to compare and contrast the aspects of mental state understanding available to children as they get older. One study of this kind (conducted by Bartsch & Wellman and cited in Wellman, 1991) compared children's first use of desire terms such as "want" and "wish", and belief terms such as "think", "know", "believe", and "understand", in their everyday speech. A distinction was drawn between those occasions on which the terms were used to talk of their own or others' internal subjective states, and those on which they referred to "external, objective aspects of behaviour and events" (p. 33). The findings were that reference to a character's desire by the term "want" was well established before the child's second birthday, but reference to belief by the terms "think" and "know" did not occur until just before the third birthday. This picture applied to the developmental progression of each and every individual child. In addition, two-year-olds showed evidence of distinguishing their own desires from those of others, but not until the age of three did they distinguish their own and others' beliefs.

Later Developments

Beyond a child's second birthday, it becomes possible to conduct systematic explorations of what the child understands or fails to understand about mental states. In order to condense this overview, I shall employ Henry Wellman's writings to frame an account of the developmental transitions that are taking place in preschool children's understanding of minds, and make only occasional references to the experimental work on which the account is based.

I shall pick up the story where we left off, with the two-year-old who is acquiring a rapidly expanding vocabulary and a more refined linguistic competence. According to Wellman (1990, 1991), two-year-olds are "internal state theorists" who attribute people with dispositions towards certain actions and objects, but not with a representational mind. With colleagues, he has demonstrated the kinds of reasoning available to these "desire psychology" two-year-olds (Wellman & Woolley, 1990). Children of this age were asked to make judgements about the actions and emotional reactions of story characters in each of three types of situation. In the first, a doll character wants something that may be in one of two locations, searches in one location and finds it. In the second, the character finds nothing in the searched location. In the third, the character finds an attractive object, but not the one that is said to be wanted. The children were asked how the character would act—and here the critical issue was whether or not she would go on searching—and how she would feel, happy or sad. The children solved these simple tasks with ease, for instance predicting sadness in both the "finds-nothing" and "finds-substitute" conditions.

Then the age of three years is something of a watershed. As Wellman expresses it: "Three-year-olds have achieved an initial understanding that people live their lives not simply with respect to an external world of objects but also with respect to an internal world of imaginings and beliefs, which complement, cause, and explain their actions" (Wellman, 1990: p. 316). So, for example, one can ask young children about the difference between a boy who has a cookie and one who has a thought about a cookie: which of these, the cookie or the thought about the cookie, could be seen by someone else, could be touched or could be transformed at will? Or one can pose similar questions about dreamt, remembered or pretended events: "Can you touch a dreamed tree with your hand?", "Why not?". When such questions were put to three-year-olds, the replies included: "No, because it's in his mind", "No, because he's just dreaming about it", "No, because he's thinking it and he can't see it" (Wellman & Estes, 1986). Children of this age already understood important differences between the mental and physical domains. Then the children were asked what a protagonist will do if she "thinks" that a desired object is in one place whereas it is really in another. Or they were required to reason backwards from a person's actions to that person's underlying beliefs and desires: "Jane is looking for her kitten. The kitten is hiding under a chair, but Jane is looking for her kitten under the piano. Why do you think Jane is doing that?" In a series of studies such as these, even three-year-olds often seemed to grasp how a person's beliefs and desires act in concert to produce actions (Bartsch & Wellman, 1989; Wellman & Bartsch, 1988). Even so, another year must pass before the children's understanding of beliefs and especially false beliefs is correctly applied across a range of contexts (e.g. Wimmer & Perner, 1983).

What does three-year-olds' understanding amount to? Wellman considers that such young children have only a "copy-container" view of the mind, whereby the mind comprises the sum of one's thoughts and one's thoughts are mirror-reflections or copies of reality. Beyond the age of three years, this rather primitive notion of representation is replaced by another in which thoughts, perceptions, beliefs, and so on are conceived of as construals or interpretations of reality. Now the mind is seen as an active processor and interpreter of reality. "What children begin to achieve at about four or five, therefore, is an interpretational or constructive understanding of representations rather than an initial understanding of representation" (Wellman, 1990: p. 244). In a similar vein, Forguson and Gopnik (1988) refer to the child's new-found appreciation of representational diversity. This relatively sophisticated concept of mental representation enables children to grasp how the same object can be represented in different, seemingly contradictory ways. From four years of age, for example, they become increasingly aware of the distinction between appearance and reality. They distinguish what an object "looks like" (it looks like a rock) from what it "really is" (it really is a sponge) (Flavell, 1988; Flavell, Green, & Flavell, 1986). The child can also understand how a person may have false beliefs about a situation, and how such misrepresentations of reality, rather than the true state of affairs in the world, may determine the person's actions. These kinds of accomplishment lead authors such as Josef Perner (1988) to identify the age of four and a half rather than three years as the point at which children acquire a concept of the "representational mind". Only now does the children's understanding of belief entail that they have a picture of the believer's mental model of a real situation.

So much for the development of mental state understanding in normal young children. How does this compare with the picture in autism?

THE CASE OF AUTISM

I shall begin by reviewing studies that have a specific focus on aspects of autistic individuals' comprehension of psychological states, and then consider the closely related issue of their awareness of self and other.

Concerning Mental States

The studies summarised in this section comprise but a limited selection of those that have a bearing on autistic children's interpersonal understanding. I am devoting the major part of a subsequent chapter to language development, and my intention here is to note how some unambiguously psychological concepts and terms function within the children's language.

One of the richest sources of data on the natural language of autistic children is a longitudinal study conducted by Helen Tager-Flusberg and her colleagues in Boston. A great strength of this investigation is the finesse with which computer-assisted analyses of the data are being conducted. Publications from the study are continuing to appear at the time of writing this chapter, and so I shall rely upon an early overview of the results provided by Tager-Flusberg (1989a). The approach was to take six high-functioning three-year-old boys with autism and six with Down's syndrome, and to record their conversations with their mothers at two-monthly intervals over a period of approximately two years. The subjects were matched for their mean length of utterance at the outset of the study. The autistic children were typical in having a marked delay in their language development, which meant that with this language-based matching procedure, they were more advanced than the Down's children in their more general cognitive abilities.

In order to study these children's spontaneous use of mental state terms such as think, know, and remember, Tager-Flusberg and her colleagues extracted from the transcripts all examples of the cognitive terms compiled in the studies of Shatz et al. (1983) and Bretherton et al. (1981), described in the previous section. Imitations, repetitions, and incomplete utterances were excluded, and the functions of the remaining utterances were coded. The findings were that the Down's syndrome children used almost three times as many mental state words (as narrowly defined), and significantly more different types of words that did the autistic children. In fact the autistic children together made a total of only four direct references to mental states such as think or know, whereas the Down's syndrome children made forty. When it came to the use of emotion terms, the group differences were not in the prevalence of the words (which in fact, the autistic children used more frequently), but rather in their relative frequency: autistic children used more "behaviour" terms such as laugh, cry, scream, or hug, whereas Down's syndrome children used more "feeling" terms such as love, happy, sad, and scared. On the other hand, autistic children used quite a lot of feeling terms to make reference to their own, and occasionally other people's, feelings—but most were either descriptions (e.g. "happy face") or reactions to an object or person (e.g. "I like this one"; "I love you"), and only a few were linked to events in a sophisticated way (e.g. "They big, and they were loud and the kids were loud and it scared me", from an autistic child with an IQ of 108). Finally, the two groups proved to be closely similar in the number and types of utterances referring to perception, except that amongst the Down's syndrome but not the autistic children, a high proportion of the terms (look, see, watch) were used to call the mother to engage in joint attention.

On the basis of these studies, then, Helen Tager-Flusberg concluded that the autistic children were specifically deficient in their ability to talk about mental or cognitive states such as thinking, knowing, and believing, even though they did not lack many of the requisite linguistic (syntatic and lexical) skills to do so. She considered that although the children's language for emotions was more advanced than their language for cognitive states, there was suggestive evidence that their understanding of affective experience in relation to events and "behaviour" was also less than fully developed.

Naturalistic studies of this kind have been complemented by more standardised investigations. We have already noted one study on autistic children's spontaneous production of emotion terms for photographed faces and recorded vocalisations (Hobson, Ouston, & Lee, 1989), and a number of tests of their comprehension of mental state terms will be described in the following section. A further linguistic study that might be mentioned at this stage employed a commonly used measure of language comprehension, the British Picture Vocabulary Scale (BPVS: Dunn, Dunn, & Whetton, 1982), to test for a specific kind of difficulty in comprehending emotion-related terms (Hobson & Lee, 1989). Indeed, the test had been administered for the purpose of matching subjects according to their general abilities in language comprehension, and it was only as an afterthought that my colleague Tony Lee and I decided to explore whether our two groups of relatively able autistic and non-autistic retarded subjects, pairwise matched for age and for ability on the test, might differ in their profile of scores when attaining identical levels of performance overall.

On the British Picture Vocabulary Scale, individuals are presented with a series of plates showing drawings arranged in groups of four. Subjects are given instructions such as "Point to...dentist", or "Show me...surprise", and they respond by indicating the appropriate picture. In order to select emotion-related and emotion-unrelated items for comparison, we asked colleagues who were unaware of the nature of our study to judge whether, in evaluating the meanings of the words with reference to the pictures, their judgements had reference to emotion (on a scale of 0 to 2). We also asked them to judge the items according to abstractness, which (following Paivio, Yuille, & Madigan, 1968) we defined as involving concepts that cannot be experienced by the senses. The emotion-related items included word-picture combinations that ranged from "horror" and "delighted" to more complex notions like "greeting" and "snarling". Although the majority of these were also included in the list of abstract items, this list also featured non-emotion terms such as "time", "pair", and "adjustable". Because the items of the test are arranged in order of increasing difficulty, it was possible to compare matched pairs of autistic and non-autistic subjects on emotion-related and emotion-unrelated items that are equally difficult for normal subjects. As expected, non-autistic retarded subjects achieved similar scores on the selected emotion-related and emotion-unrelated items, but in contrast, autistic subjects were specifically poorer on the emotion-related items. On the other hand, autistic and non-autistic subjects were equally able to judge non-emotion-related abstract words vis-à-vis equally difficult "concrete" words. This made it unlikely that the autistic children's difficulties in emotion-related understanding was simply a reflection of the greater abstractness of the words involved. Instead it seemed that on a linguistic–conceptual level, significant group differences were demonstrable specifically in the realm of emotional understanding.

There have also been two recent reports from Nurit Yirmiya, Marian Sigman, and colleagues on emotion understanding and role-taking in autistic children of normal IQ between nine and 17 years of age (Capps, Yirmiya, & Sigman, 1992; Yirmiya, Sigman, Kasari, & Mundy, 1992). These high-functioning children performed significantly less well than normally developing children on labelling emotions portrayed in videotaped stories, in reporting "empathic" feelings in response to the scenes depicted, and in assuming the protagonist's emotional perspective. On the other hand, the performance of the autistic children was often surprisingly good. The within-group correlation between task performance and IQ raises the possibility alluded to earlier, that some autistic children might use abnormal cognitive strategies in dealing with laboratory tasks of these kinds. It was also striking how the autistic children could give examples of when they had experienced both simple (happy, sad) and complex (pride, embarrassment) emotions; but they took longer, required prompts, and spoke in a more general and "scripted" (non-personal) way about the complex emotions, and less frequently made reference to the presence of others when talking of embarrassment. It remains somewhat uncertain how deeply they understood these concepts, and to what degree they experienced self-consciousness—a matter to which I have already made reference, and one to which I shall return.

The studies which follow also require subjects to understand the language in which the instructions and questions of the tasks are couched, but they adopt a more experimental style to explore the children's grasp of the concepts involved.

Experimental Studies of "Mental State" Concepts

One of the early studies in this area grew out of my own attempts to conduct a critical examination of Piaget's theory of the development of social cognition. I shall not go into the theory except to say that Piaget's claim was that young children's social adjustment and role-taking were constrained by their egocentrism. Such egocentrism was seen as a manifestation of the children's "preoperational" thought. This style of thinking was also reflected in the children's inability to understand how different people's visual perspectives are co-ordinated with one another, and their failure to grasp how (for example) quantities like number are conserved despite changes in the perceived arrangement of the numbered items. Not until thought is organised into a coherent, reversible system at about the age of seven years was there said to be a "transition from subjective centering in all areas to a decentering that is at once cognitive, social, and moral" (Piaget & Inhelder, 1969: p. 128). At this point, Piaget supposed, the child acquires notions of conservation and classification and along with these the insight that his own perspective is one of many.

Now I had already contributed to the growing literature suggesting that even preoperational normal three-year-olds have some grasp of the ways in which individuals' visual perspectives are systematically interrelated (Flavell, Botkin, Fry, Wright, & Jarvis, 1968; Hobson, 1980, 1982b). I had also emphasised how certain visuospatial tasks such as hide-and-seek might be solved by applying rudimentary principles of projective geometry (for example, by comprehending before–behind relations), rather than by focusing upon participants' "seeing experiences" as such (Flavell, 1974). This work augmented that of other researchers (e.g. Donaldson, 1978) in suggesting that the young child's social understanding, at least as evaluated by tasks that require relatively unsophisticated perceptual role-taking, was not constrained by the kinds of cognitive limitation identified by Piaget: even children who performed poorly in tests of operational thinking were able to comprehend a coherent system of relations of viewpoints independent of themselves. The question now arose, whether a group of children who were selected for their profound difficulties in the more social aspects of role-taking—namely autistic children with their insensitivity to the expectations, interests, or feelings of other people—would have corresponding disability in visuospatial perspective-taking and in operational thinking.

In order to examine this issue, I gave a series of Piagetian tests (including a number conservation task) and tests of visuospatial role-taking to groups of autistic, normal, and Down's syndrome children (Hobson, 1984). The visuospatial tasks comprised a quite complex set of hide-and-seek problems using three miniature pipe-cleaner figures, and another set of problems in which the children had to judge what one or two dolls could "see" when placed in various positions around a multicoloured cube. The principal finding was that the autistic children performed very well in the perspective-taking tasks, and better on the cube tasks than Down's children of similar verbal ability. It was clear that these autistic children had understood *something* of what it means to "see", and they were well able to co-ordinate a number of doll-perspectives at once.

I added a number of caveats to these conclusions. First, I noted John Flavell's (1974) observation that a young child might be unable to anticipate or otherwise represent to himself anyone's seeing experiences as such, and yet make sense of the question "What am I (you, he) looking at?" by reconstructing it in some such form as "What is on my (your, his) side of the display?" Second, as Carolyn Shantz (1975) had argued, a person's judgement about another's visual perspective is the least social of the various types of "social inference", for anyone and everyone who views an object or array from a particular location has an identical viewpoint. To judge what another person sees is a very different matter from discerning their thoughts, feelings, and intentions. These theoretical points, as well as the empirical findings, have been developed in subsequent studies by Alan Leslie and Uta Frith (1988) and Jacinta Tan and Paul Harris (1991) on autistic children's relative ability to understand "seeing". What remains open to question is whether there are limitations in autistic individuals' grasp that people may differ in *how* they see things, or in what they see things *as*, and even whether they have delay in acquiring such understanding as they have (for very young and retarded autistic children have not been tested on appropriate tasks). It is probable that there will be autism-specific problems in these respects. To see why, we can turn to experimental studies of other aspects of the children's social understanding.

A most important programme of research was launched with a study conducted by Simon Baron-Cohen, Alan Leslie, and Uta Frith, and published in 1985 under the title: *Does the autistic child have a "theory of mind"?* These investigators employed a task originally devised by Heinz Wimmer and Josef Perner (1983) which was designed to test children's understanding of what it means for a person to have a false belief. The importance of "false belief" is that it is a mental state in which a person entertains a representation of reality which does not correspond to "true" reality, but which nevertheless determines the person's behaviour. Therefore a child who understands "false belief" is one who understands the nature of the relationship between the representing mind and reality-as-represented, even in the specially difficult case of misrepresentation (Perner, 1991). Wimmer and Perner (1983) had already presented evidence that such understanding is acquired by normal children around four years of age—but what is the situation with autistic children?

The experimental paradigm was delightfully simple. There were two doll protagonists, Sally and Anne. There was a basket in front of Sally and a box in front of Anne. Sally first placed a marble into her basket. Then she left the scene, and while she was away Anne transferred the marble from Sally's basket into her own box, where it was hidden from view. When Sally returned, the experimenter asked the critical "belief question": "Where will Sally look for her marble?" There were two additional questions to test the children's understanding of the events and of the language employed: "Where is the marble really?" and "Where was the marble at the beginning?" Then the scenario was repeated, except that the marble was hidden in the experimenter's pocket.

The experiment was conducted with 20 able autistic children aged between six and 16 years and with a mean verbal mental age of five and a half years, 14 children with Down's syndrome who were similar in age but had significantly lower verbal ability, and 27 normal children with a mean age of four and a half years. The results were that all subjects answered the control questions about where the marble really was now, and where it was at the beginning, but clear group differences emerged on the question that hinged on an understanding of Sally's false belief about the marble's location. Approximately 85% of the normal and Down's syndrome children indicated that Sally would look in her basket, but only 20% of autistic children did so. All 16 autistic children who responded "incorrectly" pointed to where the marble really was. Thus only four autistic children, but the majority of the Down's and normal children who were generally lower in mental age than the autistic group, demonstrated their understanding that their own knowledge of where the marble really was differed from the incorrect belief held by the doll.

A second early study by Baron-Cohen, Leslie, and Frith (1986) tested subjects' abilities to order sequences of pictures according to the storyline depicted. Some of the stories involved mechanical events such as a man kicking a rock down a hill; others involved social routines like a boy dressing or a girl buying sweets from a shop; and others involved scenarios in which something happened unbeknownst to the main protagonist (for example, sweets dropped out of his bag, or a teddy was taken surreptitiously), and the figure showed an expression of surprise. The autistic children differed from control subjects in being very proficient in all but the latter form of task, the only one which required an understanding of mental states. Not only this, but when asked to narrate the stories depicted, the autistic children differed from the normal and Down's children in being relatively sophisticated in their appropriate use of physical-causal terms and yet abnormal in using very few mental state expressions such as want, believe, and know. This latter result accords with the findings from Helen Tager-Flusberg's naturalistic study of autistic children's language discussed earlier.

I shall select four further studies to exemplify the style of research conducted in what has come to be called the "theory of mind" approach to understanding autism. The first is in fact a set of three related studies in which Simon Baron-Cohen (1989b) adapted tasks designed by Henry Wellman, John Flavell, and colleagues to assess "theory of mind" abilities in normal children (e.g. Flavell, Flavell, & Green, 1983; Johnson & Wellman, 1982; Wellman & Estes, 1986). In the first task, pairs of dolls were introduced with stories of the following form: "This is Sam. He likes biscuits. He is hungry, so his mother gives him a biscuit. This is Kate. She is hungry, but she is all alone. She is *thinking* about a biscuit." There were four such stories, one each for think, remember, pretend, and dream. For each of these the child was asked questions like: (1) "Which child can eat the biscuit?"; (2) "Which child can touch the biscuit?"; and, to check that the events had been understood and remembered, (3) "Which child was given a biscuit?" The results were that approximately three-quarters of the normal and non-autistic mentally retarded subjects scored at least seven out of eight correct on the former two tasks, but only a quarter of the autistic subjects did so. This occurred despite the fact that the autistic children were at least as able as the non-autistic children on a test of verbal ability, and they passed all the tests of memory in the tasks.

The second in this set of tasks required these same subjects to answer questions about the brain and the heart. The large majority of subjects in each group could answer correctly about the location and function of the heart, and the location of the brain; but once again, whereas about three-quarters of the non-autistic subjects referred spontaneously to mental functions of the brain such as "thinking", only one-quarter of autistic subjects did so, and most of the remainder referred to the brain's role in instigating behaviour (e.g. "It makes you move", or "running and walking").

The third task involved items that required the children to distinguish between appearance and reality. For example, they were given a realistic plastic chocolate. When asked "What is it?", all the children said it was a chocolate. They were invited to handle it, and when asked "What is it made of?", the children replied that it was made of plastic. The Appearance Question was "What does it look like?", and the Reality Question was "What is it really?" The results were comparable to those already reported, with two-thirds of the non-autistic groups but one-third of the autistic children consistently responding correctly. The majority of the errors made by autistic children involved the claim that the object was really the way it appeared to be—and indeed, a number of autistic children persisted in trying to eat the plastic chocolate! In contrast, the normal and mentally retarded subjects tended to laugh at the fake food and make comments like "It's pretend chocolate!" As Baron-Cohen discusses, such findings might indicate that the autistic children were unable to conceptualise their own knowledge about the world, and instead were dominated by perceptual information.

The matter of "trickery" was at the focus of a study by Beate Sodian and Uta Frith (1992). The approach was especially inventive in comparing autistic and control children for their ability to thwart and sabotage the efforts of a nasty wolf-doll, as well as to deceive the doll-figure by influencing its "beliefs". There was also a condition in which the children assisted a friendly doll, either by acting appropriately or by providing helpful information. The most telling arrangement was one in which there was a single box that could be locked with a padlock. The child was told to hide a Smartie (M & M) in the box, and then to help a "nice smartie friend" to find it, or to prevent a "nasty smartie eater" from finding it. In the sabotage condition there was a key to lock the box, and the children were asked: "Do you want to lock the box or do you want to leave it open?" In the deception condition there was no key, and the puppets said that they couldn't see if the box was locked, and if it was, they wouldn't bother to make the long walk. The nice and nasty puppets appeared separately, and enquired: "Is this box locked or is it open?" The experimenter then asked the child: "What do you want to say? Do you want to say it is locked or do you want to say it is open?" If the child lied to the nasty puppet, or told the truth to the nice puppet, she was rewarded with a smartie, but if she told the truth to the nasty puppet, she was not. Subjects were also tested on a version of the classic (Sally–Anne-type) false belief task.

Although the results from this and complementary procedures were not entirely clear-cut (and as the authors noted, one cannot be sure of whether the elaborate language of the tasks might have been difficult for autistic subjects), one finding was that when the results were adjusted for subjects' mental ages, the autistic children's performance on the sabotage condition (locking the box for the foe, leaving it open for the friend) was as good as that of the control subjects, whereas they were significantly less likely to deceive the nasty puppet whilst telling the truth to the nice puppet. In addition, all subjects' performances on the standard false belief test (at which again, autistic subjects did poorly) predicted performance on the deception task, suggesting that both tasks were tapping the same underlying cognitive ability. It seemed to be the autistic children's understanding of the significance of beliefs that was critical, not simply a difficulty in grasping the point of the adversarial/collaborative game.

Simon Baron-Cohen's (1991) adaptation of a paradigm devised by Alison Gopnik and Virginia Slaughter (1991) provides a kind of overview of autistic children's difficulties with mental state terms, this time in the context of the subjects' recall of their own previous mental state. Tests of understanding, perception, desire, imagination, pretence, and belief all took a similar form. In the "imagination" test, for example, subjects were told to close their eyes and think about a big, white teddy bear, to make a picture of it in their head. When subjects confirmed that they had such an image, they were told to change it to a red balloon. Having done this, they were asked: "When I first asked you to make a picture in your head, what were you thinking of then? (Did you think of a white teddy or a red balloon?)" In one of the perception tasks, subjects were shown one picture and then another, and again they were asked about the first picture they saw. The pretend task involved pretending to drink orange juice and then milk, and so on.

The large majority of the subjects in each of the three groups tested (autistic, non-autistic retarded, and normal children, with the autistic subjects having somewhat higher verbal abilities) were able to recall their earlier-stated perceptions and desires. However, although the non-autistic groups performed at ceiling on the imagination and pretence tasks, only 60% of the autistic children recalled their earlier-imagined objects, and 47% recalled their prior pretence. All groups found a "belief" task more difficult—here the children found a ball within a milk carton, having believed it contained milk—but again the autistic subjects performed least well.

I hope these examples convey the current state of play in an intriguing research venture (which also includes studies by Leslie & Frith, 1988; Perner, Frith, Leslie, & Leekam, 1989; and Ozonoff et al., 1991a, 1991b). A final study, again from Baron-Cohen's prodigious body of work (1989c), is of special interest because it investigated the subgroup of autistic individuals (often 20–30% of groups tested, but varying with task and subject selection) who succeed on "theory of mind" tasks. The task involved a fairly complex story played out by miniature figures, but the crux was whether the child could judge how one doll (Mary) could predict what another doll (John) would do, when Mary had a false belief about John having a false belief (Mary wrongly thought that John incorrectly believed an ice-cream van would be in the park, whereas John had been corrected by being told that it would actually be by the church). The result was that autistic children who had succeeded in the standard tests of "first-order belief attribution" nevertheless failed on this second-order task, whereas a number of Down's syndrome and normal seven-year-olds of comparable verbal mental age succeeded. This suggests that even autistic children who manage to acquire some understanding of "false belief" may have difficulty in dealing with more taxing situations involving one person's thoughts about another person's thoughts.

"I" and "You"

I considered the early "self"-development of normal children in Chapter 3, and introduced the complexities of related phenomena in autism by presenting the views of Bosch (1970) in Chapter 4. I have postponed a more detailed consideration of autistic children's use of personal pronouns until this point, because I want to emphasise the close relation between the development of self- and other-awareness, and the earliest developments in conceptualising mental states. I say "earliest" developments, and in a way this section would be equally well-placed at the end of the previous chapter. The reason is that in normal children, the beginnings of personal pronoun comprehension and use occur very soon after the emergence of multiword utterances, towards the end of the second year and into the third year of life. Thus personal pronouns appear at roughly the same time as children begin to make references to mental states such as feelings.

This is more than a matter of temporal coincidence, however. There is an intrinsic, logical connection between understanding "self", "other", and "psychological attitude". To begin with, it is essential to the concept of a mental state that is can be ascribed to a person or animal to whom it belongs (Strawson, 1962). In other words, to *conceptualise* a mental state is also to conceptualise what it means to be a subject of experience, and this is a part of what it means to be a "self". A full understanding of self-hood entails that a child understands the range of attitudes (e.g. of embarrassment, acquisitiveness, competitiveness, jealousy, and so on) which selves may experience. The significance of all this is that we need to characterise the processes that affect self-other connectedness and differentiation in order to account for the development of mental state understanding, just as we need to analyse mental state understanding in order to account for developments in self-conceptualisation. This may seem an obvious and trivial point, but we have seen that a focus on the self draws our attention to the complex structuring of self-experience. In so doing, it highlights a range of psychological issues that are currently marginalised in discussions of children's "theory of mind".

What, then, of autistic people's concepts of self? As my concern is with the growth of interpersonal understanding, I shall not consider those aspects of self-awareness that might be derived from "I–It" transactions with the world, even though they have relevance here (Hobson, 1990a). Instead I shall concentrate on the aspect of self-expression that has received most attention to date—the comprehension and use of the pronouns "I" and "you".

First I shall provide a background to the more experimental investigations. Leo Kanner considered that for the autistic children of his original sample, personal pronouns "*are repeated just as heard,* with no change to suit the altered situation" (Kanner, 1943: p. 244). One result of the child's tendency to "echo" other people is that pronouns become misplaced, for example when the autistic child says "Do you want a bath?" to express the desire to have a bath. Observations such as those of Gerhard Bosch (1970) indicate that pronouns may also be used incorrectly in non-echolalic utterances, that sometimes the autistic child may make third-person self-references by naming himself or calling himself "he", and that the child may substitute passive constructions for what would normally be expressed in assertive first-person statements. This suggests that there is something unusual about the child's experience of himself as a self *vis-à-vis* others. One might even consider whether echolalia itself arises from limitations in self-other differentiation and/or self-conception (Mahler, 1968). As Kanner (1943) illustrates, echolalia is the use of someone else's language unmodified according to the vantage-point of the child in the child's own setting. Instead of relating the other person's utterance to that person's attitude and then identifying with the other person's stance, autistic children tend to adopt speech forms that correspond with *their* experience of the circumstances in which the words are uttered, and therefore to repeat utterances as heard (Charney, 1981). There is a failure to recognise and assume the other person's attitude-in-speaking (also Hobson, 1990a; Roth & Leslie, 1991). Thus we see how impairments in personal-social understanding might be at the root of autistic children's linguistic role-taking deficits.

In accordance with this perspective, I have suggested that autistic children's relative delay in recognising reciprocal roles in dialogue arises through their failure to comprehend the commonality between the experiences of themselves and others, and the differentiation of different people's affective-conative attitudes and perspectives. Helen Tager-Flusberg (1989a: p. 9) has taken a similar approach in pointing to autistic children's lack of understanding "that people have different conceptual perspectives—that people perceive, interpret, remember, value, and respond affectively to situations in unique ways". Together with additional developmental obstacles of a cognitive and perhaps grammatical nature (Fay, 1979), such deficits appear sufficient to encompass autistic children's difficulties in recognising people as centres of subjectivity and as the occupants of reciprocal roles in discourse.

What evidence that exists is compatible with such an account. For example, Rita Jordan (1989) recorded the responses of autistic, non-autistic mentally retarded and normal children matched for verbal mental age (between three and ten years) when given simple instructions such as "Make the doll kiss you/me". Most subjects were able to comprehend the personal pronouns in these contexts. On the other hand, the majority of autistic children were unusual in responding to such prompts as "Now the puppet's tickling...?" by giving proper names to themselves or the experimenter rather than using the pronouns "me" or "you", or they used incorrect pronouns or unusual forms of pronoun such as "I" instead of "me". The pattern of results is suggestive that the children were using abnormal forms of self- and other-reference, not merely echoing. The findings are complemented by those of Helen Tager-Flusberg (1989a), whose recordings of young autistic and language-matched Down's children's conversations with their mothers have revealed pronoun reversal errors only amongst the autistic children. Such errors occurred in about 12% of instances of pronoun use, for example where the autistic child might have been asking a question through a form of utterance that would have been appropriate had the mother rather than the child been speaking. What is also interesting about these results, is that the children were able to use pronouns *correctly* in the remaining 88% of instances! It is also of note that in a study by Kate Loveland and Susan Landry (1986), correct production of I/you pronouns by autistic children was related to the number of their spontaneous initiations of joint attention with an experimenter. This suggests that correct usage may reflect a special quality of engagement and "co-reference" between self and other.

Finally, there is a study recently completed by my colleagues Tony Lee, Shula Chiat and myself (Lee, Hobson, & Chiat, 1993). We took groups of autistic and non-autistic retarded adolescents who were closely matched for age and verbal ability. To begin with, we ascertained from teachers whether the children had current problems in personal pronoun usage. There was not a single non-autistic subject who had such a problem, but according to two independent informants, 17 out of 25 autistic subjects did so. A typical example cited was that of a young autistic boy who approached his teacher on her return from sick leave and said: "I'm better now".

We presented a series of tests to these subjects. For the first experiment, we fixed drawings of two familiar objects (e.g. a spade and a teddy bear) on either side of a sheet of cardboard. This we held upright so that the experimenter could see one picture and the child the other. Having learned what the two pictures were, the child's task was to say *who* could see each picture, or to respond to questions such as "What can I/you see?", when the cardboard sheet was rotated between trials so that the picture in front of the participants was systematically varied. Contrary to our prediction, autistic subjects were as able as control subjects both in using and in comprehending personal pronouns. This was not because pronouns were always used correctly, for in each group there were children who did not understand our questions or who employed proper names in place of pronouns. We found this a convincing and surprising demonstration that despite the teacher reports of sporadic pronoun difficulties, these relatively able autistic adolescents had achieved a firm grasp of speech-role-referring pronouns.

Like Tager-Flusberg, therefore, we found a mixture of abnormality and "normality" in personal pronoun usage. In such a developmentally advanced group of subjects, we cannot say whether there had been delay in acquiring the ability to use pronouns (in fact, we believe there often is such delay), but we can state that in some contexts these autistic individuals were as competent as non-autistic subjects of similar "general" verbal ability. The question arises: in what contexts might the reported abnormalities be revealed, and what might these tell us about the dimensions of self-awareness in autism?

Our subsequent experiments were intended to investigate how the autistic subjects of our sample employed personal pronouns when referring to photographs of themselves and the experimenter. Again our prediction was that autistic subjects would be less able to comprehend, and less likely to produce, personal pronouns in these circumstances. The method consisted of presenting pairs of photographs to subjects, and asking a simple question as the experimenter pointed to each in turn: "Who is this a picture of?", or in another condition, "Who is wearing the hat/scarf?" Although there were no errors at all in tests of comprehension (e.g. "Point to me/you"), the large majority of lower-ability autistic subjects consistently referred to themselves and the experimenter by their proper names, whereas most of the matched control subjects tended to use personal pronouns. This result was partly replicated in our final experiment, where we presented each subject with a pile of photographs of their peers, inserted amongst which was a photograph of the subject and another of the experimenter. The instructions were to "tell me who they are". There was a significant overall group difference in that autistic subjects were less likely than non-autistic subjects to call the experimenter "you", although in this case there was not a statistically significant difference in first-person pronoun usage.

These findings suggest that even amongst autistic subjects who have acquired relative proficiency in personal pronoun use, there might be something abnormal about the content of their understanding of "I"/"me" and "you", and/or something atypical in the attitudes they adopt when employing these pronouns. Such abnormalities might be reflected in unusual patterns of usage rather than in globally incorrect use. Whilst our autistic subjects had acquired the *ability* to comprehend and produce speech-role-referring pronouns, there were significant group differences in the *propensity* to use specific forms of expression in particular circumstances. In the photograph-naming tasks, for example, they were sometimes less likely to employ the pronoun "you" than to name the experimenter. This pattern was most marked for lower-ability subjects, and accords with the results reported by Rita Jordan (1989; also Silberg, 1978).

Our tentative interpretation of the results, is that they reflect abnormalities in the way autistic children sense and (probably) conceptualise self and other in relation to one another. In our own study, such abnormalities were not manifest as deficits in role-taking, because many of these particular subjects *could* comprehend and employ the pronouns "I", "me", and "you" in speech-role-appropriate ways, and "pronoun reversals" were rare. Rather, there seemed to be a relative lack of the expression of a sense of "me-ness" and "you-ness" in autistic subjects' responses. By these terms I mean the kinds of self-experience emphasised by authors such as Charles Cooley (1902), Gerhard Bosch (1970), and Daniel Stern (1985), who write of the senses of agency, appropriation, affectivity, and continuity, as well as forms of self-reflective awareness such as self-consciousness and pride. It matters if it is "me" who achieves something, or "me" who is being the object of attention. Such anchorage in self-experience may not be as secure for autistic as for non-autistic individuals (Hobson, 1990a).

If this is the case, then even when autistic individuals have achieved the *potential* for adequate speech-role-referring pronoun use, they might be subject to lapses in their propensity to identify with others in role-appropriate ways—hence the reports of sporadic echolalia and pronoun reversals—and they might be prone to experience themselves in a relatively uncommitted manner. In our own tasks, for example, autistic subjects' use of names and not pronouns for photographs might have reflected a relatively detached, almost third-person attitude to these depictions of themselves and the experimenter. In contrast, non-autistic subjects seemed to identify with the photographs of themselves, and to see and care about the photographed person as "me". The images were infused with the subjects' and experimenter's *sense* of identity as well as formal identity. Autistic subjects seemed less likely to become engaged or confer subjectivity in this way.

When considering such an account, it is essential to recognise that our experiments involved more than subjects responding to sets of materials. They also involved the current interpersonal relations (and background relationships) between subject and experimenter. In this regard, it is relevant to note that the autistic subjects had long-standing contact with ourselves, and that we were careful to make efforts to engage all subjects on a personal level during the tasks. Despite this, autistic subjects' *current* behaviour suggested emotional unengagement with the experimenter, and this may have directly influenced their relatively greater use of nouns than pronouns in the photograph tasks. In other words, the present testing situation may have highlighted deficits in the interpersonal sphere that constitute the background to autistic individuals' specific problems in acquiring, as well as using, personal pronouns.

CONCLUSION

I hope this chapter has made it clear how autistic children have specific limitations in their concepts about people's minds, and probably in their awareness of self. Normal young children are talking about feelings and using personal pronouns before the end of their second year, they are beginning to use terms like "think" and "know" by the end of their third year, and they are acquiring an understanding of beliefs as construals of reality around the age of four. Autistic children who are comparable to such children in general verbal ability, are specifically impaired in conceptualising the nature of their own and other people's mental states, and they are probably less firmly anchored in using personal pronouns correctly. For example, young autistic children are delayed in using such words as "think", "know", "believe", and "remember", and their emotion-words tend to have behavioural anchorage; older autistic children have specific difficulty in understanding and/or recalling emotion-related terms, beliefs, pretended and imagined events, and they seem not to fully appreciate the mental–physical and appearance–reality distinctions; and yet older autistic children are at least delayed in understanding one person's thoughts about another person's thoughts. On the other hand, autistic children appear to recognise something (perhaps not everything) about what it means for people to "see", and many achieve a firm grasp of *certain* aspects of personal pronoun usage.

I opened this chapter by intimating that autistic children might be constrained in acquiring concepts of mind and of the self because they have impoverished experience of interpersonal relatedness. I shall need to justify this line of reasoning. There are alternative ways to explain the conceptual deficits I have outlined. For example, Alan Leslie (1987) proposes that autistic children suffer an innate, primary impairment in the ability to represent the mental representations of people. In my own view (Hobson, 1990b), this is essentially a redescription of the phenomenon under consideration. In addition, of course, there is Leslie's claim about the

innateness of certain cognitive mechanisms that are inoperative in autistic children. This entails a claim about the inappropriateness of a further developmental explanation for such cognitive mechanisms or deficits in interpersonal-relational terms. In order to examine what is at stake here, if not to resolve the debate, it may be worthwhile to reflect on the nature and basis for knowledge of persons with minds. This is the topic of the next chapter.

CHAPTER SIX

Conceptual Issues I:
On Understanding Minds

This is the first of two chapters in which I shall be dealing with theoretical matters concerning normal development. I shall begin by taking up familiar themes on the nature of interpersonal relatedness and the growth in a child's understanding of minds. I shall turn to one especially significant psychological concept that a child needs to acquire—the concept of "belief"—and consider how an analysis of the concept might bring out what it is that a child grasps in understanding what "beliefs" are. I shall suggest that the child needs to recognise what it means to take a correct or incorrect view of "reality", where the "correct view" is that which any right-minded person would assent to. In the background to such understanding of (potentially) agreed-upon reality, is the child's awareness of and engagement with other people's attitudes towards the world and towards each other. It is only through an appreciation of what attitudes are, that an individual *could* understand what it means to agree, to be corrected, or indeed "to hold as true". The final step in the argument is that in order to conceptualise a partly covert attitude such as that of belief, a child needs to be endowed with more fundamental (and in fact, earlier-appearing) capacities to *perceive* a range of overt, bodily-expressed attitudes in other people. If the argument is valid, it reveals how an account of a child's developing conceptualisation of so-called "cognitive" states needs to invoke considerations that also have to do with the interpersonal perception and understanding of mental states that involve affective attitudes.

This discussion will lead directly on to the chapter that follows, about the nature of language and thought. That in turn will set the scene for Chapter 8, in which I return to the subject of autism and consider the cognitive and linguistic impairments that characterise the disorder. The final chapter is devoted to reviewing and reframing what has gone before.

Background

There are many levels of interpersonal understanding. I shall be arguing that the very concept of "persons" with minds is founded upon preconceptual forms of awareness that people are different from things in affording intersubjective contact. The thesis is that infants are biologically "prewired" to relate to people in ways that are special to people, and that it is through the experience of reciprocal, affectively patterned interpersonal contact that a young child comes to apprehend and eventually to conceptualise the nature of persons with mental life.

Now it is commonly supposed that human beings perceive other people's bodies in a rather detached manner, much in the way they perceive non-personal things. By way of contrast, it is acknowledged as obvious that human beings *think* about people as rather special kinds of "thing". In particular, we ascribe mental states to people, recognising that people but not things think, feel, believe, intend, and so on. Many such mental states have "mental content"—a person is known to believe *that* such-and-such is the case, or to feel unhappy *that* this or the other situation has arisen. The question arises, therefore, how it could be that the developing child moves from the perception of bodies to conceptions of mind. How does a child come to acquire the notion that "bodies" are sources of agency and centres of subjective experience, each with an individual psychological orientation towards the world?

These are matters of philosophy as well as psychology. The nature of and basis for our understanding of Other Minds has long been a topic of philosophical controversy (Malcolm, 1962). I shall be considering how the philosophical issues have surfaced in the work of contemporary developmental psychology.

Central to my approach is the following idea: if we begin with a radical division between "perceiving bodies" and "understanding minds", then we shall never put Humpty Dumpty together again. The first priority is to choose the right place from which to embark on our theorising. I think we need to start with the concept of "modes of relatedness". Relatedness has perceptual anchorage, it has cognitive dimensions, and it is motivational and emotional in quality. We can choose to describe each of these aspects in turn, but we cannot reduce relatedness to what is perceptual, what is cognitive, and so on. Or to put this another way, relatedness is not "non-perceptual" (infants relate to what they see and hear, for example); it is not "non-cognitive" (in a practical sense, infants are making categorical distinctions in relating differently to people and things, and in relating differently to different kinds of people or thing); and it is certainly not "non-motivational" nor "non-emotional" (infants become intensely engaged with the world as perceived and categorised). It is out of primary forms of relatedness that children develop what are called "perceptual", "cognitive", "conative", and "affective" psychological functions. As Martin Buber (1984: p. 18) writes: "In the beginning is relation".

This suggestion is not a counsel for conceptual nihilism. We need to make distinctions among contrasting forms and mechanisms of psychological activity. The proposal is that we may need to characterise various modes of relatedness between the infant and her world, and to examine how these contribute to development and articulate with each other. Following Martin Buber (1984), I believe there is a fundamental distinction between I–Thou (interpersonal) and I–It (person-with-things) relations (Bower,1979; Hobson, 1985; Trevarthen, 1982). I–Thou relations are constituted by specialised forms of perceptual/cognitive/ motivational/ emotional transactions with the world, and especially with other people. My thesis is that the very young child's I–Thou and I–It experiences conjoin to yield mature conceptual understanding of minds on the one hand, and a faculty for creative symbolic imagination on the other.

I have laid the groundwork for this approach in my earlier account of normal infancy and early childhood. I began by describing interpersonal relatedness in early infancy, then worked through the first few years of life towards the time when children acquire adult-style concepts of mind. In this chapter I shall take a different tack, beginning with a consideration of more sophisticated mental concepts in order to analyse the conditions that allow such concepts to be acquired at all. Before doing this, however, I shall provide a sketch of current psychological theory in this domain. My intention is to highlight some strengths and weaknesses in contemporary perspectives.

"THEORY OF MIND"

We can begin with two points that have contributed to the view that a child's understanding of minds amounts to a theory. These were first articulated by David Premack and Guy Woodruff (1978: p. 515), as follows:

> In saying that an individual has a theory of mind, we mean that the individual imputes mental states to himself and to others (either to conspecifics or to other species as well). A system of inferences of this kind is properly viewed as a theory, first, because such states are not directly

observable, and secondly, because the system can be used to make predictions, specifically about the behavior of other organisms.

Henry Wellman (1990) takes a similar stance on these matters. He emphasises how notions of belief, desire, intentions, and so on form a coherent network of interrelated concepts that combine to provide an explanatory system which serves to account for action. He, too, is impressed by the potential non-observability of mental states. Wellman (1990: pp. 94–95) provides a link between these two lines of thought, as follows:

> Ascriptions of mental states seem to be "inferences to a best explanation", inferences to a larger meaningful account. In part, mental states cannot be simple empirical generalizations because there is no set of observable activities in self or other that consistently correlates with inferred mental states. There are no actions inevitably connected to having a desire, no consistent introspectable state of conviction essential to having a belief. If no neutral observational or experiential data dictate the inferences of mental states, what does? Observation and experience play their parts but, in addition, some intervening conceptual filter seems to stand between observation or experience and knowledge of mind, a theoretical lens that organizes the latter out of the former.

I quote this passage not because I am fully in agreement with its argument, plausible though this is, but rather because it presents and attempts to resolve developmental questions that arise in connection with the two attributes of belief already identified. First, how is it that mental state concepts bear an appropriate relation to the actions that they serve to explain? Answer: because they are "inferred" from behaviour, in order to perform this very explanatory function. Second, how could it be that "knowledge of mind" arises out of "observation and experience", when the connectedness between "mind" and observable "behaviour" is so tenuous? Answer: concepts of mind do not arise in this way. Instead they are theory-generated hypothetical constructs applied to observations of behaviour. In due course I shall take issue with these suggestions.

WHAT IT MEANS
TO UNDERSTAND "BELIEF"

The next step is to characterise what it is that three- or four-year-olds have acquired in arriving at their understanding about the nature of people's mental attitudes in relation to the world. I shall follow other psychologists and philosophers in starting with a highly restricted focus on the understanding of belief. The reason for this is that I want to explicate the route by which young children have come to grasp this most quintessential of "representational" mental states. It is customary to think of adults' understanding of the mind as a belief–desire psychology, in that one frequently interprets and explains behaviour in such terms as: "She looked in the cupboard because she wanted the salt and believed it to be there". Although one might be forgiven for wondering whether quite so much of our understanding of minds is captured by this simple scheme, it does succeed in highlighting a prominent characteristic of adult reasoning in the psychological domain. If we can establish what it means to conceive of persons as having beliefs and desires, therefore, we should be able to specify the prerequisites for acquiring mental state concepts of these kinds. This will enable us to work backwards in our efforts to trace the origins of such understanding of other people's mental lives. The thrust of my argument will be that a great deal of an individual's emotional as well as cognitive life, and a great deal of the individual's specifically social experience, must enter the picture if that individual is to be in a position to understand the concept of belief.

For the moment, then, I want to pursue an analysis of the concept of "belief". To have a belief is to believe something to be true. Correspondingly, a child who understands the nature of beliefs and false beliefs understands that a person who has such beliefs holds that the beliefs represent an actual state of affairs. Otherwise, the beliefs would not be understood as beliefs, but rather as something else—merely as perspectives, points of view, fancies even. It is for this reason that Josef Perner speaks of the requirement that one who understands belief should "model the process of informational contact" between the believer and the world (Perner, 1988: p. 151). Or as Lynd Forguson and Alison Gopnik (1988: p. 235) put it: "All these abilities require that the child simultaneously consider a particular representation as a representation *and* as an indicator of how the world really stands".

At this juncture a philosophical contribution is in order. I have already stressed that beliefs have reference to what is taken to be true. David Hamlyn (1978) draws attention to some implications of the fact that an individual could not acquire concepts of knowledge or belief unless he or she was able to appreciate what it means to take a "correct" view of a state of affairs. In order to understand the notion of "correctness", the child must also grasp what it is to be mistaken or in error and what it means to be corrected. This in turn requires that he or she has appropriate attitudes both towards the person who corrects, and towards truth itself. One would not understand what "truth" is, if one did not understand the kind of respect and acceptance that truth demands.

This argument is very condensed. The first point is to appreciate that what four-year-olds have newly acquired is the notion that a given way of representing or construing a situation may be true or false. Such truth and such falsity has reference to standards of correctedness that are intimately bound up with what "they"—the human community—do or should agree upon (which is not at all to suggest that reality is socially constructed). In so far as one is attempting to characterise things as the way they are, then there is a right way and a wrong way to do so. "Appearance" has to do with "the view for me (or her, or them)"; "reality" has to do with the ways things are objectively, for the abstracted person, when the potentially misleading distractions of mere appearance or idiosyncrasies in perspective are stripped away.

The second point is that well before a child understands the concepts of appearance and reality, he or she might already grasp that different people can construe things differently, for instance in having different feelings, desires, and other psychological attitudes towards the world. It is just that the child won't understand the particular attitude: "to take as true of reality". Correspondingly, the kinds of attitude towards others' attitudes that Hamlyn deems essential if a child is to acquire knowledge, might grow out of less sophisticated but recognisably related forms of "attitudes towards attitudes" earlier in life. Therefore the developmental psychologist is faced with the dual problem of specifying what new development has taken place when a child acquires the concepts of belief/false belief, truth/falsehood, and appearance/reality, and what are the earlier-existing capacities and propensities that establish conditions within which such new developments can occur.

It is worth re-emphasising that the acquisition of a concept of belief is part and parcel of a growing awareness of what it means for: (1) something to be "correct" and "true" of reality; and (2) for someone to hold something to be true, but at times to do so incorrectly (i.e. to "misrepresent" and have a false belief). If the notions of truth and reality entail some new orientation to the way in which the world out there falls under a particular description for the "generalised other" (i.e. the other who stands as corrector and who stands *for* the individuals who apprehend things without distortion), then we should do well to respect how the four-year-old's changed perspective on reality concurs with, and may even arise from, his or her changed view of any given individual's perspective *vis-à-vis* the perspective of the "generalised other". This is the first of several instances where I shall be suggesting that a child's developing representational capacities need to be understood with reference to changes that have been occurring in the child's orientation towards the nature and significance of *people's* psychological orientations to the world. Or to put this differently, an understanding of the kind of "reality" that contrasts with "appearances" is consistent with an understanding of "the world as given to all" that may contrast with "the world for me/her/them". When the issue is stated in this way, it becomes more natural to investigate how a four-year-old arrives at a notion of reality as potentially shareable and agreed-upon by the human community, a viewpoint in relation to which any given individual's viewpoint is fallible.

However, it is with the second of the issues I raised, the already-existing capacities that lay the groundwork for the four-year-old's understanding of belief, that I shall be most concerned. Here I shall allow David Hamlyn (1978) to anticipate much of what is to follow. I have already noted Hamlyn's insistence that in order for it to be possible for a child to acquire an understanding of beliefs, she would have to understand what it is to be corrected, and for this she requires appropriate attitudes to people who correct. Hamlyn (Hamlyn, 1978: pp. 86–87) concludes this line of reasoning by addressing what "appropriate attitudes" mean in this context. Given that the possibility of agreement among people "presupposes common reactions and attitudes to the world...knowledge and experience would be impossible except in creatures which have such interests; except, that is, in creatures which have feelings, and feelings which involve each other as well as other things". One must recognise persons as sources of appropriate kinds of attitude, and one must care about the attitudes of others. The child must be endowed with those dispositions towards people and towards the world that make a common "form of life" possible. Hamlyn's conclusion is that in order to acquire the concept of belief, a child needs to have the capacity to react with feelings to the feelings of others.

The "Intentionality" of Belief

One might approach the same issues from another direction. Still the focus is on what it is that four-year-olds have come to understand when they acquire mental state concepts such as that of belief. In this case, our starting-point is Brentano's attempt to distinguish the "mental" from the "physical". Brentano (1874/1973: p. 88) drew attention to the fact a mental state has directedness towards something else as its object, but this something else that a mental state is "about" need not exist (one can have thoughts about unicorns as well as horses):

> Every mental phenomenon is characterized by what the Scholastics of the Middle Ages called the intentional (or mental) inexistence of an object, and what we might call, though not wholly unambiguously, reference to a content, direction toward an object (which is not to be understood here as meaning a thing), or immanent objectivity. Every mental phenomenon includes something as object within itself, although they do not all do so in the same way. In presentation something is presented, in judgment something is affirmed or denied, in love loved, in hate hated, in desire

desired and so on. This intentional in-existence is characteristic exclusively of mental phenomena.

Let me try to elaborate on the "aboutness" or intentionality of mental states. One popular way of characterising intentionality and representing mental states is in terms of propositional attitudes (Russell, 1940). The canonical format is: A person believes (or hopes, or fears, or intends, or...) *that* such-and-such is the case. A person can have the same attitude towards different propositions (e.g. can believe X, or Y, or...), or take different attitudes towards the same proposition (e.g. can believe, or hope, or fear...that X). The "proposition" identifies the content of the mental state. As William Bechtel (1988) cautions, one must not mistake the proposition itself to be the object of the propositional attitude: one's belief is not about the proposition, but about the state of affairs that the proposition represents. For example, my belief that I shall die is a belief not about the proposition "I shall die", but rather about an actual circumstance that falls under the description "my own death". My attitude is indeed towards the event *as represented* by me, and I could not have an attitude at all about such a future, envisaged event unless I could in some way "present" or "represent" it to myself—but to state this is not at all to equate my feelings about my own death as being feelings about my representation of my own death! Thus there remains the task of explaining how propositions or representations are *about* objects and events in the world, or alternatively, the task of providing an account of "attitudes" that accomplishes the same ends.

Here, then, is an important feature of what it means to understand representational states such as beliefs and desires. It is through such understanding that someone comprehends how a person may have mental states that are directed towards non-existing entities and states of affairs, and may misrepresent something as something else. Not only this, but the person is also recognised to represent mentally certain aspects of objects or events and, one might say, subsume them under particular descriptions "for" the person. The individual whom you know only as "the captain of the English cricket team", I know as "a fine Essex batsman"—the phrases have the same referent (Graham Gooch), but different senses (Frege, 1892/1960). What an infant sitting in the garden sees "as" a graspable and chewable soft object, his mother sees "as" a potentially poisonous toadstool. What the child finds enticing, the mother finds menacing. To understand the representational mind is to understand the variety of ways of knowing-as, seeing-as, feeling-as, etc., as well as knowing-that, seeing-that, feeling-that, and so on.

Once again, a consideration of one vital property of belief, the intentionality of mind that such a psychological attitude entails, has led us to review a *range* of intentional mental states, some of which may be understood by the child well before her fourth birthday. It is not a lack of understanding intentionality *per se* that constrains a child's understanding of false beliefs, but rather the need to grasp how a believer may wrongly take a given "description" of the world as being true of reality, whereas another description correctly applies. In order to know what a belief is, the child needs to have recognised the intentionality of mind, but this awareness may have dawned long before.

BODIES AND MINDS

I want to begin to adjust our frame of reference. Instead of restricting myself to concepts such as those of "mind", "belief", and "intentionality", I shall consider what is involved in recognising persons as persons. After all, to understand beliefs is to understand the nature of persons who have beliefs. The existence of persons is presupposed by the notion of belief. Things do not have beliefs, not even computers and robots. We have seen that in order to know what beliefs are, an individual needs to know what it means to be a person with attitudes. Not only could there be no concept of belief without an adequate understanding of the kinds of "thing" that could hold beliefs, but also the concept itself is suffused with qualities that accrue from the fact that beliefs are held (in a metaphoric and not literal sense of the word) by persons.

For example, I know what it is like to hold the belief that I shall die one day, or the belief that the world is round, or a wide variety of other beliefs. In part, what it is like depends on the content of the belief—but only in part. I also know what it is like to have the kinds of attitude that beliefs entail. For example, I experience a difference between holding a belief firmly and holding it tentatively. Admittedly, the phenomenology of having a belief is subtle and complex, and the very idea of there being a "what it is like" in the case of having beliefs is less straightforward than in the case of having sensations like itchiness or warmth, or having feelings like happiness or anger. Not all beliefs are associated with a phenomenology. It remains the case that the kinds of attitude entailed by beliefs include those that are associated with subjectively experienced qualities of conscious and self-conscious mental life.

This is true of beliefs, but it is even more true of many other mental states. In the case of beliefs, one might conceivably arrive at a partial understanding of how beliefs function, by inferring how beliefs serve as "intervening variables" between perceptual input and motoric output, rather in the way that one might infer the flexibly programmed strategies of a mobile robot adjusting to the physical features of the environment. Such an understanding would indeed be partial—it is for good reason that we do not ascribe beliefs to a machine. (In fact, as Hamlyn, 1990, discusses, it is hardly conceivable that one *could* arrive even at this level of understanding if all humans were experienced as robots whose belief states had to be inferred from input–output relations conceived in such a manner.) In cases where it is essential to mental states that they have a qualitative aspect—in the case of feelings such as anger or jealousy, for example, where amongst other things, one needs to know "what it is like" to *be* angry or jealous—it is a vital part of one's knowledge of the mental states one ascribes to people, that such states are associated with qualitatively distinctive subjective experiences (i.e. with a phenomenology).

This raises an interesting problem. Suppose one asked: "On what basis does an individual ascribe experiences and consciousness to bodies?" If we were to accept this way of framing the question, we should have to tackle another: "On what basis does an individual ascribe bodies to minds?" The point is that if a child were to acquire (or be innately endowed with) concepts of "experiencing", "consciousness", and so on, in a way that was independent of the child's capacity to perceive and conceive of "bodies", then there would need to be a route by which the child integrates the two sets of understanding in order to arrive at the concept of other persons who have both bodies and minds. In this case, the concept of "persons" would be derivative from more basic concepts of "mind" and "body".

One common sense reaction to all this, is to insist (with some exasperation) that there really is no problem. After all, I know that I myself have perceptions, thoughts, wishes, feelings, and so on. I know this directly, from observing what happens in the realm of my own subjective experience. I can also see that other people have bodies like mine, they even behave and utter sounds like I do. Therefore I have a basis for inferring that other people have minds. I simply draw on analogy from my own case, and conclude that other people are like me in being subjects of experience. True, I may not know that other people have minds in the same way that I know *I* have a mind—perhaps what I have is an hypothesis or a theory that other people have minds—but that suffices for all practical purposes, not least for understanding and predicting behaviour. And once I have made the inference *that* people have minds, I can judge *what* people feel, think, and so on from what they say, or from "cues" provided by their bodily expressions and behaviour. I can even take the role of the other person and imagine myself in the other's shoes. Then I shall understand at least the kind of thing the person is thinking, feeling, and so on.

There are good reasons why this account is so persuasive. We *seem* to perceive bodies like other physically constituted objects. We do often put ourselves in other people's shoes, and take roles or simulate their perspectives by analogy from our own case. Moreover, it is perfectly true that there are some things we know only through our first-person subjective experiences; we would not know what it is like to be angry if we had never been angry ourselves, and so it must be the case that we confer something of this on to others in order to conceptualise *their* first-person experiences. So where is the problem?

The problem is that the account presupposes too much. It presupposes that I can conceptualise my own mental states prior to and as a precondition for ascribing similar mental states to others. I do this (it is imagined) by "observing" my own subjective mental life, by noticing when the same mental states (of feeling, wishing, intending, and so on) recur in my private experience. Once I have identified thoughts, feelings, and intentions in myself, then I can ascribe similar mental states to others. Wittgenstein (1958) delivered some devastating criticisms of this way of looking at things. In particular, one needs some way of checking that one is correct in identifying this or that mental state as "the same" as another, otherwise the judgement might be entirely arbitrary. It follows that there must be behavioural criteria for at least some mental states, in order that I can reach agreement with others about how to apply mental state concepts to my own case. For agreements in judgement and correcting to be possible, there have to be public criteria for the mental states that (sure enough) correspond with particular kinds of subjective experience. Perhaps most obviously, and perhaps most significant developmentally, are the criteria for states of feeling. The meaning of "anger" has reference not only to qualities of subjective experience, but also to observable expressions in behaviour—facial, gestural, and vocal expressions as well as inclinations to behave in certain ways in response to precipitants of certain kinds. Thus on the linguistic level, for example, the young child is able to learn what "anger" means because of the ways the child hears other people using the term in relation to the child him- or herself (whom the people judge to be angry by what they observe), as well as by noticing how people use the term in relation to others who are expressing and therefore manifesting anger and/or behaving angrily. The child can be corrected if she uses the word (or concept) "anger" wrongly—providing, that is, she takes correction *as* correction.

There are further difficulties with the assumption that children could reflect on their own mental states before becoming aware of psychological attitudes in other people. In Chapter 7 we shall consider reasons why self-reflective awareness *itself* presupposes a degree of awareness of the nature of other persons with minds (Hobson, 1990a). The form of such interpersonal awareness must be such that the child has appropriate attitudes towards the attitudes of others, so that she takes the role of the other towards herself (Mead,1934). It is only once the child *is* aware of persons-with-attitudes, that she can comprehend what it means for someone else to use language to refer to things or states of mind, or to correct the child.

I shall mention a final problem with the "argument from analogy". First we need to be clear what the argument is about. There is no dispute that once one has acquired the notion of persons with subjective mental life and has grasped that others are like me in this respect, then one can take roles and infer things on the basis of analogy from one's own case. I believe that this is of major developmental significance, in that there is a great deal about other people that one only understands by virtue of one's capacity to introspect and then to imagine that other people have similar experiences, inclinations, and so on. To understand "selves" involves more than understanding that persons have subjectivity. The dispute is whether the basis for ascribing mental life *at all* arises through introspection, inference, and reasoning by analogy (Hamlyn, 1974).

Recall that the starting-point was to assume that a child perceives other "bodies" as things, and that the child infers that bodies are associated with minds on the basis of analogy from the child's own case. The trouble is that this particular analogy would have very little force. The process of analogy involves abstraction: one notes potentially abstracted features of an object or event, then one discerns that some but not all of those features inhere in some other object or event. On the basis of the shared features, one entertains the idea that some or all of the apparently discrepant features apply to the object of analogy. As Max Scheler (1954) has pointed out, however, most of a person's experiences of his or her own body seem to be radically different from that person's perceptual experiences of anyone else's body. If we were to perceive other bodies without a hint that they are sources of proprioception, sensation, emotion, agency, and so on, then those bodies would lack the very qualities that suffuse and more or less define our "observations" of our own bodies, namely the many facets of subjective experience. The contrasts between our first-person experiences of our own bodies and our third-person experiences of the bodies of others are far more striking than the experienced similarities. As Wittgenstein (1958: para 302) writes: "If one has to imagine someone else's pain on the model of one's own, this is none too easy a thing to do: for I have to imagine pain which I *do not feel* on the model of the pain which I *do feel*."

I recognise that I have presented these arguments in very schematic form (and in fact I have discussed them in somewhat more detail in Hobson, 1990c), but I hope they have served to indicate the need for an alternative way of conceptualising the foundations of interpersonal understanding. It is not the case that our (and infants') perception of "bodies" is *simply* like the perception of other things. Moreover, it is not the case that the concept of "persons" is somehow derivative from more primitive notions of bodies on the one hand and minds on the other. Instead, the apprehension of person-related meanings is a primary form of perception, and the concept of persons is more fundamental than either the concept of bodies or the concept of minds. I shall now try to flesh out what I mean.

PERSONS AND SELVES

First I had better explain what I mean by a "person". A person is that particular kind of thing that has both a body and a mind. Moreover, a person is that kind of thing that I am myself, as well as the kind of thing that you are. The ways in which I know I am a person are not exactly the same as the ways in which I know you are a person, of course: I have privileged access to my own body and mind. I have my own feelings and think my own thoughts. Nevertheless, I do know you have a mind, with as much certainty as I know you have a body. I also know that I am one among a community of persons.

In outlining such a view, Peter Strawson (1962) suggests that it is essential to the character of predicates we apply to persons, that they have both the first- and third-person ascriptive uses. They are both self-ascribable otherwise than on the basis of observation by the subject who has them, and other-ascribable on the basis of behavioural criteria. To learn their use is to learn both the aspects of their use. I know that I feel, think, or intend this or that, not (usually) because I "observe" anything, but because I have the feeling, the thought, and the intention. I ascribe feelings, thoughts, and intentions to you, because I perceive behavioural criteria that justify such an ascription. Having said this, there is much that needs to be added about how I acquire the concepts in terms of which my self-knowledge is constituted and expressed, and yet more about the perceptual underpinnings for ascribing mental states to others.

It may help to progress with such an account if we can analyse the concept of persons in greater detail. Daniel Dennett (1985) outlines the following "conditions for personhood": persons are rational; they are subjects of intentional ascriptions; a certain stance or attitude is taken towards them; they can reciprocate in some way; they are capable of verbal communication; and they have a special kind of consciousness, perhaps self-consciousness. This makes it clear that still we have to deal with how individuals understand and ascribe rationality and intentionality, but now we see these familiar problems set within a new context. The context is one in which we need to appreciate the roles of personal attitudes and reciprocal interpersonal communication, and the place of self-consciousness, in establishing foundations for an individual's understanding of persons with minds.

Let me proceed backwards from where we left off the discussion about understanding beliefs. I was suggesting that certain prerequisites for knowledge about beliefs, and in particular awareness of people's subjective attitudes and "intentionality of mind", might be features of a child's understanding well before the age of four years. Rearranging and adapting Dennett's conditions for personhood, it seems from the evidence I cited in Chapter 3 that a relatively sophisticated degree of self-consciousness is acquired by a child as young as 18 months or so. With this comes the capacity for forms of role-taking that involve an understanding of other selves, as when a child shows that she can conceptualise another person's wishes, needs, or expectations within the other's frame of reference. In due course, the child will discover that others, too, are self-conscious. As I shall discuss in the next chapter, these developments have intrinsic connections with the child's understanding of what it means for other people as well as the child herself to engage in verbal communication.

If we stick with Dennett's list as a guide to pinpointing elements in the child's developing understanding of persons, we need to move to an even earlier phase of development. At nine months of age, infants come to take a certain stance or set of attitudes not only towards persons *vis-à-vis* things, but more specifically towards the *attitudes* of other persons. Recall how during this stage of secondary intersubjectivity, the infant shares experiences of the world with a care-giver: showing objects, often looking back and forth between the object and the care-giver's eyes; seeking out and relating to the care-giver's affective relation to the world in social referencing; initiating as well as responding to games such as pat-a-cake; making and responding to gestural requests; coming to imitate meaningful actions with objects, and so on. These are examples of what I mean by manifestations of the infant's attitudes towards another person's attitudes towards the world and herself. Note how the infant perceives and reacts to both the quality of the other person's attitude, and to the overt directedness of that attitude towards a shared world. In this somewhat restricted sense, the infant treats other people as subjects of intentional ascriptions. Note, too, that the very concept of "attitude" is like the concept of "person" in that attitudes have observable manifestations as well as a potentially covert subjective dimension. Although I would question whether infants of this age have acquired a concept of persons (Hobson, 1993d), they certainly have an impressive awareness of persons as things with more-than-physical properties and with outward-looking states of being. The extra qualities that the infant experiences persons to have, are just what we try to distil out in our talk of "subjectivity", "attitudes", "psychological orientations", and the like. My point is that infants apprehend such qualities directly, in their perception of and reactions towards persons.

The remaining item in Dennett's inventory, the fact that humans reciprocate, leads us back to the earliest months of life. At least from the second month of life, reciprocal relations between the infant and care-giver are at once behavioural and experiential. The infant registers the reciprocal nature of interpersonal transactions (especially Murray & Trevarthen, 1985). Like the infant's awareness of and engagement with the subjectivity of others, her awareness of and engagement in increasingly "formatted" reciprocal exchanges become elaborated over the first year (Bruner, 1983).

In all of this, there is a special importance attached to the developmental series of forms of "sharing experiences" between infant and care-giver (Hobson, 1989b). The reason is that it is only through such episodes of intersubjectively co-ordinated experience that an infant eventually becomes aware *that* people have minds. It does not require reasoning by analogy for infants to recognise the nature of persons as like themselves in being sources of subjective attitudes, yet unlike themselves in having mental states that at any given time may differ from their own. What it does require is not only primary, biologically-given and perceptually-anchored mechanisms for establishing connectedness of mind between infant and care-giver, but also means by which the minds of "self" and "other" are differentiated and ultimately conceptualised. Or to approach the matter from a different angle, it is not that infants first perceive bodies and subsequently confer minds, but rather that they have direct perception of and natural engagement with person-related meanings that are apprehended *in* the expressions and behaviour of other persons. It is only gradually, and with considerable input from adults, that they eventually come to conceive of "bodies" on the one hand, and "minds" on the other.

It might be worth devoting some space to this matter of sharing experiences, beginning with what Heinz Werner and Bernard Kaplan (1984) call the "primordial sharing situation". We need a clear view of what early forms of sharing do and do not entail. An obvious complication here is the developmental progression towards more sophisticated forms of sharing as infants and children grow older. It is hardly surprising that different writers apply different criteria to the point at which an infant might be said to share or engage in intersubjective transactions with others. In one sense, a child would need to recognise the distinction between their own and others' experiences in order to share; one might even insist that the child should recognise how their own experiences of the world are co-ordinated with others' ways of experiencing that same world (Kaye, 1982; Stern, 1985). From very early in life, however, an infant appears to register and respond to other people in ways that lead to a co-ordination between the subjective experiences of each. Such "primary intersubjectivity" (Trevarthen, 1979) is a *sine qua non* for more mature kinds of sharing. To be more precise, some such mode of interpersonal, subjective co-ordination must provide the foundations for an understanding that people have minds, and that people are things with whom one can share experiences. It is not logically necessary that such relations exist *before* this kind of understanding develops, but it may be a psychological necessity that they do.

One of the definitions of "to share" in the *Oxford English Dictionary*, is "to perform, enjoy, or suffer in common with others; to possess (a quality) which other persons or things also have". I think we can tolerate some imprecision in characterising what the infant of two months "has in mind" when she does (as a matter of fact) respond with feelings and attitudes that correspond with the feelings and attitudes of other people. What in my view we cannot overlook, is that infants of this age are psychologically engaged with other people, in ways that co-ordinate with the other people's psychological engagements with the infants. I gave a number of examples in Chapter 3. It is not merely that we observe how infants "perform, enjoy or suffer in common with others", but also that we witness their emotional responsiveness to a particular kind of quality that other persons have in common with themselves, namely bodily expressed mental states. As the observations of Murray and Trevarthen (1985; see Chapter 3) illustrate, even young infants will make an active attempt to establish harmony in their interactions with adults. The significance of all this is that the child is perceiving and relating to persons (not merely to bodies) with emotionally charged reactions of her own. There is interpersonal linkage of subjective experiences. As Michael Tomasello (1992: p. 79) expresses it: "Almost from birth, it is clear to children when they are and when they are not in tune with an adult; and they show that they do not like to be out of tune." No doubt there are a number of perceptual channels through which a sharing (or linking, or opposing, or...) of subjective states is effected. The infant sees and reacts to faces and gestures, hears and reacts to vocalisations, senses and reacts to the qualities of touch and temporal and spatial patterns of bodily exchange, and so on (Stern, 1985). Each of these perceptual-affective capacities may come on line at different points during the early months of life. Nevertheless, infants do react to a range of other people's bodily expressions (i.e. what *we* know to "express" subjective mental life) with experiences of their own; they also seem to register what we know as shared experiences, in special kinds of ways. The critical question remains: how does the infant come to attribute experiences to persons, conceptualised as such?

There are probably two rather separate issues embedded in this question. The first has to do with the infant's ability to attribute properties (in this case, properties associated with what adults call feelings) to somethings other than itself. The second has to do with the infant's understanding that bodily-endowed persons are separate loci of mental life, beings with agency as well as feelings and a variety of other psychological attitudes. Regarding the former of these issues, there seems little reason to suppose that attributing properties to people on the basis of the experience of personal relatedness, is any more or less difficult than attributing properties to things on the basis of thing-relatedness. Just as the infant registers the difference between self-caused and other-caused events in the world of things, so the infant is likely to register the sameness or difference between self-feeling-states and feeling-states-as-observed— the registration, if not the representation, of such matches and mismatches is implied by the infant observations cited earlier (also Mundy & Sigman, 1989). If this is so, then already in infancy there are mechanisms not only for establishing psychological commonality across individuals, but also for achieving early differentiation between self and other. It is this primitive form of psychological connectedness with and differentiation from other persons that paves the way for the radical changes in interpersonal relatedness around nine months of age. For it is this inter*subjective* linkage that establishes the basis for infants to ascribe "subjectivity" of experience to others. Infants, like adults, are directly aware when they are emotionally connected with other people. Their developmental task is not to infuse bodies with minds, but rather to acquire an understanding of how different people have their own *separate* subjective perspectives and selves in relation to a common world. This returns us to the importance of being able to perceive and register the directedness of other people's attitudes, at first within face-to-face interactions and subsequently in settings where people direct their attitudes elsewhere than to the infant. It also raises the question of the genesis of self-awareness. I shall deal with these topics at a later point in this essay.

THE EMOTIONAL ORIGINS OF PSYCHOLOGICAL UNDERSTANDING

I shall try to tie up the loose threads of the argument I have presented in this chapter. I began by noting some of the tenets of the "Theory of Mind" approach to interpersonal understanding. Although there is much in this approach that I respect and agree with, I expressed my unease about the notion that mental states *en bloc* are "inferred" from behaviour, and about the suggestion that concepts of mind are theory-generated hypothetical constructs applied to observations of behaviour (I take up other contentious issues in Hobson, 1991b). I examined the implications of the fact that "belief" has reference to attitudes towards what is taken to be "true"; truth entails agreement amongst individuals about what is the case, which obviously is *not* to say that the truth is arbitrarily defined by such agreement. I suggested that other ingredients of a child's understanding of beliefs are in place well before the age of four. Beliefs exhibit intentionality in having reference to a content (that which is believed), they involve attitudes, and they are akin to other mental states in having the potential to be associated with a phenomenology ("what it is like" to experience such states).

My own proposals have concerned the nature of the conditions that allow an infant to achieve an increasingly explicit awareness of those characteristics of (infra-belief) mental states of persons, over the first two years of life. I have given prominence to perceptually anchored processes that establish intersubjectivity between infant and care-giver, and that enable the infant to apprehend both the qualities and directedness of other people's psychological attitudes. Interpersonal-affective exchanges and the sharing of subjectively patterned states are especially important here. I also stressed the importance of the new level of reflective self-awareness that a child acquires around 18 months, the time at which the child begins to express embarrassment and self-admiration before a mirror, to make self-descriptive utterances, to symbolise herself in play, and to express with full force the assertiveness of the terrible two's. At this stage children can begin to "infer" things about the nature of people's minds by conferring attributes on the basis of their own self-experience. At this relatively late stage, children *do* know that other persons are fitting recipients for a kind of analogical reasoning from their own case. They know this by virtue of long-standing and more basic non-inferential awareness of the nature of other persons.

The loose ends I want to tie up are several. First, I want to note that an adequate account of the development of self-awareness would combine a description of evolving forms of I–Thou awareness with a parallel but interleaving account of I–It awareness (Hobson, 1990a, and later chapters of this essay). Second, I need to define more precisely what is and what is not achieved in the way of interpersonal understanding, by the processes of primary and secondary intersubjectivity. Third, I should say something about what Josef Perner (1991) calls the "aspectuality" of intentional mental states, the fact that if (say) I believe something, what I believe falls under a particular description for me. Finally, I need to tag an outstanding issue about "concepts" of mind, for later consideration.

It is important to emphasise something about my account of biologically given, perceptually anchored cognitive/conative/affective capacities and propensities for personal relatedness and for intersubjective co-ordination. The account does not explain (nor explain away) the long-drawn-out growth in a child's understanding of a wide variety of mental states. It is not intended to. The account *is* intended to show how knowledge of certain characteristic and essential features of mental states has its origins. The philosophical side of the argument involves an epistemological thesis about the conditions that are necessary if knowledge of minds is to be possible at all. The psychological considerations reveal how these conditions are met in the course of early childhood. In particular, an infant is in a position to apprehend something of the subjectivity of mental states, and the young child is in a position to conceptualise how mental states are associated with a phenomenology, by virtue of the individual's direct perception of and natural reactions towards the "meanings" embodied in the appearances, gestures, and actions of other people. Basic forms of physiognomic perception (Werner) and intersubjectivity (Trevarthen) are givens of human psychology. The infant is able to perceive the outer-directedness of people's attitudes because once again, there are hard-wired mechanisms that guarantee this ability, at least if the child can see. There are probably a set of rather different mechanisms here, some that operate in face-to-face contact and others that ensure gaze-following (Baron-Cohen & Cross, 1992; Butterworth & Jarrett, 1991). Finally, the older infant and young child are able to appreciate "correction" and to enter into agreements in judgement with others, for the reason that they have appropriate kinds of attitude to the attitudes of others. As we shall see, an important additional factor is their ability and propensity to identify with others, in the more sophisticated forms of imitation.

It will be obvious that what we broadly describe as affective perception, behaviour, and experience have an especially pivotal role to play in these earliest origins of interpersonal awareness (Hobson, 1992). This is why I have subtitled this section of the chapter "The emotional origins of psychological understanding" (also Hobson, 1993b). In fact, affectively patterned interpersonal relatedness, with its cognitive and conative aspects, is a more accurate characterisation of what is foundational. Even in this early period, the child may employ Piagetian-type cognitive and perhaps inference-like processes to enrich their sensorimotor-affective grasp of the nature of persons, but the main action is taking place on a non-inferential level. Having said this, I believe that during the first and certainly in the second year of life and beyond, the child acquires insights into the nature of psychological functioning. I would join those who stress how the post-infancy child makes efforts to work out how mental states function. What I do not think is correct, is the claim that *all* mental states are unobservable and have to be inferred, nor the suggestion that our knowledge of minds is really only "theory" that employs hypothetical constructs. I think it would be to mangle language and to collapse important conceptual distinctions if I called my knowledge of the properties of an apple a "theory", and the same would be true if I downgraded my knowledge of the mental life of persons.

Perhaps it is not surprising that the Theory of Mind literature is weakest in its treatment of the fact that we know other people to be *subjects* of experience. For example, Alan Leslie (1987: p. 422) finds it "hard to see how perceptual evidence could ever force an adult, let alone a young child, to invent the idea of unobservable mental states". Josef Perner (1990: p. 122) writes: "The argument is that empathy is based on identifying another person's inner state as an emotion one is familiar with from one's own inner experience of being in that state. Empathic reactions are possible because infants project that familiar state as a *theoretical construct* onto the other person in order to understand what is going on inside her and how to alleviate her distress" (Perner's italics). I have tried to offer an alternative to these views about the pretheoretical *origins* of interpersonal understanding. I suggest children's understanding of unobservable mental states is not so mysterious once one sees that they begin by understanding mental states that are observable.

One effect of researchers' preoccupation with "beliefs" and even pretence has been to overlook the need to explain children's appreciation of and attitudes towards people as centres of consciousness. If one considers the social relatedness of nine-month-olds, one can see how they have the requisite forms of attitude well before they can conceptualise the nature of mental states. These infantile *attitudes* are the source of interpersonal understanding; it is not that understanding or "theory" comes first. So, too, for adults—as Wittgenstein (1958: p. 178) writes: "My attitude towards him is an attitude towards a soul. I am not of the *opinion* that he has a soul…The human body is the best picture of the human soul."

It remains to explain how children come to understand that given objects and events may fall under different descriptions or have different meanings for different people. In the next chapter I shall try to say how early forms of co-reference between an infant and care-giver lead the one-year-old to appreciate that what she takes an object "as" (e.g. as frightening) may be different to what another person takes the object "as" (e.g. as interesting). It is a further two or three years before the child applies such understanding to people's ways of construing what an object *really* is (I think it is a sponge, he thinks it is a rock), but this should not obscure the fundamental importance of the child's ability to recognise the differentiation and co-ordination of other psychological attitudes. Alan Leslie (1987) draws attention to the significance of what he calls "metarepresentation", the child's capacity to represent the mental representations of others and herself, for the capacity to play symbolically. We can consider this in another way, by focussing on attitudes. The child who plays symbolically adopts a novel (and creative) attitude towards the symbolic vehicle, and does so playfully. The particular attitude adopted, and therefore the meaning conferred, happens to be that which is in certain respects appropriate to something else, what we call the referent. For example, the child adopts an attitude towards a lump of plasticene (the symbolic vehicle) that is in some ways appropriate to a house (the referent), but not for-serious. I shall return to this thesis shortly. Meanwhile, this way of putting things would allow us to accept Perner's (1993) point that metarepresentation proper occurs when the four-year-old understands someone else to represent-as-reality. Even here, we should not forget that the child who understands "belief" also understands the kind of *attitude* that is fitting for belief, and much of the talk about "representations" appears to by-pass the problem of how this aspect of the child's understanding originates.

Finally, I have referred to young children's concepts about people's mental states. I have begged the question of what it means to acquire concepts of whatever kind. This is obviously a critical matter for the attempt to provide a developmental account of the acquisition of concepts of mind. In fact, it is a matter that will return us to many of the issues that have surfaced already. Therefore I shall address it forthwith, in the chapter that follows.

CHAPTER SEVEN

Conceptual Issues II: On Thought and Language

This chapter is even more ambitious than the preceding ones. I want to consider the earliest developments in children's thought and language. Once again, my approach will be to analyse what is involved in someone having thoughts and deriving concepts, and what lies behind the emergence of language. If we can set these matters in an appropriate frame of reference, we might stand a better chance of uncovering the foundations on which psychological development rests. It goes without saying that this is important for our understanding of early-rooted psychopathological states such as that of early childhood autism.

I shall begin by considering the nature of thinking, and consider the contributions of perceiving, acting and feeling to early forms of abstraction. I shall then focus on the kind of abstraction particular to symbolic functioning, proceeding from a conceptual analysis of what symbolising entails to reflections on "I–It" and interpersonal contributions to a child's developing capacity to symbolise. I shall move on to discuss certain features of interpersonal communication and language, and finally return to the business of thinking. My overall purpose is to bring out how the interpersonal dimension of early childhood experience is essential to the acquisition of certain higher cognitive capacities in the realms of creative symbolic functioning, language, and thinking.

Perhaps I should draw attention to the fact that in this chapter I shall be directing attention to the young child's own thought and language, and not primarily to the child's understanding of other people's thought and language. However, it will soon become clear that the development of the former has much to do with the development of the latter.

THE NATURE OF THINKING

What does it mean to think about things or aspects of things? What does it mean to have concepts, for example, the concept of an apple? What does it mean to abstract qualities, for example, to think about the roundness or hardness of an apple? And what does it mean to symbolise or to use metaphor, for instance to use the word "apple" to stand for an apple, or to use an apple to stand for a house in pretend play, or to think of New York as The Big Apple? Most importantly for the present purposes, what do the logical entailments of these intellectual capacities tell us about the character of the psychological processes that must play a part in development if such cognitive abilities are to be acquired?

Let us take the concept of an apple. As a preliminary, note that to perceive an apple as an apple is already to subsume the object of perception under a concept. If one had no concept of an apple, one might perceive the apple as something with fewer or different qualities (as, say, a ball or a stone), but not as something in the nature of apples. This immediately highlights the fact that to have a concept of X is to know what it is for something to be an X (Hamlyn, 1978). "What something is" depends on its relations to us. Something is an apple if it lends itself to be observed, held, eaten, cut, cooked, and so on. I would highlight two points here. The first is that the concept of "apple" involves an abstraction. It encompasses what is common to Granny Smiths, Cox's, Golden Delicious, and so on, whilst at the same time establishing distinctions from other kinds of fruit or other kinds of solid roundish object. The second point is that once one has a concept, one can "think" with it. As David Hamlyn (1983: p. 83) suggests, "concepts may be regarded as devices for thinking of the facts in a way which may be useful for some further end". To think of this object as an apple rather than a ball or simply a solid object of such-and-such a size is to accord it a set of properties and to place it in a nexus of relations to other objects, to the past and the future, and to potential desires and activities of human beings and other organisms.

We can now enquire how particular concepts are acquired. I am going to concentrate on the earliest stages of concept acquisition. Already it should be apparent that different kinds of concept may be derived from different kinds of experience of the world. At the risk of being repetitious, I shall return to my favourite concept—that of persons. The concept of persons requires that the thinker knows what a person is, and this entails that he or she has experienced the kinds of relatedness that are fitting for persons. If one always treated and experienced people like things, one would not have the concept of a person. This is a matter with developmental implications. If children did not experience something radically different in their transactions with people *vis-à-vis* things, they would not acquire the concept of persons, even though they might come to apply the term "person" to things with certain physical characteristics such as a particular form of face, two arms and two legs, independent mobility, and so on. The reason is that if a child could not become implicated in the kind of affectively patterned, intersubjective relations that can exist between persons, then the child would not know what persons are. For persons are precisely the kind of thing to afford experiences of certain personal kinds—especially the broad range of experiences we might call "sharing", but also related forms of experience such as competing, greeting, hating, conversing, and so much else that makes human relationships what they are. Persons are *subjects*, and each person is a "self".

What further is involved when we acquire *the* concept of something? To quote Hamlyn (1978: pp. 74 & 102) again:

> To have *a* concept of X is to believe something about what is is for something to be X, and this belief may or may not be right. To the extent that we can speak of the correct or right understanding of something, we can speak of *the* concept of that thing, and *the* concept is therefore objective and shareable with others...An essential stage in the acquisition of knowledge of what it is for something to be X is, through this: distinguishing X's "as *they* do".

Let us now return to the case of the apple, and to the nature of abstraction. According to the traditional theory of abstraction, concepts are formed through a process in which the person recognises similarities or identical elements in a set of objects. The person abstracts those resemblances away from the other properties of the set of objects which are not relevant to the concept. For example, an infant might notice that this object (the apple) is hard and that one (the spongy ball) is soft. The question is, what does it take for the infant to generalise from one particular to another, and so to subsume particulars under a general category? The child might notice that two apples are alike (and unlike sponge balls) in appearing a certain way and being hard and edible. The problem is that the infant could not "notice" the respect in which the two instances were alike, that both apples were hard,unless it had some intuition of the general in the perception of the particular, what Husserl (1901) called "ideational abstraction". Without this, the property in virtue of which the one particular is taken to be similar to the other (in this case, "hardness"), could not be perceived as an (abstracted) property of either particular in the first place. The critical point is that the infant comes to regard something as an example of a type according to the way the something lends itself to the infant's actions, intentions, feelings, and so on. In so far as the infant can grasp an apple and grasp a spongy ball, they are identical in terms of their "graspability". In so far as the infant can bite off and eat a bit of the apple but not the ball, "eatability" becomes a feature of *this* form of graspable object (what will ultimately become an apple) and not that form (a ball). In so far as the infant finds one kind of eatable object of this size and weight tangy and another sweet, it might start to distinguish Cox's from Golden Delicious. And so on. As Neil Bolton (1972: p. 234) puts it: "To form a concept, then, is not, fundamentally, to subsume resemblances under explicit categories, but to synthesize things through the intentions which we have towards them...the act of explicit subsumption is a secondary development and not the fundamental mode of cognition...The fundamental form of cognition is personal, therefore, in the sense that intentionality implies an involvement in an environment and not a detached attitude."

The central fact is that an individual's "detached attitude" and the kind of abstracting that this allows is a relatively late developmental accomplishment which depends on prior modes of relatedness towards and engagement with the world. The earliest forms of cognition and indeed perception need to be characterised in terms of the relations between the infant and the environment. Therefore we need to examine what these relations are like, and how they give rise to the potential for detachment that has often been seen as a hallmark of cognition. I shall address these issues by considering how they have been tackled by three "greats" of developmental psychology—Jean Piaget, Heinz Werner, and Lev Vygotsky. This approach should also elucidate how the processes of abstraction change in the course of infant development, culminating in the one-and-a-half-year-old's capacity to symbolise in a creative manner.

PERCEIVING, ACTING, AND FEELING

On the origins of knowledge, Piaget said: "I only know an object to the extent that I act upon it; I can affirm nothing about it prior to such an action" (Piaget quoted by Inhelder in Furth, 1969: p. 24). Or again, Piaget wrote: "...every perception gives to the perceived elements meanings which are relative to action, and it is therefore from action that we need to start" (Piaget, 1972: p. 20). For Piaget, thinking is interiorised action. It is therefore by way of the baby's bodily action and the older child's internalised (mental) actions that knowledge of objects is achieved. Piaget distilled the significance of action in his pivotal concept of the scheme. A scheme is "whatever is repeatable and generalizable in an action" (Piaget,

1970: p. 42). Examples are the schemes of sucking or grasping or, at a later stage, classifying or arranging in serial order. When a baby sucks the breast, or its hand, or a ball, it is applying the sucking scheme. Nor is the scheme concerned only with responses, for a perceptual stimulus cannot be active unless it is assimilated to schemes of action. That is, a stimulus acts as a stimulus if it is, so to speak, recognised by the child in terms of its propensities to action—just as food acts as food, only if and when it is assimilated by the gut and then metabolised. From the complementary perspective, a baby sucking is constructing a world of suckable things, not merely finding things in the world that it sucks (Boden, 1979). One can see how Piaget is following the pathway from the infant's capacity to generalise, to that infant's increasingly particular apprehension of different objects, as sensorimotor schemes are co-ordinated with one another. What will ultimately look like an abstracted feature of objects—suckability—is in fact a relational attribute that is perceived very early on. According to Piaget, it is only at the end of the sensorimotor period that infants are able to co-ordinate their actions freely, dissociating them from specific content, so that they can construct stable internalised representations which transcend the immediate present and form the substrate for symbolic functioning.

In Heinz Werner's (1948) approach to conceptual development, the Piagetian emphasis on action as the mediating relation between the infant and her world is complemented by a further emphasis on affective relations. In addition, and crucially, Werner and Kaplan (1984) believed that there is an intimate relationship between the evolving forms of infant–care-giver transaction and the infant's emerging capacity to symbolise. Werner (1948) cleared the ground by insisting that abstraction is not a unitary function, but rather "a process that may be effected by different functions on quite different levels" (p. 234). He proposed that "the awareness of objects during early childhood depends essentially on the extent to which these objects can be responded to in motor–affective behavior" (p. 66). He drew comparisons between the primitive mental life of young children and that of animals. Animals live in a world of things-of-action, of which the signal properties are dependent upon the biological world of the particular animal. For young children, too, affective attitudes are integral to perceptual processes: "such dynamization of things based on the fact that the objects are predominantly understood through the motor and affective attitude of the subject may lead to a particular type of perception...I have proposed the term *physiognomic perception* for this mode of cognition in general" (Werner, 1948: p. 69). More sophisticated geometric–technical perception is seen to arise out of developmentally prior physiognomic perception as the child begins to acquire more self-reflective and analytic modes of thought (Blocker, 1969).

Thus there are developmental changes in the process of abstraction itself. In primitive or concrete abstraction, things may be grouped according to the objects' "equal affective value" for the subject (Werner, 1948: p. 232), as well as by their perceptual similarity. In true conceptual abstraction, by contrast: "the quality (e.g. a color) common to all the elements involved is deliberately detached—mentally isolated, as it were—and the elements themselves appear only as visible exemplifications of the common quality" (Werner, 1948: p. 243). At the conceptual level, a person can shift his point of view in a purposeful grouping activity.

I should like to draw attention to two features of this account. Werner's point about the child understanding objects "through the motor and affective attitude of the subject" highlights the significance of attitudes and relatedness for knowledge about the world. Then there is the notion that applying concepts might involve a person in shifting points of view. This way of putting things alters our perspective on the development of the ability to "use" concepts. More specifically, we might seek the origins of higher forms of abstracting and conceptualising by studying how children come to be flexible in categorising the world according to *various* points of view (Weigl, 1941). This is exactly the route I am following.

At this juncture I turn to Lev Vygotsky. To begin with, I shall confine myself to two ideas that are central to Vygotsky's thought. I shall allow Vygotsky's own words (albeit in translation) to convey his message.

The first idea is really a composite of two points that Vygotsky makes in the opening chapter of his classic work, *Thought and Language* (1962). Vygotsky (1962: pp. 4 and 8) propounds a thesis about the appropriate "mode of analysis" in psychology, and then brings the thesis to bear on the relation between intellect and affect:

> ...[rather than analysing complex psychological wholes into elements] the right course to follow is to use the other type of analysis, which may be called *analysis into units*. By *unit* we mean a product of analysis which, unlike elements, retains all the basic properties of the whole and which cannot be further divided without losing them...Unit analysis...demonstrates the existence of a dynamic system of meaning in which the affective and the intellectual unite. It shows that every idea contains a transmuted affective attitude toward the bit of reality to which it refers.

I hope that my own approach to analysing early development in terms of "modes of relatedness" conforms with Vygotsky's recommendation concerning the proper unit of psychological analysis. Note, too, Vygotsky's view that ideas have attitudes embedded within them.

The second of Vygotsky's ideas concerns the social origins of a child's capacities of mind. In an essay entitled *Internalization of higher psychological functions* (reprinted in Vygotsky, 1978: pp. 56–57), Vygotsky considers how a gesture becomes "pointing" through the reaction it engenders from another person:

> It becomes a true gesture only after it objectively manifests all the functions of pointing for others and is understood by others as such a gesture...*An interpersonal process is transformed into an intrapersonal one.* Every function in the child's cultural development appears twice: first, on the social level, and later, on the individual level; first, *between* people (*interpsychological*), and then *inside* the child (*intrapsychological*). This applies equally to voluntary attention, to logical memory, and to the formation of concepts. All the higher functions originate as actual relations between human individuals (Vygotsky's italics).

Thus we find that in their rather different ways, Piaget, Werner, and Vygotsky are trying to understand how from primary modes of infant– world relatedness, the child develops capacities for conceptual thinking *about* the world. Indeed, each has emphasized the need for the child to distance thought from external action (Piaget & Inhelder, 1969: p. 56), from immediate experience (Vygotsky, 1962: p. 116), or from objects in the world (Werner & Kaplan, 1984: p. 42). The question is: how is such distancing effected?

I think that there are a number of different levels at which "distancing" takes place, just as there are a number of different levels of abstracting (see Werner, 1948). Nevertheless, I propose that there are two distinct mechanisms (or classes of mechanism) involved. One of these occurs as a part of the I–It developmental line, the domain of which more or less covers the sensorimotor abilities described by Piaget. The other occurs as a part of the I–Thou developmental line. This latter distancing mechanism exemplifies Vygotsky's thesis about the internalisation of social process as a means by which the child develops new psychological capacities.

I do not wish to advocate a social–determinist position, but rather to argue that the very nature and configuration of interpersonal experience is what lies behind the nature and configuration of creative symbolic functioning. I shall also consider additional language-related abilities from this perspective.

THE NATURE OF SYMBOLIC FUNCTIONING

In 1923, C.K. Ogden and I.A. Richards published their classic work, *The Meaning of Meaning* (reprinted in 1985). In this book they write:

> Symbols direct and organize, record and communicate. In stating what they direct and organize, record and communicate we have to distinguish as

always between Thoughts and Things. It is Thought (or, as we shall usually say, *reference*) which is directed and organized, and it is also Thought which is recorded and communicated (Ogden & Richards, 1923: p. 9).

The authors provide a diagram (which I have simplified for the present purposes; Fig. 7.1), and they explain:

> Between a thought and a symbol causal relations hold. When we speak, the symbolism we employ is caused partly by the reference we are making and partly by social and psychological factors—the purpose for which we are making the reference, the proposed effect of our symbols on other persons, and our own attitude. When we hear what is said, the symbols both cause us to perform an act of reference and to assume an attitude which will, according to circumstances, be more or less similar to the act and the attitude of the speaker.
>
> Between the Thought and the Referent there is also a relation; more or less direct (as when we think about or attend to a coloured surface we see), or indirect (as when we "think of" or "refer to" Napoleon)...Between the symbol and the referent there is no relevant relation other than the indirect one, which consists in its being used by someone to stand for a referent (Ogden and Richards, 1923: pp. 10–11).

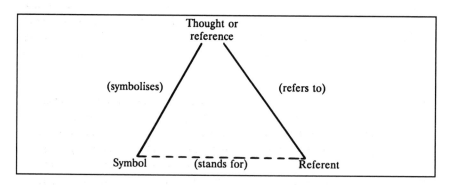

FIG. 7.1.

I shall select features of this account for further elaboration, drawing upon the writings of more recent authors.

First, Ogden and Richards catalogue a number of functions that symbols serve. Symbols direct and organise behaviour and thought; they enable a person to record something of what happens in that person's experience, and subsequently to evoke absent realities (as represented); they can be employed to communicate with others. Although in the above passages,

Ogden and Richards appear to emphasise communication in so far as one person intends to have an effect on others, they also indicate that symbols may express a speaker's attitudes and elsewhere refer to the "emotive aspects of language" (p. 10). They stress that it is only when a thinker makes use of a symbol, that the symbol stands for anything.

It is worth spending time on such a list. One reason is that we might better appreciate how far-reaching are the implications of being able to symbolise, not only for logical thought, for planning, and for the social exchange of information, but also for creative imagination and self-expression (R.F. Hobson, 1985). Another reason is that such considerations might influence our view of what is basic to symbolising from a developmental perspective—what motivates symbolising, as well as what determines its cognitive structure.

However, I need to return to the structure of symbolising. More specifically, I want to explore how the cognitive and communicative dimensions of symbolism are related to one another. What is the point of the Ogden and Richards triangle?

Ogden and Richards stress that the base of their triangle, the indirect relation between symbol and referent, is different from the direct relations between symbol and thought on the one hand, and thought and referent on the other. I think the crux is that we have to characterise how a symbol carries a thinker's *way* of thinking about and/or attitude to the referent. The relation between symbol and referent is one that passes through the thought of the person who symbolises. In fact, I am unhappy about the way in which the Ogden and Richards diagram suggests that a symbol "symbolises" a thought. Suzanne Langer expresses the relation more accurately:

A term which is used symbolically and not signally does *not* evoke action appropriate to the presence of its object. If I say: "Napoleon", you do not bow to the conqueror of Europe as though I had introduced him, but merely think of him…Symbols are not proxy for their objects, but are *vehicles for the conception of objects*. To conceive a thing or a situation is not the same thing as to "react toward it" overtly, or to be aware of its presence. In talking *about* things we have conceptions of them, not the things themselves; and *it is the conceptions, not the things, that symbols directly "mean"* (Langer, 1957: pp. 60–61, Langer's italics).

Elsewhere, Langer points out the way in which animals may use signs to indicate things, but man is unique in using them to represent. Correspondingly, words are not so much "announcers" of things, as "reminders" which "let us develop a characteristic attitude toward objects in absentia, which is called "thinking of" or "referring to" what is not here"

(Langer, 1957: p. 31). Thus a symbol is coupled, for a certain subject, with a conception that fits an object or event. The connotation of a word is simply the conception it conveys.

Let me give a simple example. I am writing this essay seated at a desk. To refer to it as a "desk" is to employ a symbol to convey a particular concept (which you, the reader, will dress up in a private conception) that relates to the piece of furniture in question. I could have selected other terms—"a table", "a heavy wooden object", "a flat-topped item of office equipment", "an aesthetic disaster", and so on—each of which would have subsumed the same object under a different, equally valid description. In Chapter 1, I used the example of a matchbox serving as a play-symbol for a car. In that case, the matchbox carried the boy's conception of "car-ness"; it stood for a car in the sense of embodying (in symbolic form) those aspects of "car-ness" that the child wanted to represent for the purposes of play. In flexible creative symbolisation of this kind, a child can only symbolise what he or she can conceptualise. On the other hand, new symbols may prompt a child to conceptualise familiar things in new ways, or to fix new meanings in symbolic form (e.g. "That car is an ambulance"). In the course of all this, symbols enormously enrich the child's store of abstractions to think with. In so far as a symbol carries a conception, it applies not only to an individual thing or event, but also to "this sort of thing" (Langer, 1957). That is why symbolising constitutes such a highly generative and intellectually amenable form of abstracting—one can articulate highly specific notions in relation to each another, within a setting that is free from the clutter of irrelevant thoughts, feelings, and other psychological goings-on.

There is a further matter to consider, before reviewing symbolic functioning from a developmental perspective. It is one thing for a child to make something refer to or even stand for another. It involves more than this when the child employs a symbol with an understanding that the symbol means the same to the child him-/herself as it does to other people. It was G.H. Mead (1934: p. 73) who expounded this point most vigorously, insisting as he did so that in order to employ "significant symbols", an individual requires a degree of self-reflective awareness. Mead writes:

> Such is the difference between intelligent conduct on the part of animals and what we call a reflective individual...in order that thought may exist there must be symbols, vocal gestures generally, which arouse in the individual himself the response which he is calling out in the other, and such that from the point of view of that response he is able to direct his later conduct. It involves not only communication in the sense in which birds and animals communicate with each other, but also an arousal in the individual himself of the response he is calling out in the other individual, a taking of

the role of the other, a tendency to act as the other person acts. One participates in the same process the other person is carrying out and controls his action with reference to that participation.

The language of Mead's social behaviorism is not very elegant, and the term "response" needs translation into more appropriate psychological language. Nevertheless, Mead's is a telling analysis of what it means to participate in communication by way of significant symbols. The individuals who communicate are sharing a set of activities and attitudes, each takes the role of the other, and their symbols have shared meanings. From the perspective of the infant learning to speak with symbols, "the signals the infant learns to produce are the same signals he comprehends when produced by others, and therefore in using these symbols he anticipates how they will be interpreted" (Kaye, 1982: p. 150). The position of the listener is that already described by Ogden and Richards (1923: p. 11): "When we hear what is said, the symbols both cause us to perform an act of reference and to assume an attitude which will, according to circumstances, be more or less similar to the act and the attitude of the speaker." Although a child might begin with but a partial understanding of what a symbol is, for example by comprehending a symbolic meaning whilst as yet unable to use the symbol adequately or flexibly, this simply illustrates that the child has some way to go before she appreciates how symbols function.

DEVELOPING THE CAPACITY TO SYMBOLISE

Now I should like to explore the thesis that there are two distinct mechanisms entailed in achieving the kind of distancing that separates Thought from Thing. This sounds deceptively straightforward. In fact, the separation involves not only a transition from signal to symbol use, but also a radical alteration in the young child's awareness of self in relation to others. We shall see how intimately an infant's developing capacity for conceptual thought is related to the infant's evolving awareness and understanding of people with minds.

The Autonomous Infant

I shall begin with the developmental pathway taken by "the autonomous infant". This is a route which an infant can follow more or less by herself. The infant acts in relation to the world-as-perceived, and drawing upon the "computational" resources provided by a rapidly maturing central nervous system, she thereby acquires substantial cognitive powers.

I shall give little by way of detail about sensorimotor developments in the first year of life. Piaget (1953, 1954) provides the classic account, and numerous commentators (Bower, 1979; Chapman, 1988; Flavell, 1963; Piaget & Inhelder, 1969; Sugarman, 1987; and chapters in Butterworth, 1981, and Liben, 1983) have summarised, amended, and extended his observations. I really only want to make two points.

The first point concerns the kinds of development in which Piaget was most interested. He followed his own three infants as they progressed towards a stage at which they could invent new means for attaining goals, they could understand the permanence of objects and could anticipate where an object might be found even after invisible displacements, and they could think through possible sequences of event. Obviously it is appropriate to class these as instances of thinking. Of special interest is the way that infants seem to be able to do something *like* reflecting on their actions, and do something *like* making one thing stand for (or at least, serve the function of) another, even before they have the capacity to symbolise. For example, "secondary circular reactions" reveal a young infant's ability to repeat an action in order to create an effect. Piaget's daughter Lucienne was just three months old when she learned to shake her legs in order to set in motion the cloth dolls suspended above her bassinet. Two months later, Lucienne was trying to grasp some spools in the same situation. Here is Piaget's account of what happened when by accident she caused them to swing:

> She manages to touch but not yet to grasp them. Having shaken them fortuitously, she then breaks off to shake herself a moment while looking at them (shakes of the legs and trunk), then she resumes her attempts at grasping.
> Why has she broken off in order to shake herself for a few seconds?... Everything transpires as though the subject, endowed for a moment with reflection and internal language, had said to herself something like this: "Yes, I see that this object could be swung, but it is not what I am looking for". But, lacking language, it is by working the schema that Lucienne would have thought that, before resuming her attempts to grasp. In this hypothesis, the short interlude of swinging would thus be equivalent to a sort of motor recognition (Piaget, 1953: pp. 210–211).

According to Piaget, we can surmise that even on the level of sensorimotor intelligence, there is some differentiation between signifiers (or "indications") and something that is signified. The sight of a certain state of affairs serves as an indication of the results to be expected if that state of affairs is acted on in a certain way (Chapman, 1988). Moreover, the child soon learns how to apply schemes as procedures to make interesting spectacles last—Lucienne would kick her legs to make other things happen. By the time she reaches eight months of age, the infant will even do something as a means of achieving a preset goal, for example pushing aside an object in order to reach another. By around one year of age, at Piaget's Stage Five of infancy, she creatively invents new schemes to achieve her ends, for instance using a stick to obtain a distant object. The child can explore new objects by applying old schemes, and can assimilate objects to several schemes at once.

My purpose in charting these changes (and observations of the infant's developing "object concept" would have served just as well), is to illustrate a form of distancing in the infant's relation with the world. Schemes are co-ordinated with each other by way of reciprocal assimilation (e.g. what is seen is also grasped), and before long they can be combined in means–ends relations. The infant *intends* to produce an effect in its circular reactions, and there is manifest creativity in the ways the infant behaves. Piaget suggests that such developments occur through the progressive integration and differentiation of sensorimotor schemes. This appears to be an appropriate and plausible form of explanation for the kinds of cognitive development described so far.

This brings me to my second point. There are many doubts one could have about Piaget's radically constructivist and individualist view of early development. For example, there are strong arguments for adopting a more realist perspective (Costall, 1981; Russell, 1981), and one might certainly question such a radically non-social treatment of what Piaget sees as the infant's "purely individual intelligence" (Piaget, 1967, quoted in Decarie, 1978). Yet Piaget may be justified in supposing that quite a lot of infant cognitive development takes place without the *necessity* of specifically social intervention. His observations suggest that simply through their own sensorimotor activities, infants might acquire what James Russell (1984: p. 61) calls preverbal "cognitive abilities in co-reference". This phrase belongs to Russell's important discussion of the subject–object division in early development. A brief summary of Russell's argument will provide a bridge to the next section of the chapter.

Russell (1984) suggests that cognitive development can be construed as children's progress in making a division between what is true of their experiences and what is true of the world. This corresponds with drawing the linguistic distinction between a mental orientation (or "intension") and "reality as falling under no particular characterisation" (or "extension"): "What constitutes the intensional is the possibility of taking up different mental orientations to one element of reality, the linguistic face of which is a plurality of words applying to one object" (Russell, 1984: p. 60). Russell distinguishes between two forms of preverbal co-reference: inter-individual co-reference, which I shall come to later, and intra-individual co-reference. Whereas Piaget describes the infant as coming to differentiate actions on objects and perceptions of objects from the objects themselves, he also shows how the infant is learning that her different actions and different perceptual accommodations can reference the same object. Here we witness an infant's own "co-referentiality of action, perception and gesture" (Russell, 1984: p. 61). This may contribute to a growing appreciation that two psychological activities may be directed towards a common object, and that what is subjective and what is objective are not the same. The world "out there" is already being distanced from the infant's own activities.

The Socially Engaged Infant

I shall now consider how Heinz Werner and Bernard Kaplan (1984) set their account of symbol formation firmly in the interpersonal domain. These authors characterise their task as follows:

> Here, then, we shall indicate how in the course of development there is a progressive distancing or polarization between person and object of reference, between person and symbolic vehicle, between symbolic vehicle and object, and between the persons in the communication situation, that is, addressor and addressee...The increasing distance or polarization of the four components in interpersonal commerce emerges slowly in ontogenesis from early forms of interaction which have the character of "sharing" experiences *with* the Other rather than of "communicating" messages to the Other...Initially, inter-individual interaction occurs in purely sensory–motor–affective terms. Sooner or later, however, a novel and typically human relationship emerges, that of "sharing" of experiences, which probably has its clearest early paradigm in the nonreflexive smile of the infant in response to its mother's smile. This sharing attitude in its true sense then becomes manifest when the infant begins to share contemplated objects with the Other...Thus, the act of reference emerges not as an individual act, but as a social one: by exchanging things with the Other, by touching things and looking at them with the Other. Eventually, a special gestural device is formed, *pointing* at an object, by which the infant invites the Other to contemplate an object as he does himself (Werner & Kaplan, 1984: pp. 42–3).

A little further on, Werner and Kaplan (1984: p. 43) continue:

> ...whereas pointing entails only reference, the indication or denotation of a concretely present object, symbolization involves differentiation and

integration of two aspects: reference to an object and representation of that object. In reference by pointing, the referent (the object) remains "stuck" in the concrete situation; in reference by symbolization, the characteristic features of the object (its connotations) are lifted out, so to speak, and are realized in another material medium (an auditory, visual, gestural one, etc).

Werner and Kaplan proceed to analyse the four types of distancing that such developments entail. First, there is distancing between person and object. This begins when the infant's early things-of-action (things of affective striving and biologically directed action) become, in addition, objects-of-contemplation. The authors describe the four- or five-month-old's new-found contemplative attitude in much the same way as does Piaget, and they point out that the object now acquires relative independence and assumes the potential status of a referent. Second, there is the distancing between person and symbolic vehicle. This involves a shift from symbolic forms that are interwoven with an infant's bodily gestures and are imbued with private experiences and personal feelings, to symbols that are more or less function-specific with regard to representational reference. Third, there is the distancing between symbolic vehicle and referential object. This occurs when the vehicle loses its thing-like status and becomes a transparent mediator through which an individual apprehends meaning, a meaning that increasingly exemplifies a general concept rather than a concrete particular. Finally, Werner and Kaplan insist that an increase in interpersonal distance between addressor and addressee profoundly affects all the aforementioned aspects of symbolic formation, not least because communication between psychologically distinct individuals requires autonomous symbols that are communal and decontextualised. In due course "names" (which are designators linked to a concrete-pragmatic sphere of action) become "words" located in a linguistic field with semantic contrasts, and two-word combinations make explicit the child's capacity to differentiate between referent and attitude in topic–comment utterances (e.g. "Ball gone").

Thus Werner and Kaplan provide a great deal to help us envisage what kinds of development need to take place for the child to acquire the capacity to symbolise. Having said this, there are many steps in the process that remain unexplained. As Werner and Kaplan (1984: p. 71) acknowledge, "there is little direct information about the stages, in the normally developing child, of this emergence of objects and symbols from an interpersonal matrix". I shall try to build upon the work of Piaget, Vygotsky, Mead, and Werner and Kaplan, to offer some additional thoughts about this process.

THE INTERPERSONAL ORIGINS OF
SYMBOLIC FUNCTIONING

Sharing Experiences

In a paper entitled *On sharing experiences* (Hobson, 1989b), I discuss how an infant's experience of primitive forms of affectively–patterned, person-with-person sharing plays a vital role in promoting the infant's recognition of what it means to share, and therefore what it means to be one amongst many persons-with-minds. I have rehearsed some of the arguments in the previous chapter, and now I want to pick up the story at the end of the infant's first year of life. At this stage of "secondary intersubjectivity", we find that the infant demonstrates an awareness that experiences of objects and events *in the world* can be shared with others. Indeed, we witness the infant's investment in bringing and showing things to friendly strangers as well as to familiar care-givers. In so doing, the child manifests relatedness towards another person's relatedness towards the world, as well as towards herself.

Let me take social referencing as paradigmatic for a specific form of interpersonal triangulation. I should like to make some rather obvious points about the particular configuration of interpersonal events I have been highlighting. For the sake of discussion, I shall refer to the visual cliff procedure of Sorce et al. (1985) which I described in Chapter 3. Here twelve-month-olds were confronted with what seemed to be a precipitate drop in the surface across which they were crawling. The typical infants noticed the cliff and looked to the mother's face. Thus they sought out the mother's emotional attitude towards the cliff and/or towards themselves at the edge of the cliff. The mother's physical orientation indicated the directedness of her attention, in this case towards the infant and the cliff. An infant's perception of the direction of a person's attitude makes a big difference in such situations—for example, the mother's mere presence is not enough (Sorce & Emde, 1981). Having "referenced" the mother's "referential attitude", the infant on the cliff then reacted to the mother's bodily-expressed emotional orientation towards what was happening. The infant's own emotional attitudes and actions *vis-à-vis* the cliff were altered correspondingly. When the mother posed fear, for example, the infant froze or turned back; when the mother posed happiness, the infant crawled forward.

I shall restate my way of capturing these events. The infant manifests an altered attitude in response to the mother's attitude towards a particular, visually-specified circumstance. There is nothing here to justify saying that the infant has a "representation" of the care-giver's "representation" of the situation. On the other hand, there is every reason to say that the infant has an environmentally focussed emotional reaction to the mother's behaviour *both* as emotionally expressive (in adult terms) *and* as directed to something "out there" in the child's own external world. My goal is now to explain how infants travel from this point towards the end of the first year, to another point six to nine months later (i.e. at around 18 months of age) when they can symbolise and use language.

The Relatedness Triangle

I am going to refer to the infant–person–environment configuration of social referencing, joint attention, and so on, as the "relatedness triangle". I shall set a diagram of the relatedness triangle (Fig. 7.2) alongside Ogden and Richards' "meaning triangle". My aim is to describe how the latter cognitive triangle emerges out of and embodies the interpersonal events depicted by the former kind of social triangulation.

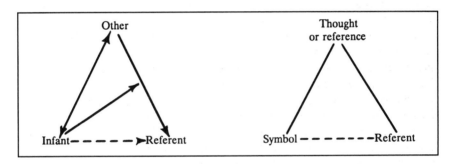

FIG. 7.2.

The most important thing about my relatedness triangle is the nature of the relations that exist among the fixed vertices of infant, other person, and referent. In particular, the arrow within the triangle represents the infant *perceiving* the quality and directedness of the other person's attitude towards a referent that is or can become the focus of the infant's own attitude. More than this, the infant relates to the other person's bodily-cum-mental relation with that object or event. We have already seen that infants of around one year can distinguish their own attitude from that of another person—why else would they show things to anyone, if not to align or co-ordinate their body/mental states? What is special about the triangulation I have described, is that the infant has the opportunity to register that the self-same object in the visually-specified world (e.g. the visual cliff) has one meaning-for-self and a *different* meaning-for-other.

This configuration of events establishes conditions in which the child can apprehend that meanings are person-dependent. Or to redescribe this from the complementary perspective, a given object or event may have more than one meaning-for-persons. Most evidently in the case of social referencing, but also in other situations involving joint attention, affective and conative meanings are central to the infant's concerns. In the former case, the meaning of the environmental circumstance is often of paramount importance; the visual cliff has one emotional meaning for the infant (it is anxiety-provoking), another for the care-giver (it is quite safe). In episodes of joint attention, the object or event is less important than the other person's attitude or goal-directed actions towards it, as well as the person's attitudes towards the child who is sharing the experience. Note that at this stage, the event referred to falls under a single description for infant and care-giver—for instance, something like "infant-at-cliff"—but this has more than one "value" attached to it. In becoming aware of this multiple-meanings feature of events in which they are already implicated, infants are making a momentous discovery about person–thing relations, not merely about things in the world. To repeat: one thing may have more than one meaning, and a single person can have more than one meaning-conferring attitude. Insight into all this constitutes a major advance in the distancing of Thought from Thing, and of Self from Other. Not merely the separateness, but also the connectedness, of self, other, thought, and thing is being apprehended.

This suggestion raises many problems. Setting aside the controversial claim that an infant registers (and assumes an attitude to) someone else's *attitude*, what is there to suggest that the infant can simultaneously entertain the idea of two contrasting attitudes to the same object? My response here is to point out that at the end of the first year, infants are already busy influencing their care-giver's actions (e.g. in requesting) and inducing the care-giver to become attentively engaged with themselves in relation to this or that object or event (e.g. in showing or pointing to things); the infant is both able and motivated to follow the care-giver's gaze, and in situations of uncertainty, will look to the care-giver to see what the latter's reaction is. So infants not only ascribe a "contemplative attitude" to another person, they also recognise that at any moment the other may have a particular attitude that differs from their own. My suggestion is that conditions are ripe for the infants to acquire the insights that a given object may have multiple meanings, and that persons can confer meanings.

I need to say more about what these propitious conditions are, but perhaps I should first explain why I think all this is important for developing the capacity to symbolise (I shall also need to explain why it takes some months before the capacity is acquired). I am trying to show how the distancing of Thought from Thing occurs through the interiorisation of a configuration of interpersonal events. The first step is for infants to distinguish (distance) attitudes from thing(s) towards which attitudes are directed. The intermediate step is for infants to realise their own potential for assuming another person's attitude towards an object or event—and knowingly so. This leads to the capacity to adopt multiple attitudes to things and, with this, to confer multiple meanings. The final step is for infants to discover that given, interpersonally negotiated meanings can be assigned to symbols that can then be used to carry the meanings. This discovery creates new realms of communicative exchange and intellectual adventure. Rita Leal (1993) has been exploring related themes from a psychodynamic standpoint, and has also referred to the triangulation involved as the child negotiates and constructs symbols to capture aspects of shared interactions *vis-à-vis* things in the world.

Having established the drift of my argument, I need to return to the relatedness triangle, in order to complicate it.

The Referent as Pivot.   In one sense it is obvious that the process I have described pivots around the object or event in the world. It is important to recognise that from the infants' point of view, the object or event has a privileged description and a specific location. The infants apprehend the visual cliff "as" a cliff (albeit not in those terms), and they relate their care-giver's attitude to this same cliff. Especially within the structured but ever-shifting infant–care-giver games described by Bruner (1983), but also in many other everyday situations, there will be recurrent episodes of referencing the same kind of object or event, and more than one other person will simultaneously or successively serve as "referencing-points". Therefore the relatedness triangle needs to be altered (Fig. 7.3):

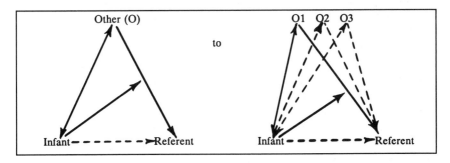

FIG. 7.3.

A further embellishment to the picture is that in many cases of joint-attention, the referent may be a "something" that can be assimilated to various of the infant's schemes of action and feeling. In this case, the referent might already have a number of infant-centred meanings, as described by Piaget.

The "Other Person" as Pivot.   Once again, it is clear that a range of referents crop up as the foci for infant–care-giver sharing and referencing. This alters the triangle (Fig. 7.4):

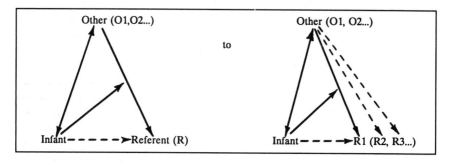

FIG. 7.4.

Infant and "Other".   The relations between infant and "other" are complicated by the fact that each is a person with attitudes, and each can assume the other's attitudes. For the present purposes, the infant's capacity to move into the other person's psychological position is most significant (Fig. 7.5):

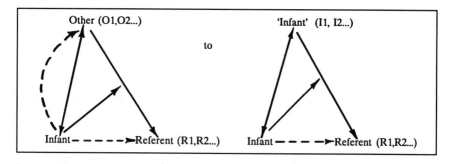

FIG. 7.5.

If infants can maintain a sense of the duality between their own alternative positions, the one originating in their initial view and the other arising through identification with the other person's attitude, then they can now relate to their *own* relatedness to the world.

It remains an empirical question which attitudes the infant can relate to in this way, either now or later in development. Consider the capacity to pretend. There is much to indicate that even during the first year of life, an infant comes to appreciate the significance of a playful attitude in her transactions with others. Jerome Bruner (1975) has described the spontaneity as well as the structuring of increasingly elaborated "formats" of infant–care-giver play during infancy, and Vasu Reddy (1991) has provided some delightful descriptions of infants under one year old teasing and mucking about with grown-ups. It is around the end of the first year that an infant begins to enact pretend sequences such as falling asleep or driving a car. What develops over the first half of the second year is children's ability to relate the "pretend attitude" to situations in which they apply novel attitudes to objects or events, whilst maintaining an awareness of their non-pretend relationship with the world-as-given. According to this account, the child makes one thing stand for another by playfully conferring a particular kind of person–referent attitude on to a new (symbolic) referent which is also recognised in its non-pretend status.

The purpose of my relatedness triangle(s) has been to illustrate how the infant's experience of self–other–world relations promotes this cognitive development. The requirement is that the infant should distance person-to-world attitudes from the infant's own immediate, first-person apprehension of events. The infant needs to recognise that, being a person, she can be the source of a variety of attitudes; that is, the infant can assume the attitudes of an infinite number of other persons (represented in my diagrams as O1, O2...). So, too, the infant can apply these attitudes to an infinite number of referents (R1, R2...). In other words, any given person-to-world attitude is distanced from particular persons and from particular referents; a care-giver's attitude-to-X can become the infant's attitude-to-X, and a given attitude-to-X can be applied as a pretend attitude-to-X to Y, without undermining the infant's veridical attitude-to-Y. In terms of the Ogden and Richards triangle, the symbol now anchors or carries the child's conception of the referent. It is only in this sense that a symbol itself "symbolises" and "refers" to anything, by encompassing and embodying a meaning-for-the-symboliser. So it is that a person comes to refer to things-as-conceptualised through the use of symbols.

What, then, are the essential ingredients of my proposal? I am suggesting that an infant's experience of co-reference with others is a prerequisite, not merely a precursor, for creative symbolic function. It is essential that the infant can *perceive* how other people have evaluative attitudes to objects and events that are also the foci of the infant's own attitudes—the relatedness triangle. More than this, the mechanism by which the infant comes to symbolise is through insight into the shifts in perspective that may occur through identification with other people's (or potential other people's) attitudes. Infants realize that they themselves can confer person-dependent rather than world-specified attitudes and meanings to things and events. They can knowingly pretend-take this as if it were a "that".

The remaining ingredients of my account are those that pertain to the infant's capacity to relate to other persons *as* persons with their own subjective attitudes to the world. For example, the infant needs to perceive attitudes as attitudes, and to recognise persons as beings with whose attitudes they can identify. The infant also needs a basis for achieving the kind of self-reflective insight I have described. I shall deal with these issues in the following section.

The Interpersonal Dimension

If it is the case that symbolising involves the ascription of person-to-world attitudes detached from their original person-specific and target-specific anchorage; if it is through their experience of referring to the world in ways that conflict as well as agree with other people's attitudes towards that same world, that infants come to recognise how different people have different attitudes towards things and events, and different ways of seeing-as; if, moreover, infants' capacity simultaneously to adopt multiple attitudes to given objects and events depends upon their ability to identify with alternative standpoints and attitudes, and to adopt a special kind of attitude to themselves and their own attitudes; if all this is so, then it becomes clear how interpersonal understanding is integral to the developing capacity to symbolise. The levels of interpersonal understanding most relevant for symbolising are those concerned with perceiving the outer-directed attitudes of people on the one hand, and with conceiving of self and other as separate but similar centres of consciousness on the other.

What I am calling the interpersonal dimension begins with the infant–care-giver face-to-face interactions of the early months of life (Newson & Newson, 1976). As I discussed in an earlier chapter, co-ordinated exchanges of affect establish a primary connectedness of subjective experience between infant and care-giver. The infant perceives and relates to the other person as a "thing" with special properties that call out the infant's own emotionally patterned reactions. Then by the age of nine months or so, the infant perceives the other person's emotional attitudes as having directedness to things and events in the world. The infant begins to imitate other people's actions and attitudes, and can reproduce those actions and assume those attitudes even after a delay of weeks or hours. At the same time, the infant continues to be the focus of many of the care-giver's attitudes; the infant can begin to assume evaluative attitudes towards him- or herself as a source of attitudes. This is the final element of the relatedness triangle—the double arrow between infant and other person that becomes a double arrow between infant and the infant herself. I imagine it is also this aspect of the situation that, coupled with progress in brain maturation and no doubt other cognitive abilities, has a considerable bearing on the time taken for infants to acquire the insight that they themselves are a source of subjective attitudes, separate from other persons but linked with them by virtue of the kinds of attitudes that persons have in common. Presently I shall come to additional, specifically communicative factors that also contribute to these developments.

The outcome of all this is a totally new way of being self-conscious: in relating to their own ways of relating to the world, children become aware of their own subjectivity. At this point they can reflect on their own experiences and knowingly attribute to other "selves" the kinds of experience they now conceptualise in themselves. In the last chapter I argued that this reflective and conceptual form of perspective-taking is not the origin of interpersonal understanding, but it certainly enriches the child's capacities for sensitive social engagement as well as affording vital insights into the mental life of others.

I have just referred to "other cognitive abilities" that enter the developmental picture. Any account that emphasises the interpersonal dimension of development needs to respect the role played by abilities that are relatively non-social in origin. As Vygotsky (1978) stresses, it is often in the convergence of practical and social intelligence that we may find an explanation for emergent properties of mind. One important example concerns the transition to secondary intersubjectivity at around nine months of age. For example, Susan Sugarman (1984) has presented evidence that the same cognitive–developmental hurdle acts as a constraint on object–object co-ordination (e.g. using a support to reach an object) and on person–object co-ordination (e.g. using someone else to reach something). Only once children are able to effect instrumental co-ordination with objects at around eight to ten months of age, are they able to "use" people to obtain things or to use an object to solicit the attention of a person. On the other hand, the capacity to subordinate the use of one physical object to manoeuvre another differs from the co-ordination of an object in relation to a person, in so far as the infant will cue the adult (often smiling and vocalising) without physically manipulating her. Elizabeth Bates and her colleagues (Bates et al., 1979; Bates, 1979) also consider "tool use" to be a requisite for intentional and ultimately symbolic communication. If this is so, then it seems to indicate that the infant has an understanding of other persons as agents and as beings with their own subjective attitudes, prior to (or at least alongside) non-personal means–ends co-ordination. It is through specifically intersubjective understanding that "instrumentality" finds unique application in the interpersonal domain. The fact that the child signals intent to someone else implies that the someone else is recognised as such, to be "used" as a very special kind of means in this new means–ends nexus. Moreover, requesting of others is not the same as sharing experiences with others; as Luigia Camaioni (1992) has recently emphasised, to engage with someone as a communicative partner is quite distinct from the ability to attribute agency (in the sense of autonomous behaviour) or instrumentality to others. Juan-Carlos Gomez (1991) describes how the young gorilla masters tool-use several months *before* she is able to communicate requests to another person—and we have noted how there is a similar developmental progression in autistic children. What normal infants (but neither gorillas nor autistic children) seem to have ready and waiting for linkage with generalised means–ends understanding, is some sense of other persons as subjects of experience with their own capacity to register and react to events. This is the interpersonal dimension.

Thus there is a need to specify exactly what does or does not implicate which kinds of interpersonal understanding, at various stages in cognitive development. The present thesis concerns creative symbolic function, specific aspects of language, and conceptual thought. As Janellan Huttenlocher and E. Tory Higgins (1978) argue, there are phenomena in animal as well as early child development that might seem to imply symbolic functioning, but which actually entail less complex and less productive psychological processes. A child may categorise one thing as another, or may exemplify one form of behaviour in relation to novel (inappropriate) objects, without this entailing that the child *designates* something by something else. To substitute one thing for another is not enough; rather, the child must grasp the fixed functional relation between a symbol and what it signifies, so that (for example) a symbol is both understood correctly and used productively, outside any particular context in which it was originally learned. Elizabeth Bates (1979) writes that the vehicle–referent relationship needs to be "objectified", and this corresponds with my emphasis on the child's insight that person-to-world attitudes can be detached from their original settings, and anchored elsewhere. The corollary of all this is that quite sophisticated, symbol-*like* substitutions of one object for another might be accomplished without interpersonal input, if the child can operate with alternative modes of representational functioning. What such processes will lack, is the generativity and motivational investment that issues from the kind of interpersonal perspective-taking I have described. This will be important to bear in mind when considering autistic children's limited capacities for symbolic functioning.

I have just characterised symbolic functioning as a form of perspective-taking. Dennie Wolf and Howard Gardner (1981) highlight this aspect of the structure of early symbolisation. Indeed, the present account of the origins, development, and implications of children's understanding of their own and others' orientations and attitudes to the world might be reframed in terms of role-structuring as described by Wolf and Gardner. These authors argue that a child's capacity to use "a set of understandings about the distinct situational roles that objects and persons can play in events" provide the child with a critical point of entry into language and other modes of symbolisation (Wolf & Gardner, 1981: p. 315). They provide details of the transition from the point about nine months of age to a stage at 18 months, when children can play from the vantage-point of any of several roles, not only in games such as hide-and-seek but also in sociodramatic play. I take it that Wolf and Gardner's (1981: p. 303) account in terms of "the crystallization of understandings latent in tool use and social interaction into a set of concepts about roles" would easily map on to my description of a young child's insight into the transferability and transposability of person-to-world attitudes.

Before moving on to consider communication and language, I should like to end this section of the chapter on a more personal note. Just as Vygotsky (1962) alerts us to the affective attitude buried within each and every idea, I have tried to analyse the interpersonal relatedness triangle that lies behind, and gives life to, the seemingly impersonal process of symbolising. One of the experiences that persuaded me of this account, was to witness my oldest son's first ventures into symbolising. I am no longer sure what he used to symbolise what, but I vividly remember the setting (our kitchen at meal-time) and the atmosphere of the moment. James was in his high-chair when he picked up something, probably a spoon; he looked at it and looked at me, bright-eyed, and with a slightly mischievous and delighted expression (as if to say: "So you think you know where I'm coming from...!"), he gestured and vocalised to communicate to me that this was now...a car! I felt I could almost see his movement into a someone else's attitude, and I was left in no doubt that he was aware that I would be aware of what he was doing—and that this was *his* creation of an alternative reality which I would (when I caught up) enter with him. I see no better way of describing this than in terms of an insight into the nature of self, other, thought (or attitude), and thing. The intense pleasure we both derived from the event was both interpersonal and intellectual—as perhaps is true of all symbolising.

COMMUNICATION AND LANGUAGE

Language functions in diverse ways. Not all words refer to things; for example, many words accompany or replace more natural expressions and gestures. This may be true not only for early performative words such as "Hi" or "Bye-bye", but also for later and more complex expressions such as

"I am in pain" (Huttenlocher & Higgins, 1978; Wittgenstein, 1953). One influential attempt to capture early linguistic functioning *en route* to the emergence of word meaning, is the scheme outlined by John Dore (1985). Dore divides the single-word period into four successive but overlapping phases. The first phase is that of protocommunicative signals which are almost always accompanied by affectively salient vocalisations, gestures, and facial expressions. These are not always directed towards others, but are often interpreted by adults as signals of the infant's affective states. The second phase is that of indexical signs, which are usually directed to someone and applied to some aspect of immediate context, but lack clear referential intent to designate particular objects or actions. The next phase of denotative symbols involves adult word-like forms that are not only used referentially, but are also semantically contrastive and exhibit displacement of reference outside the immediate context. They may be used in a variety of speech acts, whether to label, to question, or whatever. It is during this phase that there occurs an "explosion of naming", a rapid spurt in vocabulary growth. Finally, in the phase of predicative syntagms, children produce one word about part of a situation for which they have other words that they might have chosen. They can use words to comment upon topics supplied by the non-linguistic context or by other utterances. Martyn Barrett (1985) skilfully portrays how similar phases may be discerned in the accounts of other major contemporary theorists.

In explaining these transactions, Dore's focus is on the social and emotional interaction that occurs within the infant–care-giver dyad. For example, when an infant expresses some inner state, the care-giver routinely attunes to it by sharing the same state and articulating it in a conventional way. When the infant adapts to such an expression, this is not so much an imitation as an appropriation of the new expression for their own original experience. In such an occurrence, the cross-personal sharing of a state is one critical ingredient. It is through interpersonal transactions such as these that the child moves from the stage of emitting more or less reflex signals which are interpreted by care-givers as communicative, to that of predicating properties of entities which are presumed to be topics shared by interlocutors.

I am going to use Dore's descriptive scheme as a background against which to foreground just four points about the emergence of language. These points are intended to fill major gaps in my account thus far.

The first point concerns children's intention to communicate, and their ability to recognise others' intentions to communicate in return. There would seem to be two potentially separate components here: one to do with having and perceiving intentions or agency, and the other to do with the kind of goal being intended, namely that of communication. In order for children to intend to achieve this particular goal, they must clearly have some sense of what it means to communicate. I have argued that a fundamental prerequisite for this, is a sense of what it means to be intersubjectively engaged with someone else, and of what it means to share. Infants must have the means to register that their own affective expressions and motoric strivings are registered by someone else. What I have argued for the case of sharing, Susan Sugarman (1984: pp. 63–64) expresses for the case of communication: "Before children can use language to communicate they must learn what communication is. They must learn that there is a purpose not only to making clear their experience, but to intentionally presenting that experience for, or as though it were for, someone else."

This leads to my second point. Let us suppose that infants' experience of intersubjective co-ordination with someone else is primary. Such modes of sharing and making contact with another person may become integrated with infants' growing sense of their own and others' agency, such that more systematic and determined forms of "intending to communicate" emerge towards the end of the first year of life. The picture becomes further complicated when one recognises, following Grice (1957), that in mature symbolic communication, a speaker not only intends X to designate Y, but also intends that the listener recognise that he or she intends X to designate Y. Further varieties and embeddings of intentions-to-induce-readings-of-intentions become possible and indeed vital for effective communication, for example when a speaker intends to induce the listener to recognise the speaker's playful or metaphorical intent in using a given expression.

My third point concerns a particular line of development within the class of having and recognising others' intentions to communicate, namely that concerned with "referring" and commenting on a shared focus of attention. Once again, there is a distinction to be drawn between infants' ability to perceive that another person's behaviour and gestures express a directedness of attitude towards the world, and the infants' ability to perceive that the person *intends* to communicate something of his or her attitude, in a referential manner. So, too, infants need to discover the indicating potential of their own actions and gestures, and to proceed from deictic or pointing gestures to the capacity to denote classes of items in contrast to others, and finally to comment on shared topics. I suggest that here we need to distinguish among three different classes of psychological process or mechanism. These underpin respectively: (1) the perception of outer-directed (and in a particular sense, referring and meaning-attributing) subjective attitudes in others; (2) the perception of goal-directed behaviour; and (3) the awareness of a person's intention *to* refer and/or to comment, communicatively. I think that processes involved in category (3) presuppose others in categories (1) and (2). I further suggest that the psychological capacities required for category (1), the perception of others' outer-directed attitudes, need to be further subdivided into a cluster of abilities that have to do with perceiving the *directedness* of another person's bodily orientation, eye-gaze, and so on, and other abilities that have more to do with perceiving the affective *meanings* in the expressions of others. I trust the significance of these proposals will become clear when we review the abilities and disabilities of autistic individuals.

Turning to the progressively more differentiated modes of referring, Jerome Bruner (1978; 1983) has provided a rich description of the ritualised "joint action formats" within which infants learn to take turns with their care-givers, to evolve a sense of interchanging roles, and to co-ordinate intentions and mutual attention. Bruner makes a convincing case for supposing that such formats serve as a Language Acquisition Support System by providing a topic–comment structure into which words may be woven when infants and care-givers share a target of joint attention (and see Tomasello & Farrar, 1986, for evidence that such joint attention episodes can contribute towards vocabulary learning). Each member of the dyad may infer the referent of the other's referring acts by judging the significance of the acts (e.g. utterances) within highly familiar and constrained contexts. Bruner believes that an infant's intent to refer is unlearned, and so too is the recognition of that intent in others. He writes: "Some basis for referential intersubjectivity must exist before language proper appears. Logically, there would be no conceivable way for two human beings to achieve shared reference were there no initial disposition for it" (Bruner, 1983: p. 122). The question remains, of course, what form(s) the "initial disposition" takes, and I have suggested that certain psychological primitives posited by Bruner—in particular, "that there is a world 'out there' that is shared by others" (Bruner, 1983: p. 122)—might be subject to further developmental analysis. However, Bruner's principal thesis is unaffected (also Bruner, 1975a, 1975b): ritualised games between infant and care-giver structure a meeting of minds and a mutual co-ordination of intentions and attitudes, and in so doing they provide a scaffolding for the care-giver to pass to her infant the forms and uses of language.

My fourth point concerns the conventionalisation of language. As Bruner (1983) again describes, the care-giver becomes intent on getting the child to appreciate that there is a standard vocalisation for a given referent or speech act; or as Dore puts it, the child is held accountable for her utterances. This has great significance. As we noted earlier, a true symbol is one that a symboliser recognises to designate for both speaker and listener. Early performative expressions that accompany action (e.g. "Bye-bye") may become conventional without being referential, but true symbolism entails knowledge of what and how a symbol represents (Zukow, 1984). Despite the controversy that surrounds the idea, I think that

McShane (1980) is right about the child achieving an insight into the nature of referring to things by names. Indeed, my own hunch is that the insight that gives rise to the "naming explosion" (when it occurs) is not simply that *a* word can be used to stand for this or that, but rather that there is "the" word—a mutually agreed-upon word (which the care-giver has been stressing for, as well as seeking from, the infant)—for each instance of a given thing or event. At this point the child becomes eager to discover not merely the names for things, but also the things for names. The child has reached a new level of understanding of what it means to refer; the child not only knows when to make utterances, but also appreciates how people use words to name. The relatedness triangle has yielded insight into language.

Why Talk?

In a beautiful paper with this title, Susan Sugarman (1983) questions the parallels that have been drawn between the "language" of apes and humans. Apes may be trained to perform symbol-like operations in order to bring about desired states of affairs. On the other hand, even very young children "use" language for a broader range of purposes, not least for communication, for sharing, and for the free expression of ideas. Sugarman's point is that what we have called protodeclaratives are expressions of an entire complex of motivations and intentions. The fact that children choose to employ language in order to indicate things to others, and that they elaborate language so creatively, suggests there is something uniquely human about what people are doing when they talk.

So, too, Suzanne Langer insists that human beings have an impulse to express ideas which is irreducible to anything more fundamental:

> How else shall we account for man's love of talk? From the first dawning recognition that words can *express* something, talk is a dominant interest, an irresistible desire. As soon as this avenue of action opens, a whole stream of symbolic process is set free in the jumbled outpouring of words—often repeated, disconnected, random words—that we observe in the "chattering" stage of early childhood...There must be immediate satisfaction in this strange exercise, as there is in running and kicking. The effect of words on other people is only a secondary consideration (Langer, 1957: pp. 43–44).

It is obviously difficult to know whether this claim is congruent with or antithetical to Macmurray's proposal (1961; cited in Chapter 3, p. 34) that the impulse to communicate with others is primary. The phenomenon of infant babbling might also make us wonder whether such productive expressiveness is essentially symbolic. I am inclined to believe that there is *something* social about symbolic forms of expression, from the outset. It is certainly of psychological significance that children find joy in symbolising and communicating, and that one source of joy (and reassurance) is for a child to establish and maintain psychological connectedness with others. Even in the private domain of a person's own mind, symbolic activity seems to involve a kind of internal communication.

If this is so, then the creativity of symbolic activity may have much to do with the means by which it is acquired. The processes of intersubjective co-ordination and differentiation, of identification and role-shifting, are integral to the creativity of social exchanges in general, but also to symbolic activity in particular. Correspondingly, if what *looks* like human symbolising is acquired by some alternative means and operates by some different psychological mechanism—whether we think of apes or autistic children—then for this very reason, it should lack the exuberant generativity of normal human symbolic activity.

RECAPITULATION

It is time to complete the circle by returning to the nature of thinking. Perhaps I should do so by reviewing the progress of this rather lengthy chapter. I began by considering what it means to achieve the kinds of abstraction entailed in acquiring concepts. To have the concept of something involves more than discriminating one thing from another. As Hamlyn (1978) describes, it is to know the principles according to which Xs are classified—and this amounts to knowing what it is for things to be X. Concepts are also distinguished by the roles they play in human forms of thinking, judgement, knowledge, and the like. My aim has been to explore how capacities not only for conceptual thought but also for symbolic imagination and language emerge in the first two years of life.

I have proposed that we need to begin by considering infants' modes of relating to and with their environment. To put this another way, we need to consider infants' capacities to perceive what the environment affords, as well as their abilities to engage with persons and things through corresponding forms of action and feeling. It is in virtue of the actions and attitudes called out by the people and objects in the environment that infants commence on the path to understanding the very nature of persons and things.

I have then tried to characterise how infants become able to distance themselves from their immediate sensorimotor–affective engagements with the world. Such distancing is necessary if infants are to think about the world around them, and in due course to reflect upon their own and other "selves". I proposed that we might distinguish two distinct lines of development. The I–It pathway is that followed by the autonomous infant who is endowed with more differentiated perceptual–relational capacities than Piaget allowed, but who nevertheless proceeds along a Piaget-style developmental trajectory as the infant negotiates her transactions with the non-personal world (which includes people-as-things). The I–Thou pathway follows a somewhat separate course as the infant's capacities to perceive and respond to person-related meanings establishes psychological connectedness with others and enables the infant to experience and register early forms of sharing.

Towards the end of the first year of life, concurrent developments in the child's dealings with the non-social and social world suggest that important cross-linkages are being forged between advances in I–It and I–Thou understanding. On the one hand, I–It means–ends understanding (or something related to this) appears to facilitate new forms of person–person–object interaction. On the other hand, these more elaborate modes of intersubjective relatedness are going to launch the infant into a cognitive revolution. Through new-found capacities to relate to another person's relation with the world, and through the ability and propensity to assume another's attitude and psychological stance towards a visually-specified and shared environment, the infant begins to learn "through" other people (Tomasello, Kruger, & Ratner, 1993). Not only this, but the very origins of creative symbolising are to be found in these propensities to identify with, yet recognise the distinctiveness of, the attitudes of other persons. Here is a route by which the child can acquire insight into the relationship between "attitude" and "focus of attitude". Once this insight is acquired, children can apply novel attitudes (symbolic meanings) to familiar things (symbolic vehicles) in creative symbolic play. They also advance to conceiving of themselves as selves in relation to other selves. At this point children can deliberately take roles and ascribe their own introspected states of mind to other selves and to the figures of symbolic play.

Finally, there is the issue of how symbols come to be conventionalised. The young child needs to recognise the meaning of any given (linguistic) symbol, a meaning that applies whether the symbol is produced *for* someone else or *by* someone else. For this there has to dawn a further insight, no doubt facilitated by a care-giver's efforts to correct the child and hold her accountable for what she says, into the nature of agreed-upon meanings for symbols. Having already understood what it is to intend to communicate, the child comes to grasp what it is to refer by means of words.

Now we get back to the nature of thinking. Perhaps it is self-evident that my story of the development of linguistic reference and predication is also a story about the infant's growing capacities for abstraction and thought. "For a thought to be a genuine thought it must be about something, and something else must be thought about that something; so there is in that thought something corresponding to the distinction between subject and predicate that becomes explicit in language itself" (Hamlyn, 1978: p. 76). In accordance with this, I have been trying to tease out how a child comes to realise that attitudes have "aboutness", and how people can intend to convey their attitudes about the world to others in subject–predicate communicative acts.

In order to communicate by symbols and to think creatively, and in order to acquire concepts and knowledge, a child needs to relate to other people in ways that not only achieve distancing of thought from thing, but also allow for interpersonal correction and agreement. There are close parallels between understanding *the* concept of something and understanding the word for something. It is not that "correcting" itself needs to happen very often, but rather that the child must come to grasp what it means to be correct (in principle, not on any given occasion), and for this the child must see correction *as* correction (Hamlyn, 1982). These requirements for mature cognition point towards the developmental significance of a child's reactions and attitudes towards the world—reactions and attitudes that the child must have in common with others—and the child's attitudes towards the attitudes of other people who (amongst other things) perform the functions of correctors and agreement-givers.

Therefore let us accept Wittgenstein's (1958) suggestion that language-users need to enjoy a "form of life" that is centrally one of interpersonal sharing and conflict, agreement and correction. This means that basic to our account of cognitive and linguistic development is a further account of the nature and origins of a child's experiences of sharing, agreement, conflict, and the like. I have tried to indicate how innate mechanisms operate to yield interpersonally co-ordinated attitudes between an infant and others, such that appropriate kinds of sharing, agreement, and so on become possible. I have also suggested that several of these same mechanisms are needed for an infant to develop creative symbolic functioning. If all this is valid, where does it leave the individual animal or human who for one reason or another cannot enter into intersubjective relations of the relevant kinds? Well, even chimpanzees and prelinguistic human infants may be capable of seeing things in respects other than those that have immediate relevance to their behaviour. They may sometimes treat one object as indicative of, or of relevance for, the potiential presence of something else. This is especially the case if they are trained to do so by human beings. Yet without the potential for becoming initiated into the use of interpersonally created and socially sanctioned symbols and concepts, individuals would demonstrate a marked impoverishment in creative imagination, flexible thinking, and language. So it is with non-human species. It is time to consider the case of autism.

CHAPTER EIGHT

Thought and Language: The Case of Autism

The purpose of this chapter is not to conduct a detailed survey of the forms of cognitive and linguistic ability and disability in autistic individuals. Instead I shall focus on some prominent and characteristic features of the psychology of autism, with a view to exploring how far a *social–developmental* account might explain the typical profile of cognitive abnormalities. In fact, I shall be trying to integrate much of the thinking of the previous chapter in my approach, hoping thereby to follow the tradition of developmental psychopathology in pursuing universal principles of child psychology through a consideration of abnormal development.

A preliminary caveat is in order. In Chapter 1, I explained how we need to distinguish between deficits that are autism-specific, and those that reflect coincidental general mental retardation. Although there is undoubtedly a complex story to unravel concerning the social dimensions of cognitive development in non-autistic mentally retarded individuals, I shall be setting this matter to one side in order to dwell upon the special considerations that apply in the case of autism.

A CLINICAL EXAMPLE

Two years after Kanner's paper of 1943, Martin Scheerer and his colleagues (Scheerer, Rothmann, & Goldstein, 1945) published an account of an idiot savant whom they called L. In this case the manifestations of characteristically "autistic" intellectual deficits appear all the more striking for their juxtaposition to exceptional abilities in circumscribed domains.

L was first seen at the age of 11 with a history of severe learning difficulties. He was said never to have shown interest in his social surroundings. At times he would run up and down in a stereotyped manner, slapping his sides and waving his hands. He presented as an inattentive person rubbing the four fingers of each hand in a drumbeat against his thumbs, displaying a friendly poise and stereotyped politeness. Although he had an IQ of only 50 on a standardised (Binet) test of intelligence, L was capable of telling the day of the week for any given date between about 1880 and 1950. He could also recount the day and date of his first visit to a place, and could usually give the names and birthdays of all the people he met there. He could spell forwards and backwards. He could play melodies by ear. L's background history included the fact that in his fourth and fifth years, he rarely offered spontaneous observations or reasons for any actions or perceived event. Nor would he imitate an action of others spontaneously. He was unable to understand or create an imaginary situation. He did not play with toys, nor did he show any conception of make-believe games. He was unable to converse in give-and-take language. He frequently displayed laughter out of keeping with the situation. He barely noticed the presence of other children, and appeared emotionally indifferent to others, even if they cried or took away his toys. He was, however, very attached to his mother. He was said to have "little emotionality of normal depth and coherence".

Up to 15 years of age, L was unable to define the properties of objects except in terms of egocentred and situational use. For example, he defined orange as "that I squeeze with", and an envelope was "something I put in with". L could neither grasp nor formulate similarities, differences or absurdities, nor could he understand metaphor. At the age of 15 he defined the difference between an egg and a stone as "I eat an egg and I throw a stone". Once, when the doctor said "Goodbye my son", L replied: "I am not your son". When asked "What would happen if you shot a person?", L replied: "He goes to the hospital". L was unable to tell who was the older and the younger of the two persons confronting him, even when a great age discrepancy was present, and this in the face of L's just having figured out the weekdays of their respective birthdays. He showed no shame in parading naked through the house. Even at 15 his emotional responses and human attachments remained shallow and perfunctory.

I have chosen to edit this account in such a way that the more obviously cognitive aspects of the patient's condition are set alongside his social-emotional disabilities. After all, my overriding aim is to show how autistic individuals' social impairment is integral to the development of their cognitive abnormalities. Many of the features of L's social relatedness are already familiar to us: his lack of interest in the people around him, his unusual affectivity and apparent emotional indifference, his seeming lack of interest in reasons for actions, his lack of self-conscious shame, his apparent incomprehension of age groupings, his failure to imitate, and yet despite all of these, his attachment to his mother. I shall take up the most striking and characteristic facets of L's cognitive and linguistic difficulties in turn, citing as I do so some of the relevant literature on autism. As I shall be offering an interpretation of the deficits as I proceed, I shall set the stage by summarising my theoretical perspective. This perspective arises naturally and perhaps rather obviously from my earlier discussion of conceptual issues. It is not just "my" perspective, by the way—important elements of the approach are common to a number of recent writings on autism (Baron-Cohen, 1988; Frith, 1989a; Happé, 1991; Hobson, 1989a; Leslie, 1987; Paul, 1987; Sigman & Mundy, 1987; Tager-Flusberg, 1992; Wetherby, 1986).

A THEORETICAL PERSPECTIVE

The essentials of this account are really quite straightforward. What we need to explain, amongst other things, is why many autistic children fail to acquire language, and why those who do so rarely use language normally, showing peculiarities such as echolalia, personal pronoun errors, and idiosyncratic word forms, and often failing to adjust linguistic forms so that these accord with the social and communicative needs of the moment. Why is the children's thinking "concrete" and inflexible, and like their symbolic play in being seriously constrained in creativity and imaginative breadth? Finally, why are certain cognitive abilities spared?

The crux of the matter is that autistic children do not fully understand what it means for people to share and to co-ordinate their experiences. For example, they have but a partial grasp of the manifold ways in which people employ and adjust language in order to refer to things, to communicate their own attitudes, and to influence the attitudes of others. It is because autistic children's thinking is relatively unsocial in form as well as content, that their imaginative capacities are so severely compromised. That is the theory, in a nutshell.

Perhaps it is simplest to begin with language. Autistic children fail to comprehend how language functions as communication. In the most extreme case, the lack of comprehension is almost complete—the children understand little of others' speech, and speak hardly at all themselves. More commonly the failure is partial, affecting some but not all of the various forms and functions of language. Most important here is the fact that language is the most exquisite means of expressing a speaker's attitude both to the listener, and to whatever is being talked about. Autistic children are (relatively) insensitive to the infinite variety of ways that language embodies a speaker's psychological orientation to the listener and to the topic(s) of conversation. One underlying reason is that they fail to understand how people have a set of intentions-in-speaking, a repertoire of speech acts (Searle, 1969), and how speakers select from a limitless set of co-referential expressions the one(s) that capture the particular aspects of meaning that are to be communicated or thought about. At root is a fundamental limitation in comprehending what it means for a person to have a range of psychological attitudes to other people, to things and to events, and moreover to have a variety of communicative motives and attitudes in speaking at all. Difficulties of these kinds infect some meanings more than others: deictic terms such as personal pronouns which shift meaning according to speaker–listener roles are especially vulnerable, so are metaphors. Echolalia is one notable instance of the failure to adjust linguistic forms according to speaker–listener perspectives. Yet the problems are ubiquitous—all utterances convey nuances of "speaker's meaning" that will be lost on autistic individuals.

How does this tie in with the deficits in symbolic play? Simply that in order to symbolise, and to apply (say) the notion of "a horse" to a wooden block, one has to achieve a form of co-reference or dual-track thinking in which a pretend meaning (that is, a potential meaning which is currently inapplicable in a literal or "concrete" manner) is applied to and therefore carried by a symbol. My thesis is that the source of this capacity in fully developed, flexible form is to be found in a normal child's experience and understanding of *interpersonal* co-reference *vis-à-vis* the world, and that it is in this regard that autistic children are seriously handicapped.

Finally, what of those cognitive capacities that are spared in autism? Simply put, these are abilities that develop in a manner that does not require a sensitive appraisal of the subtleties of differentiated yet co-ordinated co-referential meanings.

So much for an outline of the theory. How does the theory find application in explaining the character of autistic children's cognitive and linguistic capacities and incapacities? Given that much of language presupposes infralinguistic cognitive and symbolic abilities, I shall first deal with impairments in the latter respects, then turn to specifically linguistic disabilities, and finally consider deficits in higher cognitive function.

THE CAPACITY TO SYMBOLISE

In the previous chapter we observed how for the normal child, creative symbolic play appears around the middle of the second year of life. Yet L was unable to understand or create an imaginary situation. He did not play with toys, nor did he show any conception of make-believe games. How typical of autism is such a lack of imaginative symbolic play?

We might begin by returning to the epidemiological research of Lorna Wing and Judith Gould. Wing, Gould, Yeates, and Brierley (1977) found that even non-autistic mentally retarded children with a language comprehension age under 20 months did not demonstrate symbolic representational play that was flexible and varied in theme. Here, then, we land on a kind of intellectual floor, at the level of which neither symbolic play nor language will have developed far, whatever a person's diagnosis. When the researchers focussed on individuals with a non-verbal mental age of over 20 months (and, one presumes, with the cognitive potential for imaginative play and more advanced language, all being well in other respects), those who failed to demonstrate symbolic play also manifested autism-like conditions. Whereas many of the non-autistic retarded children exhibited creative symbolic play, none of the autistic children did so. Similar findings emerge from experimental research. For example, the study by Candace Riguet and her colleagues (Riguet, Taylor, Benaroya, & Klein, 1981) with relatively low-ability autistic, Down's and normal children confirmed that autistic children differed from the other groups in showing less and lower-level play with few substitute symbolic uses of objects, a performance that was out of keeping with language ability and that improved only modestly when the children watched play being modelled by the experimenter. Clearly the association between autism and deficits in symbolic play goes beyond what might occur through general intellectual retardation alone.

What is the character of the early stages of play in young autistic children? This is another topic that has been explored in some detail by Marian Sigman, Judy Ungerer, and their colleagues at UCLA (research that is well reviewed by Sigman & Mundy, 1987). The autistic children studied were between two-and-a-half and six years of age, and they were compared with non-autistic mentally retarded and normal children of similar levels of general intellectual function (with mental ages between about 16 months and just over three years). For example, Ungerer and Sigman (1981) and Sigman and Ungerer (1984b) presented children with a set of toys which included three dolls of different sizes, doll furniture, a tea set, a dump truck, a garage, a telephone, a brush, and a mirror. The session began with the experimenter modelling four different symbolic acts with toys while the child sat on the mother's lap. Following this, the experimenter and mother sat in diagonal corners of the room while the child was permitted to play alone with toys for sixteen minutes, and the child's behaviour was recorded through the use of a systematic checklist. The prime focus was upon the presence and frequency of functional and symbolic play. Four different types of appropriate acts with toys were counted as functional play: object-directed (e.g. pushing the truck into the garage), self-directed (e.g. brushing one's hair), doll-directed (e.g. feeding a doll with a spoon), and other-directed (e.g. holding a telephone to the mother's ear). There were three categories of symbolic pretend play: substitution play, defined as using one object as if it were another different object (e.g. using a teacup as a telephone receiver); agent play, defined as the use of a doll as an independent agent of action (e.g. propping a bottle in a doll's arm as if it could feed itself); and imaginary play, defined as the creating of objects or people having no physical representation in the immediate environment (e.g. making pouring sounds and saying "tea" as imaginary tea is poured from the teapot into a cup). The diversity of play was measured by the number of different instances recorded for each of the categories. In a second, more structured play assessment, the experimenter presented the child with toys one at a time, or in small meaningful groups.

The results were that although the autistic children demonstrated a range of different functional acts and some symbolic play, the non-autistic children tended to engage in relatively more frequent, more varied, and more integrated acts in both play categories. The group differences were greatest with respect to object-directed and doll-directed play. A subsequent study by Mundy et al. (1987) provided additional evidence that autistic children are unusual in rarely using a doll as an agent in structured play, as well as rarely directing play outward to other people and dolls.

The research team were also concerned to explore the relations among the play, joint attention, and language deficits of their young autistic subjects (Mundy et al., 1987; Sigman & Mundy, 1987). Although the small number of autistic children who showed toys to the experimenters were also those who engaged in more elaborate symbolic play, there were a number of autistic children who showed very few instances of joint attention but some functional and symbolic play acts, and there were several autistic children who demonstrated little symbolic play but engaged in joint reference with the experimenter. There was also evidence for correlations between the children's sensorimotor abilities and their play skills. The investigators concluded that "representational play seemed to involve a cognitive factor that was less associated with joint reference for this sample of autistic children" (Sigman & Mundy, 1987: p. 43). On the other hand, when the frequency with which a child pointed and made eye contact with an examiner was considered along with a measure of diversity in symbolic play, this combination bore a close correspondence with the child's performance on a test of language comprehension.

The researchers at UCLA (Mundy et al., 1987) tentatively concluded that their measures of functional and symbolic play on the one hand, and non-verbal communication involving joint-reference on the other, reflected independent psychological factors associated with language development in young autistic children. It is certainly impressive that the children's language development correlated with the ability to engage in joint attention (a situation that may be compared with the case in normal children; Tomasello & Farrar, 1986). However, it remains an open question how far play (and specifically symbolic play) is independent from joint attention in having a relation with language development. Although only four out of the sample of 16 autistic children exhibited two or more symbolic acts, and only eight of the children exhibited at least one such act, the correlation between responding to joint attention and the frequency of symbolic play acts approached significance. The number of spontaneous acts of symbolic play was also correlated with expressive as well as receptive language skills. Communicative abilities might be necessary if not alone sufficient for the development and spontaneous expression of creative and symbolic forms of imaginative play, just as they may be necessary but not sufficient for language development. As Mundy et al. (1987) discuss, the contribution of various factors associated with functional and symbolic play, and the bearing of such factors on language development, remains to be evaluated.

My emphasis just now on creative forms of imaginative symbolic play was deliberate, but also question-begging. What is to count as "true" creative play? It is already evident that many autistic children are able to engage in *some* forms of symbolic play, even though this may appear mainly in structured situations and rarely in spontaneous play (Baron-Cohen, 1987; Gould, 1986) This becomes even more clear when one considers older and more able autistic individuals. Vicky Lewis and Jill Boucher (1988) studied a group of able six- to 16-year-old autistic children, together with non-autistic retarded and normal children, in spontaneous and elicited play with conventional toys and "junk" objects such as bricks, paperclips, or tinfoil. In the elicited condition, children were given either a toy–junk pair or a toy–toy pair and asked: "What can these do? Show me what you do with these." Although the autistic children produced less functional (reality) play in the spontaneous condition, the proportion of children producing at least one act of spontaneous play was similar for all three groups (approximately 50 per cent of subjects). More important still, the autistic children displayed quite a lot of symbolic and functional play when this was elicited. Indeed, when the autistic subjects were compared with control subjects who were matched for performance on a test of language ability (the Renfrew Action Picture Test, 1972), there was little to distinguish the groups in the number of toys used either singly or in combination, nor in the detail and realism of the play elicited (further impressive examples being provided by Boucher & Lewis, 1990). Note that, as the authors emphasise, these results concern children who had acquired a level of conceptual and linguistic attainment well beyond the minimum at which symbolic play normally occurs.

When reviewing data such as these, it is always important to weigh up whether autistic children might have had special difficulties on the test that is used for matching subjects. If the matching procedure poses specific problems for autistic children, and especially if the procedure taps processes (such as those of flexible symbolic thinking) that are subsequently tested in the experiment proper, then perhaps there is little wonder if subjects are equally "matched" when it comes to examine performance on the experimental tasks. In the present case, the results suggest that at least certain autistic subjects may have found as much difficulty in the Renfrew Test as they did in certain aspects of symbolic play. The Renfrew Action Picture Test requires subjects to provide grammatically correct answers to questions about what is happening in pictures, and Lewis and Boucher (1988, Table 1) provide data to suggest this might be more difficult for autistic children than a standard test of vocabulary comprehension, the British Picture Vocabulary Scale. This in turn might mean that the control subjects were *less* able than the autistic children in task-relevant respects. Nevertheless, these researchers' point about autistic children's *potential* ability to make one thing stand for another in play, and even to play out a sequence of events, is well-taken. Lewis and Boucher suggest that if one is studying autistic children who have well-developed language skills, then the observed dearth of spontaneous play (which in their study applied to functional as well as creative forms of play) reflects a motivational rather than cognitive abnormality. They also allow for the possibility that an initial delay in the development of play might arise out of some form of "symbolic deficit".

This study returns us to the problematic question of what is to count as true creative play. Which characteristics are distinctive to one or another form of play, and what is missing or abnormal in the case of autism? Certainly, the delayed onset of symbolic (and possibly functional) play is important to consider here, so is the stereotyped play that characterises many autistic individuals (Gould, 1986; Wing & Gould, 1979). Then there is the specially marked abnormality in spontaneously produced as opposed to elicited play. Why do so very few autistic children seem to have fun in playing? As Sharon Wulff (1985) describes, an autistic child who is left to his or her own devices in a playroom full of toys is very likely to ignore the toys and continue rocking or hand-flapping, or will spin moveable parts rather than becoming engaged in a meaningful way. This surely prompts us to enquire not only about the cognitive (symbolic, representational) functions that are required for normal symbolic play, but also about the meaning that play itself has for normal children. Why do toys and other symbolic artifacts *engage* us so?

I do not have an adequate response to this rhetorical question. Certainly, the reworking of social scenarios and interpersonal conflicts has a role;

certainly, too, the more pervasive process of imbuing objects with personal significance, sometimes unconsciously through what psychoanalysts call sublimation, is powerfully motivating. Autistic children seldom appear to be moved in these ways. In Chapter 7, I proposed that there may also be something in this very exercise of the symbolic function, developmentally grounded as it is (according to my thesis) in interpersonal experiences, that excites a sense of social interplay. To paraphrase Vygotsky (1962), every act of creative symbolisation contains a transmuted affective attitude towards the aspect of interpersonal relatedness from which it is derived. This does not seem to be the case for autistic individuals, even for those who have (somehow) come to appreciate that one thing may stand for another. The very psychological processes underpinning "symbolic play" may be fundamentally different in autistic and non-autistic children.

LANGUAGE

In the passage I quoted from Scheerer et al. (1945), the authors' statements about their autistic patient's lack of play were immediately succeeded by the observation that L "was unable to converse in give-and-take language". I shall now explore the thesis that here is the very essence of autistic individuals' characteristic abnormality in language comprehension and use. If we can conceptualise what it means to be unable to give-and-take in communication, and if we can elucidate both the sources of and developmental sequelae to this special kind of interpersonal impairment, then we may be in a position to understand why a certain profile of linguistic abnormalities is so prominent a feature of the clinical picture of autism.

To start with, here is a brief overview of typical abnormalities in the language of autistic people. Leo Kanner (1943) noted that besides a lack of communicative speech that may amount to muteness, the autistic child commonly displays echolalia (an "echoing" of words or phrases the child has heard spoken by others, either in the immediate or more distant past), confusions in the use of personal pronouns "I" and "you", idiosyncratic utterances that can only be understood with reference to the contexts in which the child acquired the words, and a literalness of speech that seems to show a restricted grasp of connotative meanings. Amongst other features one may add to this list are abnormalities in the tone and rhythm of speech (which may be flat and monotonous, or sing-song) and difficulties in initiating or sustaining a conversation with someone else, partly through insensitivity to the knowledge and interests of the listener (e.g. DSM-III-R; American Psychiatric Association, 1987).

Here, then, are a number of quite striking and perplexing abnormalities in language use. Not only this, but the degree of linguistic handicap is an important predictor of an autistic child's subsequent social as well as intellectual development (Rutter, Greenfeld, & Lockyer, 1967). It is hardly surprising that for some years, a number of investigators (e.g. Churchill, 1972; Rutter, Bartak, & Newman, 1971), considered language disability to be *the* cardinal feature of autism. However, a more detailed examination of both the quality and the boundaries of the deficit has led to a marked shift in perspective. Rather than underlying the handicaps of autism, language might constitute an especially refined and vivid reflection of the children's limitations in interpersonal relatedness and understanding, and more specifically in their notions of sharing, referring, and communicating. As Gerhard Bosch wrote of autism many years ago: "...it is in the language and through the language in particular that the success and failure of the constitution of the common and own worlds are most impressively revealed" (Bosch, 1970: p. 61). I shall indicate how several lines of research justify such a view.

First, it is remarkable that several facets of language development in autism follow a relatively normal course, albeit one that is often delayed. Two excellent reviews by Helen Tager-Flusberg (1981, 1989b) summarise the evidence. For example, verbal autistic children do not show serious problems with articulating words, and the pattern of their phonological development is essentially normal (e.g. Bartak, Rutter, & Cox, 1975). By and large, too, autistic children do not seem to be deviant in the development of syntax and grammar (e.g. Cantwell, Baker, & Rutter, 1978), even though they may show more restricted uses of the grammatical structures they have available (Tager-Flusberg, 1989b). On the other hand, as early writings on autism captured well (Kanner, 1943, 1971; Pronovost, Wakstein, & Wakstein, 1966), autistic adults as well as children show marked abnormalities in speech intonation, rhythm, stress, and other prosodic features that convey important information about a speaker's attitudes and meanings, not least with regard to the person's feelings.

When we turn to consider autistic children's comprehension of word meanings, again there is evidence for surprisingly normal abilities in at least certain domains. For example, in a very well-controlled experiment on the conceptual basis for referential word meaning in high-ability subjects, Helen Tager-Flusberg (1985) examined the range of referents to which matched autistic, non-autistic retarded, and normal children applied particular words. All the words referred to concrete objects—for example, kinds of birds, boats, food, or tools. The children's task was to select from an array of pictures those that belonged to the category named. The experiment was designed so that the ways in which children overextended and underextended the use of the words could be studied. The results were that the pattern of performance was the same in all three groups of children. In these semantic domains, therefore, autistic children at the same general level of vocabulary as non-autistic children were not applying idiosyncratic word meanings. So, too, when my colleague Tony Lee and I examined the profiles of closely-matched autistic and non-autistic subjects on the British Picture Vocabulary Scale (Hobson & Lee, 1989), we found they did not differ in the ability to point to pictures that corresponded with abstract *vis-à-vis* concrete words.

There are several qualifications that need to be added here. The first is that we have hardly begun to map the kinds of word meaning that seem to present little difficulty to autistic individuals, and those that pose problems of a more or less serious degree. We have already seen how terms referring to mental states (as well as emotion-related words, and also the word "friend") may not be acquired until relatively late in development, and even then with only partial understanding. Second, we have to study whether autistic people appreciate all the kinds of connotative and associative meanings that so enrich our language; some of their "concrete thinking" suggests not (Frith, 1991; Tantam, 1991). Third, and partly related to this, there is considerable doubt whether autistic children are normal in the ways they mentally co-ordinate and apply meanings. It is difficult to define this problem adequately—writers refer to an abnormal "use" of meaning and language, although this phrase over-emphasises language-as-a-tool rather than language-as-expression (or even language and thought as something that just happens or occurs to us)—and so perhaps an example would help.

Beate Hermelin and Neil O'Connor (1967) tested autistic and non-autistic retarded children for their recall of structured and unstructured verbal material. Each subject was presented with three types of word sequences for recall. These were sentences of words that occur frequently in the language of mentally retarded subjects (e.g. "The bird builds its nest"), randomised lists of equally frequent words (e.g. "Home give down red fall"), and sentences with less frequent words. There were sequences of different lengths, and subjects were tested for the ability to recall the items in the correct order. The results were that the non-autistic subjects had lower recall scores than did the autistic subjects, but unlike the latter, they performed significantly better with sentences than with random sequences. Thus the autistic children had good immediate memory, but they did not seem to draw upon the structuring of language to aid remembering (also O'Connor & Hermelin, 1967a). In a second experiment, subjects were tested for free-recall of eight-word lists that were beyond their memory span. One list consisted of two categories of words, colours and numbers ("Blue three red five six white green eight"), another was a short sentence with digits interpolated between the words ("Nine this one tea four is ten cold"), another featured three names of table utensils (pot, cup, spoon) interspersed with random words, and the fourth contained random words. The results were that there was no group difference in the number of items recalled, but autistic subjects were significantly less likely to give a response in which conceptually related items were clustered together.

Helen Tager-Flusberg (1991) has recently replicated the finding that autistic children have specific deficits in recalling semantically related word lists, and she has extended this work by testing subjects' ability to benefit from cues involving meaning or rhyme (e.g. "I said a word that sounds like...What was that word?") to assist in retrieving unrecalled words from memory. Autistic and control subjects were similar in the use they made of such prompts to memory. This suggests that the meaningful words had been encoded properly, but that autistic subjects were less able spontaneously to use linguistic information to facilitate retrieval (also Boucher & Warrington, 1976). In conversation, too, autistic children have difficulty with the spontaneous recall of events they have experienced over recent months (Boucher & Lewis, 1989). Tager-Flusberg (1981) also reported evidence that in understanding sentences, autistic children may fail to use a semantically based comprehension strategy because of a partial inability to map real-world knowledge about relationships between people and objects (for example, knowledge that "the truck carries the box" is a more likely circumstance than "the box carries the truck") on to language.

These studies provide evidence for autistic children's failure to apply word-related meanings in recall "on demand". As we have noted, their spontaneous speech is even more remarkable for abnormal uses of language. Lawrence Bartak, Michael Rutter, and Tony Cox (1975, 1977; also Cantwell, Baker, & Rutter, 1978), compared a sample of able four- to 10-year-old autistic boys with dysphasic boys of similar age and non-verbal IQ. Not only were the autistic subjects more markedly impaired on standard language-based IQ tests (to be discussed later), but so too there were few autistic children who showed imaginative pretend play, few who chattered spontaneously or gave an account of their activities as often as twice a week, and few who were able to sustain a conversation. In addition to showing a high prevalence of echolalia, personal pronoun difficulties, idiosyncratic language, and stereotyped utterances, the autistic boys were less able to use gesture to describe the use of objects or to mime actions named by the tester, and less able to name the tester's mimed actions. The researchers concluded that "in autism the disability extends beyond spoken language into gesture and "inner language"...even when comparable speech was available, the autistic children were less likely to *use* it in a social context" (Bartak, Rutter, & Cox, 1975: p. 137 and 139).

It is time to move away from word meanings considered in the abstract, towards a concern with the uses of language in context, or what is called pragmatics (Bates, 1976). Communication between people is the setting within which language is learned, and in which most speech takes place. Perhaps it is only once we have reviewed how language functions or fails to function in the communication of autistic people, that we shall be able to resolve the issue of why it is that certain word meanings are especially problematic, and why certain "uses of language" are more aberrant than others.

Language as Communication

An early informal but insightful study of the pragmatic deficits of five able autistic adolescents was conducted by Christiane Baltaxe (1977). Baltaxe examined the dialogue that took place when she gave her subjects a semistructured interview. She considered that three classes of deficit were characteristic: in appreciating speaker-hearer role relationships, in following the rules of conduct governing a dialogue, and in foregrounding and backgrounding information.

The notion of speaker and listener "roles" is a critical one for characterising conversation, in that both the forms and contents of speech are constantly modified and adjusted according to the respective positions and perspectives of the people talking. The most obvious example is the use of personal pronouns "I" and "you", where the very same person is addressed as "I" by the speaker but as "you" by the other person, and where "I" refers to one person this moment and to another the next. Baltaxe noted that confusions in the use of these pronouns were common in the dialogues she recorded. One example was: "But this time you [meaning I] couldn't get back into the children's unit". Yet this was not an isolated phenomenon, there being numerous other instances in which the autistic subject's speech seemed overly formal in taking the form of written rather than colloquial speech, or in containing direct quotations from the experimenter or others: "Well, I asked my parents. I told my parents I'd be good at home, but I feel you're too old to be at home, we feel you should be away." Baltaxe reflected that in instances such as these, the adolescent was reporting an event as if he were still the hearer in the original dialogue, without adequate accommodation to the speaker role.

A further element which lent a "sense of pedantic literalness" to the exchanges was the autistic person's relative failure to background old information, for example in repeating fully specified noun phrases instead of using pronouns ("they", "she", "it", etc.) to refer to people and things already mentioned. These adolescents appeared to display a lack of differentiation between old and new information, and a difficulty in discriminating what was relevant or irrelevant to the listener. Finally, contravention of the rules of conduct that specify what is polite and appropriate in a given dialogue seemed to occur without apparent intent:

Question: "Tell me, what are you going to do now?" Answer: "None of your God damned business." When Baltaxe and Simmons (1977) studied the bedtime soliloquies of an autistic child, again these exhibited a lack of the dialogue structure characteristic of normal children, and instead seemed to comprise a monologue spoken from the hearer's perspective alone.

The kinds of pragmatic deficit which Baltaxe illustrates in her paper have been further documented and defined by numerous clinical and experimental studies of autistic individuals. A paper by Ricks and Wing (1975) is replete with illuminating (and often moving) examples. One was the following question–answer sequence: Question: "What did you have for dinner?" Answer: "Meat and cabbage and potatoes and gravy and salt and jam tart and custard and orange juice and cup of tea." Another concerned an autistic child who always referred to the dog's dinner plate as a "dish"; when asked to put some scraps in the dog's "bowl", she gave food to the dog in the washing-up bowl. "Non-reciprocal speech" was a prominent feature of the conversation of a large group of very able autistic adolescents described by a 1974 panel of parents and professionals (Dewey & Everard, 1974). These commentators gave the example of how an autistic person may talk on for far too long without regard to the interest (or lack of interest) of the listener, or alternatively may stop short; when one young man participating in a conference for autistic people was asked from the audience: "Do you have a hobby?", he replied simply "Yes". The to-and-fro of normal conversation is striking by its absence.

Systematic studies of selected aspects of such difficulties allow a more precise definition of the abnormalities specific to autism. For example, the narrative language of autistic individuals reveals a tangle of pragmatic deficits. Kate Loveland and Belgin Tunali (1993) have recently discussed how there are various kinds of narrative, ranging from story narratives through script narratives (the way things usually happen) and didactic narratives, to recitations and performances. Each may be examined not only for language content, but also as a form of speaker–listener interchange. In telling a story, for example, a person must understand the meaningful aspects of the events to be discussed, and these will often involve one or more protagonists who have feelings, motives, mistaken beliefs, and the like; but more than this, the person must select, organise, and present information in a way that enables the listener to follow what is happening, and must more or less respect the conventions of the rhetorical mode.

In one study, Loveland, McEvoy, Tunali, and Kelley (1990) presented language-matched autistic and Down's subjects with a puppet show involving animals or a videotape sketch involving humans, in each of which a theft occurred. The subjects' task was to tell the story to a listener and then to answer some follow-up questions. The majority of these high-ability subjects could produce recognisable narratives, and the groups did not differ in the number of story events or characters mentioned, nor in factual recall in response to questioning. However, the autistic subjects had a greater tendency to produce bizarre language and to adopt an externalised point of view in which puppets or actors were seen as objects rather than characters, and they often seemed not to capture the story as a representation of fictional events. For example:

> "That hammer over there...[prompt] That egg and the nest and the puppet...[prompt] They opened their mouths, they talk...[prompt] The animals say something...[prompt] The puppets...[prompt] the green and the red...[prompt] They are called animal puppets" [etc] (p. 15).

Or again, Loveland and Tunali (1993) give the following as an example of how a more able autistic adolescent (S) spontaneously retold the videotape story to his mother (M) during a free interaction session, one hour after the experiment just described:

> S: "I saw that there was a kid stealing someone else's wallet." M: "There was?" S: "Yeah, and they, she had an umbrella." M: "Was it make-believe or did it really happen?" S: "It really happened. Why do you have to hit an umbrella you take the money?" M: "What?" S: "Why to you have to hit the umbrella?" M: "Who hit an umbrella?" S: "That was the lady did." M: "Who had the umbrella?" S: "The robber...the robber was taking the money" M: "From who?" S: "From the secretary." M: "And what did the secretary do?" [etc] (p. 253).

The authors point out that in addition to deficiencies in grammar and organisation, the narratives also seemed to reflect the subject's difficulties in understanding what a story *is*.

A further study illustrated how autistic children have problems with what is called "referential communication" (Loveland, Tunali, Kelley, & McEvoy, 1989). When autistic subjects were asked to explain to a naïve listener how to play a simple board game, their narratives contrasted with those of Down's subjects in being uninformative and including irrelevant material (for example, leaving out how the game begins or ends, or how the pieces were used, but including extraneous comment), even though the subjects could reply correctly when asked specific questions about the missing information. They did not seem to register or adjust to what the listener knew or needed to know. Or again, Tager-Flusberg and Anderson (1991) reported that in the earliest stages of linguistic development, young autistic and Down's syndrome children were rather similar in their ability to maintain a topic of conversation. As development proceeded, however, the Down's children showed an increase in the proportion of their utterances that provided new information but the autistic children did not. Nor was it usual for those with autism to ask questions to elicit new information from their mothers. Even though their language was becoming more complex, they failed to evolve these new dimensions of conversation.

ANALYSING COMMUNICATION

Discovering what Communication is

In the previous chapter, I tried to characterise some of the features of non-verbal as well as symbolic communication. For communication to be communication, the sender must be able to register that the receiver registers the message. The idea of "registration" implies some degree of psychological (i.e. mental) involvement on both sides—one does not communicate with a robot or a computer. The idea of "message" implies some kind of intent to transmit something ("information" in the very broadest terms, if this may be taken to include feelings and other attitudes); communication proper entails an intent to communicate *that* as well as *what* one is communicating. I have argued that communication between persons with minds presupposes that the persons can share or otherwise co-ordinate their experiences, and that a person who communicates is (necessarily) aware of this. The modes of communication available to infants correspond with infants' levels of awareness of "other minds": in six-month-olds, for example, such awareness is on the preconceptual level of registering the degree of bodily-cum-mental attunement and co-ordination that is achieved with others. Communication *about* the world requires more, in that the communicator needs to have grasped the nature and directedness of psychological attitudes. Symbolic communication entails additional insights into people's intentions in communicating, and into the nature of symbolising itself.

The first question, then, is whether autistic children have difficulty in discovering what communication *is*. Many autistic children never acquire a proper use of language. A major reason for this appears to be the children's lack of awareness of how communication functions to connect people psychologically. Or to put this another way, the forms of speech act that are presupposed by the very fact of communication—conversing, describing, requesting, demanding, reassuring, asking, answering, and so on—can only occur between people who know that persons have psychological states and attitudes towards each other and the world. Moreover, the motive to communicate at all is frequently that of becoming psychologically connected with others in ways that are pleasurable.

Autistic children who have a profound disturbance of affective engagement with others seem to be lacking in motive as well as understanding when it comes to communication.

I say that they seem to be lacking in these respects, and it has to be admitted that the evidence for this account of failing-to-speak is circumstantial—and obviously, other kinds of cognitive and motivational deficit, especially those associated with mental retardation, enter the picture. However, suggestive evidence arises from what happens when the chidren *do* learn to speak, in that they are usually restricted in when, in how, and in what they communicate. The pattern of their restricted "uses" of language is compatible with the suggested reasons for delay in using language at all. Another piece of evidence comes from a particular kind of asynchrony in autistic children's development. As I have already described, the work of Bates et al. (1979) and Sugarman (1984) suggests that in normal infants towards the end of the first year, the means–end ability to make one object serve as an instrument for acting on another (for example, to use a stick in order to reach an object) is a cognitive achievement that emerges at the same time as the infant's ability to "use" an adult to obtain something in their transactions with the environment (for example, to gesture towards an adult to request help in procuring something out of reach). A plausible explanation is that the same cognitive– developmental constraints operate on social and non-social "instrumental co-ordination". What is of interest here, is that young autistic children (and, according to Juan-Carlos Gomez, hand-reared gorillas) develop competence in non-social means–end instrumental tasks *before* they request people to do things (Wetherby & Prutting, 1984). Even when they *do* come to request things of people, autistic children (and gorillas) are unlike normal children in rarely showing things or pointing things out to others. These observations suggest that whereas in normal children, it is something related to means–end abilities that constrains the emergence of person–object co-ordination—which implies that some understanding of the subjectivity of other persons is already in place, ready and waiting, as it were—in autistic children (and gorillas), it is understanding *persons* that is the constraint.

Indeed, Susan Sugarman (1984) gives a brief account of some impressive therapeutic work she conducted with a two- to three-year old autistic boy. At the beginning of treatment, the child would treat the therapist's hands as though they were objects; by the end, he would look at the therapist's face to request things. It was midway through therapy before the child would respond to routine questions and commands, and it was shortly after he began to co-ordinate non-verbal person- and object-oriented bids that he began to speak spontaneously. Sugarman stresses how this autistic child showed the same progression as normal children: "Specifically, he did not build person–object coordination from his already complex involvements with objects. Instead, he developed a separate domain of social exchange, and gradually integrated that domain into his transactions with the physical environment" (1981: p. 58). The autistic child's awareness of persons is hard-won, even at this level.

Intentions in Communicating

How might an analysis of communication clarify what these deficits mean? One very helpful approach pioneered by Ted Shapiro and developed by Amy Wetherby and Barry Prizant (Prizant & Wetherby, 1987; Shapiro, 1977; Shapiro, Roberts, & Fish, 1970; Wetherby, 1986), is to analyse autistic individuals' utterances and gestures for communicative intent.

The first lesson to be learnt from this research is that we should be wary of supposing that autistic children are non-communicative. What might at first appear to be failures to use speech and gesture for communicative purposes may often turn out to have significance for the children's interpersonal transactions. For example, the autistic child's use of idiosyncratic or "metaphorical" expressions may reflect an attempt to communicate, but one that is ineffective in so far as the message is not adapted to the listener's perspective (Wetherby, 1986). Echolalia may seem (and sometimes be) meaningless, but it can also serve a variety of purposes such as to curtail a social exchange (Shapiro, 1977), to maintain an interaction in the face of a failure to comprehend another person (Fay, 1973), or to fulfil a variety of other functions such as requesting, protesting, affirming, and so on (Prizant & Duchan, 1981; Prizant & Rydell, 1984). Incessant and repetitive questioning may be intended to initiate or to maintain social contact rather than to request information (Hurtig, Ensrud, & Tomblin, 1982). Correspondingly, autistic children vary in their wish or ability to communicate with different individuals, and may be more communicative with teachers than with children or with familiar than unfamiliar adults (McHale, Simeonsson, Marcus, & Olley, 1980; Bernard-Opitz, 1982).

On the other hand, the functions of speech and gesture appear to be different for autistic than for non-autistic children. In Chapter 4, I cited the seminal study of Wetherby and Prutting (1984) in which small groups of autistic and normal subjects were reported to display distinct profiles of communicative functions. The autistic children used a high proportion of communicative acts that led to an environmental consequence which satisfied a physical want or need such as requesting objects, requesting actions, and protesting. On the other hand, there were few communications that fully acknowledged the other person and drew attention to the children themselves, few that involved requests for information and permission, and few that commented on objects for the adult (as by pointing, describing, and so on). The autistic subjects' initial attempts to obtain a social end mainly involved requests for a game-like interaction, rather than to engage the attention of another as a person. It was also observed that these young autistic children almost never used utterances in the labelling-for-self and self-regulatory ways that occur in normal young children, who thereby identify and focus their attention to salient features of a referent or direct and control their own actions.

Drawing upon this and other studies, Prizant and Wetherby (1987) discuss how a sizeable proportion of young autistic children's communicative acts may be re-enactments in which they replicate a situation or aspects of a situation to accomplish a goal, as when they use an adult's hand to open a door. This is one example of indexical communication (delayed echolalia is another), in which the meaning of the communicative act is embedded in the original event being replicated. When the anchorage is in particular events or situations not shared with the listener, the result is often unconventional and idiosyncratic (Ricks & Wing, 1975). As the authors note, "one may speculate that the development of idiosyncratic and unconventional means to communicate results from the autistic child's limited participation in social exchanges from early in life" (Prizant & Wetherby, 1987: pp. 476–477).

Apprehending Others' Intentions in Communicating

Thus far, I have dwelt upon the autistic individual's intentions-in-communicating, what they seem to be trying to achieve by speaking. Evidence has emerged to suggest that there is something unusual about the autistic person's experience of the other who is being communicated with. The other person is rarely called upon to share experiences or to witness showing-off, and he or she seems to be unacknowledged or at least misjudged as a source or recipient of opinion or knowledge, or as a conversational partner. This reminds us that the give-and-take of communication involves two-way traffic. What do autistic children "take" another person's speech to express, or "take from" a conversational partner? Commenting on autistic adolescents' lack of the to-and-fro of normal conversation, Dewey and Everard (1974: p. 348) elaborated thus: "At best, the autistic person is a poor listener, and sometimes he seems to be completely unaware of the fact that somebody is trying to talk to him". The question arises, how far the autistic individual apprehends another person *as* a person who has intentions-in-speaking.

This is a profound question. Consider how the normal child comes to understand what speech is. One route is to recognise what other people are doing with sounds when they speak, and not least, how they are using sounds to refer to things (Baldwin, 1991; Tomasello, 1992). If the child manages to achieve this much, he or she can identify with the other person and come to express similar things in similar ways. If the child fails to understand what the other person is using language for—what the other intends, and especially what the person intends the child to understand—then he or she will be enormously handicapped in acquiring speech at all.

Autistic individuals' understanding of other people's intentions-in-speaking, or "speaker's meanings", have received relatively little systematic study. Obviously the issue is relevant for much of the pragmatic disability of autism, as already outlined. The following two studies illustrate how more focussed investigation not only on social exchanges, but also on the very content of language itself, may yield important insights.

The first study was conducted by Rhea Paul and Donald Cohen (1985), and concerned autistic adults' comprehension of indirect requests. The setting was a colouring-in task, and the indirect requests took the form of questions such as: "Must you make the circle blue?", implying that the experimenter would prefer an alternative, "Shouldn't you colour the circle red?" and "I'll be very sad unless you make the circle blue". Because the intended force of such utterances—the speaker's illuctionary intent in making them—does not match the surface form of what is framed as a question, such requests can be used to establish a listener's appraisal of "speaker's meaning" as well as "utterance meaning".

Subjects were groups of autistic and non-autistic retarded young adults who were of similar age and performance IQ. There was a structured session in which subjects were told what to do ("I'm going to ask you to colour some circles. Colour them either red or blue, according to what I say"), and were presented with a set of indirect requests (e.g. "Why not colour the circle blue?"). At a later time, subjects were involved in a free-drawing session in which the indirect requests were made at moments when a drawing had just been completed (e.g. "I'll be happy if you colour this house blue"). The results were that the autistic subjects performed less well in the structured and especially in the unstructured situation, during which negative sentences (e.g. "You shouldn't colour the circle blue") were least responded to. The authors concluded that the autistic subjects were having difficulty in deciding what the speaker had in mind, and specifically in inferring the intention behind the indirect speech acts. If one asks an autistic child: "Can you tell me about your home?", the answer may come back: "Yes".

My second example is very different. This is drawn from recent (not yet published) work by Francesca Happé (1993). Alongside her colleague Uta Frith (Frith, 1989b), Happé has been exploring how far Relevance theory (as developed by Sperber and Wilson, 1986, on the basis of work by the philosopher Grice, 1957) might contribute to our understanding of autism. The crux of this approach is an analysis of the many levels on which speakers and listeners understand each others' communicative intentions. Happé offers the proposal that individuals who could not infer a speaker's intentions would be left with trying to decipher the code of what was being said from the words alone (Baron-Cohen, 1988; Hobson, 1989a; Paul, 1987). If they failed to apprehend speech as expressive of an intent to communicate, they might even remain relatively oblivious to language *per se*. The question arises, how far this might explain the language handicap of autism.

Happé's empirical approach has been to examine breakdown in comprehension when a speaker's (or implicit speaker's) attitude must be taken into account in modifying the literal meaning of a sentence. She selected metaphor and irony as candidates for study. Happé argued that whereas metaphor requires a "first-order theory of mind"—an understanding of the speaker's non-literal thought behind the word—irony requires second-order understanding of the speaker's ironic attitude towards his or her own expressed thought. Therefore she divided a sample of able autistic adolescents and young adults into three groups according to their performance on "classic" theory-of-mind tasks (as described in Chapter 5); those who failed these tests (no ToM), those who could understand false beliefs about the world (first-order ToM), and those who could also understand false beliefs about beliefs (e.g. "Mary thinks John believes the marble is still in the basket": second-order ToM). Although the latter two groups were roughly equivalent in verbal ability on standard IQ tests, Happé's prediction was that they would differ in their ability to judge irony.

The first task was for subjects to select from a list of target words, the correct words to complete five sentences in each of three conditions: (1) synonyms which could be interpreted literally, e.g. "Jane was so pale and quiet. She really was..." [unwell]; (2) similes, e.g. "Carol gazed at Nicola. She was so cross. Her eyes were like..." [daggers]; and (3) metaphors, e.g. "Michael was so cold. His nose really was..." [an icicle]. To balance out the effects of variable semantic content, each set of five sentences appeared equally often in each of the three conditions. A second task involved the presentation of stories which involved one character addressing another with metaphor (e.g. "Your head is made out of wood!") or with irony (e.g. "What a clever boy you are, David!"). In each case, subjects were asked what the speaker meant (e.g. "Does she mean David is clever or silly?").

The results from the first task were as predicted: all three autistic groups performed relatively well on the synonym and simile conditions (although there was a trend towards lower scores in the "no ToM" group), and only the "no ToM" autistic subjects performed poorly on the metaphor condition. The results on the second task were again in line with the predictions, and only the "second-order ToM" autistic subjects were consistent in interpreting the ironic remarks correctly. A further group taking part comprised non-autistic mentally retarded control subjects who were of low IQ but at the "second-order ToM" level. Despite their poor language, these individuals with relatively sophisticated Theory of Mind abilities performed well throughout. All in all, therefore, this elegant study provides impressive evidence for the significance of successive levels of understanding (or levels of "metarepresentation") for the comprehension of metaphor and irony.

COGNITION REVISITED

We have come almost full circle. Even if one begins by considering "cognition" in the abstract, as a function of an individual's intelligent dealings with the world, soon one reaches a point at which communication between and among persons is seen to be integral to the very fabric of thought. It is not simply that thinking finds expression in social contexts, but rather that cognitive and social aspects of mental functioning reflect one another. This is not the case for *all* levels or facets of intellectual function, a fact that becomes obvious when one considers that certain cognitive abilities are required for an individual to experience interpersonal events *as* social in the first place. Nevertheless, we might now reconsider how far the cognitive deficits characteristic of autism can be explained by reference to underlying social/interpersonal sources of deficit (Hobson, 1989a).

Recall the observations of Scheerer et al. (1945) on L's difficulties in defining objects, in locating absurdities, in understanding metaphor, in thinking abstractly, and in wresting himself from a fixed and rigid point of view. The ways in which autistic children perform on standard tests of language and language-related abilities bear out the prevalence of problems of these kinds. A number of studies (e.g. Bartak, Rutter, & Cox, 1975; DeMyer, 1975; Lockyer & Rutter, 1970; Tymchuk, Simmons, & Neafsey, 1977) have demonstrated that it is particularly on the Peabody Picture Vocabulary Test (or its British counterpart, the British Picture Vocabulary Test), in which subjects have to point to a picture corresponding with a word, and on specific parts of the Wechsler Intelligence Scale for Children (WISC), that autistic children show marked impairment *vis-à-vis* their relatively intact non-verbal intellectual abilities. For example, when Bartak et al. (1975) tested able autistic and dysphasic boys on the WISC, the autistic subjects had specific difficulty with those items that test general comprehension (e.g. "What is the thing to do when you cut your finger?" and "What is the thing to do if a boy much smaller than yourself starts to fight with you?"), vocabulary (e.g. "What does fur mean?"), and similarities (e.g. "In what way are a cat and a mouse alike?"), whereas tests of digit span and information (e.g. "How many days in a week?") were answered adequately. We have seen how Lorna Wing (e.g. Ricks & Wing, 1975; Wing 1969, 1981b) and others have offered numerous examples of autistic children's concrete thinking and failure to understand metaphor. When one autistic child was asked if he had lost his tongue, he anxiously started to search for it; whenever another was instructed to put something down, he always had to put it on the floor.

This set of cognitive impairments needs to be considered with reference to a further set of cognitive functions that are relatively intact in autistic people. When the effects of general retardation are taken into account, even quite young children are relatively unimpaired in such abilities as visuospatial pattern recognition (Bartak et al., 1975), the understanding of means-ends relations (Curcio, 1978; Wetherby & Prutting, 1984) and the awareness of the permanence of objects (Dawson & McKissick, 1984; Wetherby & Gaines, 1982). As Kanner wrote in 1943 (pp. 247–248): "The astounding vocabulary of the speaking children, the excellent memory for events of several years before, the phenomenal rote memory for poems and names, and the precise recollection of complex patterns and sequences, bespeak good intelligence in the sense in which this word is commonly used." I have already given many illustrations of the impressive cognitive abilities of older and less retarded autistic individuals, not only in certain restricted modes of inferential thinking, but also in quite extensive domains of conceptual and linguistic functioning. Indeed, there are also cases of *idiot savants* such as L in whom particular facets of intellectual or even artistic function are exceptionally developed (Hermelin & O'Connor, 1986, 1990a,b; Hermelin, O'Connor, Lee, & Treffert, 1989; O'Connor & Hermelin, 1989).

How are we to explain this impressive dichotomy in the modes of impaired and unimpaired cognitive functioning in autism? By now an answer more or less suggests itself. The answer has reference to two separable lines of normal development—corresponding with what Buber (1984) called I-Thou and I-It relations—only one of which is selectively and specifically disordered in autistic individuals (Hobson, 1990a). If for the moment we set aside the influence of general mental retardation, and also make allowance for some additional considerations which will qualify the account (Chapter 9), it is plausible to suggest that the greater part of autistic children's *characteristic* cognitive and language disabilities arise as sequelae to the children's relative failure to engage in I–Thou relatedness with others. What results from this failure are difficulties in understanding and identifying with the subjective orientations and mental states of other people, in recognising the nature and varieties of interpersonal sharing and communication, and in appreciating and adapting to the range of co-referential attitudes that people may adopt towards a shared and objective world. This account is one that applies not merely to autistic individuals' problems with pragmatic aspects of language or to their inflexible, one-track lines of thinking, but also to their impoverishment in the very sources of higher cognitive functioning—the capacities for creative symbolisation, for "as–if" thinking and for self-reflective thought. In the remarkable discussion of their 1945 paper, Scheerer et al. attributed L's difficulties to "an impairment of abstract attitude" (p. 27). They considered the abstract attitude to be a "common functional basis" for the following (amongst other things):

> to behold simultaneously different aspects of the same situation or object, to shift from one aspect to another; to understand a general frame of reference, a symbolic meaning as relation between a given specific percept and a general idea; to evolve common denominators, to reason in concepts, categories, principles; to assume different mental sets...to plan ahead ideationally...to behave symbolically (e.g. demonstrating, make belief, etc.); to reflect upon oneself, giving verbal account of acts; to detach one's ego from a given situation or inner experience; to think in terms of the "mere possible", to transcend the immediate reality and uniqueness of a given situation, a specific aspect or sense impression (Scheerer et al., 1945: p. 37).

It is my contention that the forms of abstract attitude and detachment that are missing in autism, are precisely those for which appropriately patterned intersubjective experience is necessary. This formulation has its basis in the arguments and theory of earlier chapters, and I shall try to recapitulate and extend the reasoning in the final chapter that follows. What is important for the present purposes, is to respect how *much* some autistic individuals achieve in their intellectual life. A part of this will be explicable in terms of the partial, rather than absolute, degree of their limitations in intersubjective co-ordination, and in their corresponding social-developmental arrest. After all, many autistic children do learn to communicate with language, and it is difficult to see how this could happen without some awareness of the nature of communication between persons. On the other hand, as I discussed in the previous chapter, there appears to be an "I–It" cognitive-developmental line that a young child can follow with minimal input of a specifically interpersonal kind. This is a route available to autistic as well as non-autistic children.

If this oversimplified description has some validity, then in certain (I–It) respects but not in other (I–Thou) respects, autistic people will inhabit the "same world" as those of us who are not autistic. Even if autistic people do not fully grasp what it means to share an objective reality, there will be some congruence between their own perspectives on the world and those of other people. Once again, this must necessarily be the case if they are to learn language at all. When one considers language, there are many different ways in which words are embedded in the patterns of conduct and "forms of life" of children and adults (Wittgenstein, 1958). Whether or not an autistic child grasps particular kinds of linguistic and/or conceptual meaning will depend upon the extent to which his form of life corresponds with that of the people from whom he learns to speak and think. Perhaps this allows us to interpret Kanner's (1943: p. 247) suggestion that the autistic children of his sample were "endowed with good cognitive potentialities". The kinds of ability (such as pattern recognition) that Kanner noted in those children are sometimes viewed as mere "splinter skills". An alternative proposal is that many autistic children do have far greater "potentialities" than one observes, but that these cannot be fully realised because the children lack *experience* of intersubjective co-orientation and co-reference with others. The neurological machinery for sophisticated cognitive function may be there, ready and waiting, but the cognitive materials with which the mind works—especially, what we reify and refer to as "symbols"—are never adequately forged in the crucible of interpersonal relations.

I shall conclude this account of thought and language in autism with an extended quotation from my old favourite, Gerhard Bosch (1970: pp. 110–11):

...the particular aspects of intelligence and of intellectual life that develop in the autistic child are precisely those that are only to a limited extent dependent on the prior constitution of a common world. Husserl has discussed the interesting question to what degree a solipsistically conceived subject, i.e. a perceiving and thinking subject without the least idea of another and thus also oblivious to itself and without any awareness of itself, can arrive at the constitution of a world. The subject can succeed in perceiving, i.e. in distinguishing between shapes and, under certain circumstances, separating appearance and reality, in so far as perception in individual sensory areas is not confirmed by perception in others. Consequently the subject is unable to see a thing "differently", with the eyes of others, i.e. intersubjective objectivization is not possible for him...Only such experience as can be objectivized by logical-mathematical laws does not depend on confirmation by the other person, or on intersubjective objectivization; it could be the constitution of a physical thing according to dimensions, number, weight, i.e. physically determined, measurable properties, or it could be the comprehension of a mathematical principle or the laws behind a series of numbers. All these constitutions, which are confirmed by logic and mathematics, contain their own objectivization and are independent of place, time, and human community.

If we consider from this angle the interests and achievements that come to the fore in autistic children, we find that they may all be classified as being of the type that to a large extent requires little or no objectivization within a common world.

CHAPTER NINE

The Development of Mind and the Case of Autism

The purpose of this chapter is both to review and to supplement my attempt to frame an understanding of the normal development of mind. This perspective on normal development provides the context within which I set a developmental theory of autism. I hope that in covering this ground we shall encounter nearly all of the issues I introduced in the Prolegomena of Chapter 1.

It goes without saying that my account leaves out a great deal. In particular, I regret that I have not dealt with psychoanalytic insights into the nature of those intra- and interpersonal psychological processes that take place early in a child's life to facilitate or disrupt the formation and integration of mental structure, especially as this relates to the mental representation of persons (Alvarez, 1992; Bion, 1962; Kernberg, 1976; Ogden, 1983; Sandler & Sandler, 1978; Tustin, 1981). However, I believe that my emphasis on the centrality of personal relatedness for the development of interpersonal understanding and symbolic functioning accords with the spirit of "object relations" psychoanalytic theory (Hobson, 1993e). Indeed I am hopeful that this essay might enable some readers to reappraise psychoanalytic thinking with a greater degree of tolerance and interest than might otherwise have been the case.

THE NORMAL DEVELOPMENT OF MIND—
THE THEORETICAL CHALLENGE

I shall divide the chapter into two parts, in accordance with the two parts of its title. I begin with the case of normal development, concentrating upon the ways in which a young child's acquisition of "mind" is bound up with her growth in understanding "other minds". This is only part of the story, of course, but in my view it is central to the process of becoming a mind-endowed person.

What do we need to explain? Crudely put, we need to understand how over the first four years of life, a child becomes aware that people differ from things in having minds. Minds have properties that are not shared by physical objects. *Inter alia*, they involve subjective experiences and they are directed towards something other than themselves—they have "aboutness" or intentionality. Indeed, they are representational, so that something that truly exists may be misrepresented, or something that does not exist may be (re)presented. Moreover, things are represented *as* such-and-suches, and what a given object is represented "as" may differ from mind to mind.

A turning point in mental development occurs when the very young child acquires a first insight into the nature of "representation" by becoming aware that there is a distinction between subjective orientations to things and events, and those things and events themselves. The somewhat older child understands that in addition, people represent the world in ways that may be adjudged in relation to that which is true or correct. Knowledge and true belief accord with what is objectively the case; false belief and misperception (or perception of deceptive appearances, combined with a mistaken belief that the appearances are veridical) do not. At least in certain respects, knowledge might be said to entail that the knower justifiably holds certain "mental representations" of the world to be true. Therefore one aim is to describe how a child comes to know what it means to know or believe.

In fact, of course, children come to know what it means for *people* to believe. A mind is the property of an embodied person. It is not merely that mental states may serve to explain behaviour, but also that mental states are apprehended through the bodily expressions as well as the behaviour of people whose mental states they are. On the other hand, a given mental state on a given occasion may be covert; a person may have thoughts that others could never guess. Therefore we need to explain how the child comes to ascribe such private experiences and mental states to persons whose bodies may or may not express those states at any given moment. There is also something to respect about the nature of the conviction with which a child conceives people to have minds. There is no possible evidence that could shake that conviction. The child knows that people have minds, no more nor less than the child knows that objects exist.

There are additional things to learn about the nature of persons with minds. The child recognises herself to have her own interests, concerns, desires, intentions, beliefs, and so on, and acknowledges others to have similar kinds of mental state which may differ in content. She not only conceptualises her first-person experiences as her own, but also ascribes similar first-person experiences to others. The child is self-conscious, and takes others to be self-conscious. Persons are also selves. Therefore the individual acquires knowledge that she is like others in having a mind, but unlike others in so far as the contents of others' minds differ from her own. The problem is to say how such knowledge is acquired.

In all of this we need to conceptualise how the development of a child's own mind is bound up with her increasingly sophisticated awareness of other minds. The task is not simply to describe the evolution of particular contents in the child's mind (for instance, contents that have to do with the concept of persons). Rather, the very structure and functioning of the mind may alter as a result of new understandings about the mind itself. In particular, a child comes to symbolise in a creative manner, to acquire language, and to think with imagination and foresight. We should like to know how specifically interpersonal experiences contribute to these cognitive developments.

It remains to identify the degree to which cognitive development can proceed in a manner that is (relatively) independent of social engagement and interpersonal commerce. I shall say little further about the mechanisms of this I–It line of development, and take it for granted that there are important ways in which such initially non-social cognitive abilities articulate with and contribute to interpersonal relatedness and understanding.

A THEORY OF DEVELOPMENT

The theory begins by positing some psychological "givens". The givens are features of early infancy. They do not necessarily appear at birth, and they have their own developmental histories. Nevertheless, they function as the bedrock upon which interpersonal understanding is founded.

Personal Relatedness and "Thing" Relatedness. The first "given" concerns an infant's capacity for manifesting and experiencing different forms of relatedness to people and to things. There are two complementary perspectives here. The one is to consider the child's own contribution, her own propensities to engage in "personal relatedness" and "thing relatedness". For example, the child requires appropriate mechanisms for perceiving, for feeling, and for acting towards persons and things in different ways. The second perspective is to consider what transpires between the child and others. If personal relatedness involves intersubjective exchanges that are co-ordinated between the infant and others (e.g. through affective communication and through imitation), then we shall need to think in terms of the structure of *inter*personal events. Even if one wishes to maintain a focus on the individual infant, it is still necessary to consider how specifically interpersonal patternings of behaviour and experience are generated and registered.

The nature of the very young child's experience of personal relatedness has to be such as to underpin the older child's concept of persons. This consideration from genetic epistemology is a major impetus for positing and seeking a special quality of personal relatedness from early in life. The point is that specific forms of interpersonal communication and coaction are essential for children's ability to constitute the kind of concept of persons that they acquire. More specifically, the argument goes, a child's experience of affectively patterned personal relatedness is constitutive of that child's understanding of the nature of persons with minds. It is therefore appropriate that in their helpful discussion of the development of the distinction between people and inanimate objects, Rochel Gelman and Elizabeth Spelke (1981) emphasise how young children communicate with persons, focus on their intentions and feelings, and engage with them in reciprocal actions. The pivotal issue is how the child's capacity for personal relatedness is realised in such a way as to effect interpersonal engagement and communication with persons, and ultimately to yield an ability to focus on the subjectivity and outer-directed psychological states (including thoughts and beliefs) of other selves.

The account runs as follows. Personal relatedness is characterised by the potential for forms of behaviour and experience that promote "primary intersubjectivity" (Trevarthen, 1979). The starting-point for interpersonal understanding is a primitive form of sharing, most clearly manifest in patterns of behavioural and affective co-ordination between the infant and others, but also experienced by the infant in special ways. As Charles Cooley (1902: pp. 84 and 102) writes: "The immediate social reality is the personal idea...The personal idea in its more penetrating interpretations involves sympathy, in the sense of primary communication or an entering into and sharing the mind of someone else...". There are forms of reciprocal relation between persons that entail a linking of subjective experiences.

What might these forms of reciprocal relation look like? Affective communication, including that involved in early forms of imitation, is especially important. One reason is that in an infant's perception of the "bodies" of others, personal meanings may be apprehended directly (Scheler, 1954; Wittgenstein, 1980). Or to put this more accurately, the infant's perception is not so much of bodies, but rather of "somethings" that draw out of the infant modes of feeling and action that have a degree of specificity for the somethings (people) related-to. Thus in a philosophically inclined discussion of social relations in early childhood, Merleau-Ponty (1964) quotes Husserl as saying that the perception of others is like a "phenomenon of coupling", and proceeds to stress the "simple fact that I live in the facial expressions of the other, as I feel him living in mine" (p. 146). Non-inferential empathy, the direct perception of and affective responsiveness to the bodily affective expressiveness of others, is a principal mode of intersubjective communication.

There are several matters that deserve emphasis here. First, affective communication refers not only to perception and responsiveness to so-called universal emotions such as happiness, sadness, and anger, that have relatively constant expressions across cultures and can be recognised by all peoples of the world (Izard, 1977; Ekman, 1984). There are also less easily specified patterns and intensities of bodily feelings, what Daniel Stern (1985) calls vitality affects, that would qualify in this category. In the present context, the essence of affective communication is that behavioural co-ordination between individuals is also psychological co-ordination.

Second, there is no radical developmental disjunction between the perception of "bodies" or "behaviour", and the apprehension of "mind". A fortiori, it is not a matter of the infant beginning with the cool perception of thing-like bodies, and only subsequently interpreting or theorising that behind bodily behaviour there might be "mind". On the contrary, aspects of mind are perceived in aspects of expressive behaviour. This is true of adult perceptual experience just as it is of infantile experience. As Wittgenstein (1980: p. 100e) writes: "We do not see facial contortions and make the inference that he is feeling joy, grief, boredom. We describe a face immediately as sad, radiant, bored, even when we are unable to give any other description of the features." Or as Woodruff Smith (1989: p. 134) puts it: "I not only see 'her', I also see that 'she is feeling sad'...Such an experience we feel intuitively is a direct awareness of the other's grief...And such is our acquaintance with others." To perceive personal meanings is also to have the propensity to react to such meanings in appropriate ways. Perception is relational; in the early stages of personal relatedness, perceiving has intrinsic connections with feeling and acting.

All this takes us some way towards appreciating why minds are ascribed to bodies, and why children as well as adults know for sure that people have minds. The fact is that with regard to certain mental states, the subjectivity of others is perceived (and reacted-to) in bodily expression and behaviour. There is direct perception of "personal meanings" anchored in people's bodies. This form of perception is not reducible to nor supervenient upon the perception of bodies *as* "bodies". The starting-point for the I–Thou developmental line is interpersonal and intersubjective engagement, in its infantile forms. This special mode of engagement is necessary if the child is to understand what a person is—a special kind of thing with a body and a mind.

However, there are complications to all this. Does not the idea of communication or sharing already imply that self and other are differentiated? Is not the leap to adult cognition, with references to "she" and "the other", begging the very developmental question we are trying to answer—namely, the origins of the concept of the other? I think that part of the answer is "Yes". The kind of communication witnessed in two-month-olds is not the same as communication in two-year-olds. The kinds of experience that a two-month-old has of other people does not entail that the infant has a concept of people with whom experiences can be shared. On the contrary, it is partly from early experiences of "sharing" (in inverted commas) that a child's concept of persons is derived. It is to bodily-expressed *attitudes* that a young child responds, often with (sharing) attitudes of her own. The infant does not have to impute mental life to bodies; rather, concepts of "body" and "mind" are derived from a child's experience of persons. At the risk of overdoing it, let me repeat once again: persons are experienced as special in virtue of the child's capacity to perceive and to react to attitudes in others, attitudes which have and are perceived to have *both* an external–behavioural and an internal-subjective dimension.

There are further ingredients that we need to add to the primordial soup of infancy. In particular, we need to establish how "self" and "other" are differentiated out of what Werner and Kaplan (1984) call the "primordial sharing situation". Note how the drift of this account is *from* interpersonal relatedness (in terms of co-ordinated experiences as well as behaviour) *to* an increasing awareness of the distinctions among persons, *from* intersubjectivity *to* individual self-reflective awareness. Yet an infant's awareness of people's subjectivity is only part of the story. The infant also becomes aware of the directedness of people's mental attitudes, and in due course the child has to grasp the representational nature of mind.

Before I take up these matters, I should stress once again that not all cognitive development takes place on the I–Thou developmental line. On the contrary, there are all kinds of perceptual capacities and sensorimotor-affective propensities that are directed to the inanimate world. There is much that the Piagetian or Gibsonian infant can achieve by herself. In addition to manifold forms of categorisation and sensorimotor co-ordination, practical understandings of means–ends relations and object permanence are cases in point. It is through the articulation of such abilities with developing forms of interpersonal awareness that

between the later months of the first year and the early months of the
second, an infant crosses the Rubicon into reflective self-awareness and
language.

Mind, Self and Symbol.   My thesis is that the relatedness triangle is
critical for a child's developing capacities to symbolise, to reflect on her own
mind, and consciously to assign selfhood (including a self's forms of mental
state) to other people. Instead of retracing all the steps of the argument, I
shall try to state my case for the plausibility and potential validity of this
view.

The story goes like this. Towards the end of the first year of life, infants
not only register the emotional meanings of and subjective background to
the bodily expressions of other people, but they also perceive the
directedness of another person's psychological attitudes. There may be one
or several distinct mechanisms operating when the infant follows another
individual's line of eye gaze or orientates to other features of the person's
bodily orientation, target of action, direction of movement or gesture, and
so on. The important point for the present purposes is that on the basis of
already-established intersubjective connectedness, the child *perceives* the
person's bodily orientation to be expressive of a psychological orientation.
Correspondingly, the infant not only relates to the same things and events
as does the care-giver, but now also relates to them *as* shared things and
events. So, too, the infant relates to the care-giver as one who shares
experiences of the world. On the other hand, a common focus of attention
may be the target of different attitudes; the infant may feel differently
about an object or event than does the person with whom it is shared. In
addition, the child herself is often the focus of another person's attitudes.

There is a further important characteristic to the one-year-old's
interpersonal relations. This is that the child is able to identify with
another person and assume as well as respond to the other's attitude. Here
is what Michael Tomasello and his colleagues have identified as the
beginning of "cultural learning", a means of cognitive advance that is
unique to humans: "…the cognitive representation that results from
cultural learning includes something of the perspective of the interactional
partner…[an] internalization or appropriation of perspectives" (Tomasello,
Kruger, & Ratner, 1993: p. 6). These authors emphasise that when an infant
reproduces an adult's novel behaviour in both its form and function, she
must have understood what the adult is perceiving and intending. The
reason is that she needs to grasp the purpose of the adult's behaviour. One
profound implication of such imitative processes is that humans can learn
new ways of acting, thinking, and feeling by cultural means—as
Tomasello nicely expresses it, they can learn "through" others. We can see

an early instance of this when an infant under one year old assumes the agent role in such adult-created games as peek-a-boo or give-and-take (Bruner, 1983).

What all this means is that the child can both recognise and adopt alternative attitudes to any single, specific object or event. This is our adult description of what is happening, not the child's. However, the child has the experiential basis for acquiring insight into the nature of person-directed attitudes *vis-à-vis* the multiply-referenced world. The child can also begin to assume as well as to register alternative attitudes to him- or herself as a source of attitudes—she has the basis for acquiring reflective self-consciousness.

It is not yet possible to know what conditions are necessary and sufficient for this intellectual leap to conceptualising "thought" *vis-à-vis* "thing". There may well be contributory factors to do with brain maturation and others that stem from developments in I–It understanding. There is certainly intense communicative input and scaffolding from the child's care-givers and siblings who join the child *in* "relatedness triangles". The child is pushed as well as led to realise that persons find and confer alternative meanings in and on the world. The interpersonal negotiation of attitudes and intentions is an intense and sometimes fraught affair. Yet for all that is speculative and uncertain here, I am suggesting that the relatedness triangle provides the child with a configuration of experience that is necessary for and essential to self-reflective awareness, creative symbolisation, and referential aspects of language. Why am I suggesting this?

The first consideration has to do with the logic of what it means to symbolise and to refer by means of words. For mature communicative symbolic functioning, children need to be self-consciously aware that they are using a symbol or word to stand for something else, and that another person will understand that symbol or word to mean what they intend it to mean. The reason is that the child has to know what it is to designate. Designation is necessarily designation *for* someone, and the designator needs to have a sufficiently elaborated concept of what it means to represent something "for someone" in this way. More than this, *the* meaning of a symbol, word, or concept is necessarily a "correct" meaning, and this means that more than one "someone" is involved or potentially involved in establishing or confirming the meaning. Children need to understand that they and others are selves in relation to whom symbols and speech acts have appropriate kinds of significance. Therefore the child *must* be self-conscious to an appropriate degree, and must be able to take the role of the other, in order to designate by means of symbols. Designation-for-self presupposes the possibility of designation-for-other. Having said this, there are ways of using language which do not require this degree of self-consciousness—for example, using language to accompany or take the place of action or gesture, to express feelings, or to simply get things done by others. There is a corresponding range of circumstances in which one thing may be associated with (and in *this* sense, "stand for") another. On such occasions, the child does not need to have grasped the relationships among persons, symbols, and referents. Quite simply, they need not know that they are making one thing stand for another. Only from our adult perspective are they "symbolising".

Of course even if these logical considerations are correct, they do not establish anything about how a child acquires self-consciousness and the capacity for the mature use of symbols. What they help to do is to sensitise us to what such development entails. Although the relatedness triangle provides the right kinds of input for a child to recognise the relations among self, other, symbols, and referents, what is there to indicate that it has developmental as well as logical significance?

First, there is rather weak evidence from normal development. In earlier chapters I charted some of the major advances in social and cognitive functioning over the first two years of life. Broadly speaking, the unfolding sequences and coincidences of interpersonal, communicative, and more specifically "cognitive" development correspond with what one would expect from the account I am giving. The most significant parallels concern the 9- to 18-month-old infant's increasingly sophisiticated configurations of personal relatedness, their growing communicative abilities, and their passage from presymbolic to symbolic intellectual functioning. Considering the final stage of this transitional period, for example, the onset of creative flexible symbolic play coincides with a new quality of self- and other-consciousness in the child's personal relations. The observations from the work of Kagan and Hoffman that I cited in Chapter 3 reveal how the child of 18–24 months can conceptualise what it is to experience oneself *as* a self with a mind, and moreover can knowingly attribute similar or corresponding forms of experience to other "selves". I say that such evidence provides only weak support for my account, and the reason for this is that there are many possible explanations for coincidences in developmental change. Even when there are intrinsic links between different domains of development, it is usually hazardous to say what those links are—for example, there are many options for explaining how symbolic and social functioning are related.

However, there is a second line of evidence that bears upon these matters. This comes from developmental psychopathology. Before I review such evidence, I need to consider how a child progresses from apprehending persons to conceptualising the mind as a potentially private domain which is characterised by representational states such as those involving beliefs.

Certain requirements are already in place. The child has established the capacities to symbolise, to reflect on his or her own "self" as a source of world-directed attitudes, and to confer self-anchored mental states on to others (and on to dolls). Earlier I stressed that although perceptual-affective bases for intersubjectivity are needed for the child to become aware *that* persons have minds, and in particular *that* persons are centres of subjectivity, they do not account for the child's understanding of all aspects of mind. This is why the acquisition of reflective self-awareness and the accompanying forms of role-taking are so critical. Now the child becomes able to introspect and to conceptualise a great deal about her own mental life. She can reflect on what it is like to be a self, and ascribe such psychological characteristics to others who have long been recognised as persons on the basis of primitive kinds of interpersonal co-ordination, but who are now also conceived of as "selves". The child has acquired a radically new way of expanding her knowledge about minds. From the child's point of view, persons have become bodies-with-minds. The child can draw upon the experience of him- or herself-as-experiencer in order to understand that whatever their current bodily expressions, people go on having a range of psychological states and attitudes. Not only may particular mental states remain covert, but also the very character of mental states can be fully discerned only if the covert dimension of mental life is understood.

The child is well-placed to infer more about the mind over the coming months and years. Note that only once the child is aware of her own cognitive processes does it make any sense to think of her as "theorising" about minds, because it is only now that she can formulate and test out hypothetical possibilities in accounting for people's behaviour. Even here, where the role of theorising may or may not be important in comparison with other ways of inferring things about mental processes, the child's increasingly sophisticated understandings and concepts about persons are better seen as progress towards *knowledge* of the mind, rather than as "theories of mind". The child comes to know that people have feelings, thoughts, beliefs and so on, and does so through a combination of her own first-person experiences and reflections, and her judgements about the (third-person) minds-cum-behaviour of others.

Finally, then, what of the child's understanding of "belief" and "knowledge"? We have already reached the stage at which the child recognises the perspectival nature of subjective attitudes and orientations towards the world. As Josef Perner (1988) rightly emphasises, however, there is a vital distinction to be drawn between understanding that a person represents something *as* something (for example, an event as frightening, or a matchbox as a pretend-car), and understanding that a person holds a representation to be a representation of reality, i.e. as being "true". How does the child come to evaluate a person's attitude as that of "holding a representation to be true of reality"?

Concepts of knowledge, belief, and false belief, as well as the distinction between reality and mere appearance (for a person), pivot on the notion of what is "true" or "correct". It seems to me there are at least two things that the child has to grasp in order to acquire the concept of being "true" of reality. The first is that if an individual has a true version of reality, then that person will be correct in his or her expectations about the fruits of action. Given certain aims, the person and/or others will behave appropriately in relation to that reality. In so far as a person acts in accordance with a false belief, on the other hand, that person will behave inappropriately. The second thing is that truth corresponds with what *anyone* would give as a description of a state of affairs, if that person were in an appropriate position to pass judgement. This is my way of putting the point about truth having reference to the possibility of agreements in judgement among individuals. Correspondingly, someone with a false belief is wrong to suppose that his or her "description" of a state of affairs corresponds with that which would be espoused by any right-thinking person, and wrong to think that in accordance with this, the belief can be used as the basis for planning appropriate action.

These considerations from logic point to the possibility that, in psychological development, children's progress towards understanding the nature of knowledge, belief, and so on, may arise in two conceptually separate but not wholly dissociable ways: (1) by inferring something about the status of their own and others' (imputed) "representations", namely that they may be categorised as "true" or "false", by observing how such ways of representing arise through perceiving situations appropriately and issue in successful or unsuccessful action; and (2) by recognising the status and implications of agreed-upon descriptions of what is the case ("I'm telling you that *this* is true—try it out for yourself, and you will agree!"). Note that in order to acquire a concept of belief by the first of these routes, a child would need to be engaged with and focussed upon her own and others' ways of representing the world; to follow the second route, the child would need to be struck by the significance of what people assert and agree to be the true or correct perspective. My suggestion is this: not only does a proper understanding of truth and knowledge entail an implicit acknowledgement of something that corresponds to the view of the generalised other, but also the *acquisition* of these concepts and respect for truth may be promoted by experiences of appropriate kinds of agreement and disagreement with others. Some recent studies by Josef Perner and his colleagues (Perner, Ruffman, & Leekam, 1993) do suggest that children with many siblings may arrive at "false belief" understanding earlier than those in small families. Once again, a child's intersubjective experience as well as her judgements of "behaviour" appears to be essential to the development of concepts of mind.

THE CASE OF AUTISM

I promised to consider a second line of evidence in support of my suggestions concerning the formative influence of the relatedness triangle. Here the perspective is that of developmental psychopathology. I shall focus on two abnormal conditions, although I suspect there are others that could shed light on the issues. The two conditions are early childhood autism and congenital blindness. I shall concentrate on the former condition, and then deal with the latter rather briefly.

The Theoretical Challenge

There are many difficult things to understand about autism. As I stated near the beginning of this essay, I am restricting my discussion to a certain level of psychological explanation. The question I want to tackle is: why is the syndrome of autism characterised by a particular kind of impairment in interpersonal relations, patterns of communication (including language) that are frequently delayed but also abnormal in form and usage, and a typical profile of cognitive deficits that include severe restriction in symbolic play and imaginative activity?

A Theory of Autistic Children's Development

Personal Relatedness and "Thing" Relatedness.   The principal thesis is that the essence of autism is severe disturbance in intersubjective personal engagement with others. Autistic children are profoundly limited in their capacity for and experience of personal relatedness. I believe that Kanner (1943: p. 250) was more or less right when he suggested that these children "have come into the world with an innate inability to form the usual, biologically provided affective contact with people". I say "more or less right", for the reason that the condition does not always seem to be constitutional in origin (it sometimes results from postnatal organic insult), and we must not assume that there is complete homogeneity to the quality or depth of the children's underlying affective disability. What autistic children appear to have in common is severe limitation in their experience of interpersonal relations *as* interpersonal. Their sense of psychological connectedness to and affective engagement with other people is seriously impoverished. The emphasis on affective impairments serves to highlight the domain in which bodily interco-ordination between people is also mental co-ordination between people, and in which intra-individual configurations of bodily expressed feeling are potential sources of inter-individual patterns of social experience.

There are a number of ways in which one might justify this way of putting things. However, no amount of evidence and reasoning could ever be decisive in establishing the account as correct. It is always possible that what appear to be "primary" features of autism, seeming to arise *sui generis* early in development and apparently responsible for subsequent secondary effects, might yet turn out to be caused by prior disabilities of a more fundamental kind. In addition, of course, *any* aspect of a disorder is related to dysfunction in or disorganisation among lower-order processes, even though these latter processes may not explain the origin and nature of the higher-order deficits.

I would simply highlight the following. First, we recognise impairment in interpersonal engagement as a *sine qua non* for the diagnosis of autism. Our clinical judgement of whether a child's social disability is of a kind to justify the diagnosis, is heavily dependent on the "feel" we experience when relating to the autistic individual. True, this "feel" changes with the individual's development; true, non-autistic individuals can sometimes give one a rather similar "feel", even though their condition is very different from autism in other respects. It is also the case that not all autistic individuals are reported to be abnormal in their social relations during the first two years of life, and it remains uncertain whether an organic insult after this period could abolish those abilities established through I–Thou developmental processes (it is extremely rare for non-autistic adults to become autistic). Nevertheless, there is *prima facie* plausibility that the deficits in interpersonal attentiveness and engagement which are universal in autism occur on the levels of what in normal infants one calls primary and secondary intersubjectivity. If one wishes to explain autism as the outcome of disability in what are normally later-appearing cognitive abilities, then one needs to give a convincing account of how such deficits have such a devastating effect on these most basic aspects of non-verbal communication and interpersonal body-mental co-ordination. Moreover, impairments in personal relatedness are apparent in many young and/or very retarded autistic children who have not yet attained the developmental stage(s) at which such relatively mature cognitive functions would be expected to appear, so it would seem that abnormality in such functions is unlikely to be the cause of these deficits (Klin, Volkmar, & Sparrow, 1992).

Second, there is the experimental and observational evidence for abnormalities in autistic children's perception of and responsiveness towards the meanings in other people's expressions of emotion. The children's own emotional expressiveness is also abnormal. It appears that this quality and level of impairment captures a facet of autism that cannot be explained in narrowly cognitive terms. As Margaret Mahler (1968: p. 3) writes, there is often "a most striking inability, on the part of the psychotic child, even to see the human object in the outside world, let alone to interact with him as with another separate human entity". Once again, the problem seems to affect processes implicated in primary intersubjectivity.

It may be worth noting that autistic children's deficits in very basic, early infantile forms of I–Thou relatedness, expressed for example in their lack of mutual eye gaze, their failure to attend to and orientate towards others, and their dearth of interco-ordinated affective and motoric exchanges with other people, might be described as "motivational" or even "cognitive" in nature, and not merely "affective". This is why I emphasise the structure of "relatedness". Normally to perceive affective expressions *is* to be grabbed by the experience, in a sense it *is* to categorise "input" according to meaning, it *is* to be motivated to make a response in feeling and action. In such circumstances (though not in all circumstances), it is wasteful to spend time arguing whether autism involves a cognitive *or* a motivational *or* an affective deficit. The critical question here is which forms of cognitive-conative-affective processes are derailed, and our task is to trace the implications of the deficits for what we identify as the somewhat more separable cognitive, conative, and affective aspects of later life.

This brings me to autistic children's capacities for "thing relatedness", for here too there are interwoven cognitive, conative, and affective dimensions. As Kanner (1943) observed, many autistic children have relatively good attentiveness to objects and they can often apply themselves to mechanical tasks, particularly those that suggest their own solutions and do not need the child to apply social–dependent meanings. On the other hand, Kanner also noted how autistic children show impaired relatedness towards people *and* objects from early in life, and we should beware of oversimplifying matters. Whatever component deficits there are to the children's impaired personal relatedness—and these may well vary from child to child—there is no guarantee that all of these will have effects that are restricted to the interpersonal domain. It should come as little surprise that the majority of children have significant general intellectual handicap, or that in some individuals, particular facets of thing relatedness are disrupted. In addition, of course, much that a child comes to understand about things is mediated by the way that other people scaffold and augment the child's learning, so that autistic children will be partly deprived of this interpersonal input to I–It cognitive development. Notwithstanding these caveats, autistic children are *relatively* proficient in acquiring at least certain I–It capacities which may include aspects of visuospatial pattern recognition, the understanding of simple means–end relations, and the awareness of object permanence. They even seem to be able to follow and draw inferences from the direction of eye gaze and probably from other behaviour exhibited by people, although this has not been studied in very young children. Here we see that there is specificity to the children's strengths and weaknesses. They are relatively successful in following the I–It developmental pathway, and they can even respond to aspects of people when such exchanges are not intrinsically "intersubjective" in nature. It is specifically in I–Thou interpersonal relatedness that we find the abnormalities characteristic of "autism".

Mind, Self, and Symbol. We can now consider the evidence for autism-specific deficits in secondary intersubjectivity. Autistic children rarely manifest the protodeclarative gestures of giving and showing things to others, they appear to have difficulty in understanding such gestures as used by others, and they rarely engage in other forms of social referencing. The tendency to imitate others is striking for its relative absence. It is especially when a normal child would be attending to, registering, evaluating, and identifying with the *subjective orientation* of another person, that the autistic child is most abnormal. For example, autistic children are relatively more likely (albeit not that likely) to request things of others by proto-imperative gestures; they are sometimes inclined to "imitate" aspects of other people's behaviour (as in echolalia), but only when this does not entail that they assume the other person's psychological orientation and attitude. This profile of ability and disability certainly suggests that the problem lies in the processes that lead to awareness of others as subjects of experience. What was missing initially on the level of primary intersubjectivity is missing again on the level of secondary intersubjectivity. The evidence is far from conclusive, but we seem to be tracing the developmental implications of early-onset impairments in psychological connectedness between persons.

Now we come to the relatedness triangle. The reason that the relatedness triangle of normal development and the phenomena of autism are relevant for each other, is that each seems to be the negative image of the other. I have already suggested that autistic individuals lack something essential for the capacity to relate to other people's psychological relatedness to themselves and to the world. This capacity is *the* defining characteristic of the relatedness triangle. It follows that if a non-autistic child's experience of the relatedness triangle is foundational for a range of subsequent developmental accomplishments, then the autistic child's impoverished experience in this respect should result in corresponding psychopathological sequelae. Foremost among these should be impairments in creative symbolic play, abnormalites in language whenever an awareness of and adjustment to psychological attitudes is involved, limitations in self-reflective awareness, problems in context-sensitive thinking and conceptualisation, and a restricted understanding of the nature of mind.

It is hardly necessary for me to state that these are exactly the areas of cognitive and motivational functioning in which autistic children are most markedly impaired. Let me consider them, one by one. Even in those older and more able individuals who do acquire some capacity for making one thing stand for another in symbolic play, there appears to be neither the emotional–motivational investment in shifting among alternative symbolic meanings (a process I have suggested is tantamount to a form of flexible and even adventurous role-taking), nor the involvement in acting out social scenarios which involve the attribution of personally significant "meanings" to play materials, including the ascription of subjectively experienced attitudes to dolls and other figures. Although we can distinguish cognitive from motivational aspects of symbolising, the autistic child has abnormality in each respect. There is good reason for this—if the root cause of the deficit is to be found in the child's failure to *engage* with others psychologically within the relatedness triangle, and then no wonder that what follows as a result is both a cognitive problem (the failure to understand what it means to designate by symbols) and a motivational problem (the failure to be drawn into adapting alternative psychological roles and perspectives, and to be invested in the kinds of role relationships that normal children live out in their creative symbolic play).

Autistic children's language impairments spring from the same source. The children are limited in their experiences of sharing and therefore communicating with others; as a consequence they are slow to appreciate what it means for they and others to intend to communicate; and they are especially handicapped in coming to grasp what it means to refer to something *for* someone else by means of interpersonally agreed linguistic symbols. It is the very essence of language that speakers intend not only to indicate what they are referring to, but also to convey that aspect of meaning that they have in mind. Speakers also convey that they are trying to communicate their message. There are several ways in which language captures the *attitudes* of a speaker, both in relation to the listener and to the topic that is spoken about; this is the pragmatics of language. Deictic terms such as "I" and "you", "this" and "that", and "now" and "then" are especially clear examples in which the appropriate terms are anchored to the position and stance of the speaker; metaphors are especially clear instances where the habitual meanings of words are altered according to novel meanings determined by the speaker's attitude. It is in the comprehension and production of linguistic forms reflecting such pragmatic aspects of language that autistic individuals are most at sea.

Autistic children are also limited in their capacities for self-reflective awareness. They are at best only partially aware of themselves in the minds of others. I have given a number of clinical illustrations in earlier chapters. Not only do the children show a relative lack of shame and pride, and a lack of coyness when seeing themselves in a mirror, but so too they appear to contrast with normal one-year-olds in having little sense of themselves as agents and possessors. As Gerhard Bosch (1970) portrays most vividly, many autistic children show little possessiveness or sense of property, little competition or focussed self-defence or counterattack, and they may be delayed in saying "No" and "Yes". This kind of list illustrates how a child's awareness of self is sharpened by awareness of other selves, and *vice versa*; for example, normal possessiveness and competition are experienced in relation to rival possessors and competitors. Once again, to speak of "self-awareness" is to express the matter too blandly. Normal young children are passionate in their pride and possessiveness, their self-assertiveness and opposition, their disagreements and their alliances with others. In many autistic individuals, such motivational and emotional investment in the self *vis-à-vis* others seems hardly there at all. I believe that children with autism do have difficulties in *conceiving* of themselves as "selves", but this cognitive difficulty is closely allied to their lack of engagement not only with other people, but also with themselves *as* "selves".

Not surprisingly, the restrictions in autistic individuals' thinking conform with the pattern of their limitations in symbolic play and language. They are slow to develop the higher cognitive functions. Almost certainly, such delay is only in part a reflection of general mental retardation directly caused by brain damage. The discrepancy between autistic children's superior visuospatial performance and inferior linguisitic–conceptual abilities, especially as these apply to concepts and meanings with high "social loading", suggests that the children have a degree of cognitive potential which cannot be realised. Even when they have adequate cortical "hardware" in the brain, they are partly deprived of those forms of social experience that are needed to acquire the *conceptual* apparatus for the "hardware" to support effective and creative thought.

Having said this, many autistic individuals do eventually achieve a relatively sophisticated level of thought and language. Although their thinking tends to be "concrete", in that particular concepts may be applied in a stereotyped way with little adjustment to context, they do come to apply many conceptual categories in a relatively normal manner. Not only have these individuals some understanding of being corrected so that they learn the conventional meanings of words, but in addition there are many respects in which their natural ways of mentally partitioning the world seem to correspond with those of other human beings. Their manner of perceiving and understanding demonstrates an impressive capacity for abstraction, even though the areas of weakness (for example, concerning emotion-related and other mental state concepts) have only begun to be charted. These facts seem to underline how different kinds of abstracting support different kinds of thinking. Charles Fernyhough (1992) has contrasted the computer-like "monologic" thought of autistic individuals, even those who are able to calculate in highly abstract domains such as mathematics, with the "dialogic" mode of flexible thinking that stems from the capacity to bring alternative perspectives into relation with one another. This exactly parallels my own point about the kind of socially derived symbolic functioning necessary for creative imagination.

Finally, we come to autistic individuals' restricted conceptions of mental functioning. There is evidence that although they have at least some notion of what it means to "see", they have considerable difficulty with a number of emotion-related concepts, with understanding pretence and imagination, and perhaps especially, with concepts of belief and knowledge. For example, they have difficulty in understanding how another person may behave inappropriately on the basis of a false belief about a situation. They are also unclear about the distinction between appearance and reality.

My account of this aspect of autism is best summarised by reference to the characteristics of propositional mental states such as that of "belief". In believing, a person adopts the attitude that a given description (or "representation") of a state of affairs is true. In order to understand what beliefs are, one has to understand: (1) that states of affairs can fall under different descriptions for people; (2) that people have attitudes towards things and events as "represented"; and (3) that one kind of attitude (belief) is "to hold as true of reality", which implies a kind of commitment to respecting what is true. We can see how autistic children face a *number* of hurdles in acquiring the concept of belief, and in making the appearance/reality distinction. They are partly debarred from those experiences in the relatedness triangle that normally lead a child to understand what psychological orientations and attitudes are, and what it means for the world to fall under different descriptions for people. Even those autistic individuals who achieve some such understanding, who have a degree of self-reflective awareness, and who are in a position to infer things about the relation between people's "representations" and their behaviour *vis-à-vis* the world, are still at a disadvantage in at least two respects. First, they remain little concerned with or focussed upon their own and others' attitudes. This lack of attentiveness to people's ways of representing is part and parcel of their failure to engage with and to identify with others. One implication is that autistic individuals will be

less likely to *notice* the special status of "representing as reality". Second, they will not fully appreciate the force of agreements in judgement, and will be slow to register the significance of the "world for anyone (who is not misled)". They will partly miss out on the interpersonal process by which a particular form of shared perspective is branded as "reality".

There is something additional to note about beliefs, in comparison with other mental states. Beliefs are special in the sense that their intentionality—their directedness towards a content "as represented"—often does not have direct and immediate behavioural expression. Recall that intentionality and subjectivity are precisely the aspects of mental states for which processes of primary and secondary intersubjectivity (and the relatedness triangle) establish the foundations for understanding. To appreciate beliefs is to have a relatively advanced form of such understanding. The notion of "belief" entails a kind of sophisticated distillate of what is earlier perceived as the "intentional aspect" of psychologically expressive bodily states and actions. Whereas an able autistic child can acquire *some* understanding of what "happiness" is from observing behaviour that others call "happy" and even from introspection, it is very difficult for him to arrive at *any* understanding of "belief" until he is able to appreciate the nature of psychological attitudes, including the fact that attitudes may involve commitment to a particular way of seeing things. Therefore it is to be expected that the person with autism finds "beliefs" less comprehensible than "feelings". It is to be expected even if impairments in affectively co-ordinated personal relations lie at the source of his difficulty in understanding people's minds.

Further Perspectives

I have been emphasising the social-developmental contribution to the pathogenesis of autism. I have hardly touched upon the ways in which impairments that are not *primarily* social in nature might impinge upon both social and non-social psychological function. Indeed, I have set to one side a range of clinical features that are characteristic of autism, most prominently the autistic person's repetitive routines and restricted range of interests. I shall not attempt to correct these omissions at this late stage, but I should like to illustrate how the foregoing account needs to be set in a wider context.

Let me take the issue of "routines" as a case in point. Kanner (1943) remarked on the way in which many autistic children seem to have a "desire for sameness", and indeed they manifest a spectrum of repetitive activities from motor stereotypies at one extreme through to elaborate preoccupations with restricted and often idiosyncratic topics at the other. What approaches might we adopt in trying to explain such phenomena? A first approach might be to point out that if autistic individuals have deficits in symbolising, perhaps associated with abnormality in more basic mechanisms for establishing affective/motivational links among items of the world (as in Werner's physiognomic perception, or in what psychoanalysts call sublimation), then one would anticipate a restriction in their interests and a narrow channelling of their behaviour. A second approach, which has in fact been adopted by many authors, is to point out that autistic children and adults have to cope with a world which is frequently incomprehensible and at times overwhelming, so little wonder if they do so by imposing a rigid structure on their attitudes and behaviour. A third approach is to view this aspect of autism as a direct expression of primary abnormality in cognitive functioning.

There are several versions of this third, cognitive approach. For example, perseverative behaviour is often prominent in patients with neuropsychological disorder in the frontal lobes of the brain. Recently, evidence has been emerging that autistic subjects perform poorly on tasks that are generally considered to assess frontal lobe function (Ozonoff, Pennington, & Rogers, 1991a). One such task is the Wisconsin Card Sorting Task, which requires a subject to shift strategies of sorting and inhibit prepotent responses; another is the Tower of Hanoi, which requires a subject to plan a strategy of moving discs among upright supports. With these observed deficits as a neuropsychological starting point, Sally Rogers and Bruce Pennington (1991) mount a well-considered argument that dysfunction of the prefrontal cortex and/or its connections with the subcortical limbic system of the brain might account for autistic individuals' deficits in "executive function" on tasks requiring foresight, flexible planning, and the inhibition of responses. They hypothesise that this same dysfunction might also be responsible for deficits in "forming and co-ordinating social representations of self and other" (Rogers & Pennington, 1991: p. 157), an abnormality expressed in autistic individual's impairments in imitation, emotion sharing, and "theory of mind". A variant on this theme of disability in executive function has been proposed and given empirical backing by James Russell and his colleagues (Hughes & Russell, 1993; Russell, Mauthner, Sharpe, & Tidswell, 1991). Such abnormality might well contribute to the repetitive and routine preoccupations of autistic people.

I cite these approaches as three among several, in order to illustrate how difficult it is to judge which kind of explanation is appropriate for any given aspect of the clinical picture of autism. For example, one might argue that *certain* aspects of planning and flexibility of thought require just those abilities in self-reflective awareness, hypothetical (multi-perspective, as–if) thinking, and symbolic functioning that autistic children lack for social-developmental reasons. It would follow that when applied to autistic subjects, the supposed tests of frontal lobe functioning may not be tests of frontal lobe functioning after all. Or again, there might be a complex mix of social-developmental and (relatively) non-developmental sources of frontal-type disorder. This problem for the builder of theories is quite general. In the area of autistic children's language, for example, Robert Goodman (1989) has made a persuasive case for the existence of primary language disabilities, and there is every likelihood that such a disorder interacts with deficits in linguistic and symbolic functioning which have social-developmental origins.

Fortunately, there are many ways forward in deciding among competing theories or among alternative emphases within theoretical perspectives. These range from neurophysiological and neuro-imaging studies of the brain, through genetic studies of associations among deficits within and across generations, to the experimental dissection of autistic subjects' abilities and disabilities on carefully designed tasks. There is much to be gained from detailed appraisal of the *quality* of autistic people's behaviour, whether in natural or in testing situations. Equally, one sometimes needs to step back and consider the development of the clinical picture as a whole, rather than picking off a given psychological function and supposing this to result from disorder in a part of the brain which specialises in the function. We need more than adequate brains if we are to think and to talk.

I want to illustrate what I mean by "stepping back" here. Already I have dwelt on the need to explain how a particular combination of impairments in personal relatedness, symbolic functioning, and language occurs as the syndrome of autism. Suppose we could identify another condition where there is a similar and equally perplexing constellation of problems. The character of that condition, perhaps especially its psychological causes and its natural history, might assist us in weighing up alternative accounts of autism, just as autism may help us decide among rival theories of normal development. I believe there exists at least one such condition—congenital blindness.

CONGENITAL BLINDNESS

In a remarkable paper entitled *Self-representation in language and play*, Selma Fraiberg and Edna Adelson (1977) describe three intelligent and non-autistic congenitally blind children whose development of symbolic play was delayed until after they were three years old. In each child, moreover, the emergence of representational play corresponded with the earliest correct usage of the self-referential pronouns "me" and "I".

One case report concerned a child called Kathie. When Kathie was two years old, her general language competence compared favourably with that of a normal child of the same age. On the other hand, Kathie's confusions in personal pronoun use were unusually marked—"Want me carry you?" she said to her mother when she herself wanted to be carried. Then between the ages of two-and-a-half and three years, it became clear that Kathie "could not represent herself through a doll or a toy. She could not recreate or invent a situation in play. She could not attend to a story or answer questions regarding a story or tell a story herself" (Fraiberg & Adelson, 1977: p. 256). She would sometimes echo requests (e.g. "Give it to her!" when requesting an object for herself), and she appeared to lack a concept of time. When tested at the age of just over three years, Kathie could neither pretend that playdough was a cookie, nor understand personal pronouns: when the interviewer asked: "Can I have a bite of the cookie, Kathie?", Kathie put the playdough in her own mouth and said: "This cookie different". It was not until after she reached the age of four that Kathie began to represent herself in doll play and, in parallel with this, to master the use of personal pronouns. By six years of age, she had become inventive in imaginative play, mischievous and fun-loving, independent and responsible as well as socially and linguisitically accomplished. Kathie was clearly *not* autistic.

Although this description is by no means typical of congenitally blind children, it is nevertheless striking for the coincidence in impairments in symbolic play, confusions in the use of personal pronouns and other deictic expressions, echolalia, and difficulties in producing and comprehending narrative. There are additional ways in which children with congenital blindness show similarities to those with autism—they are frequently delayed in achieving external reference and in giving and showing things to others, as well as in pointing (Mulford, 1983; Rowland, 1983). They are sometimes slow to say "No" and "Yes", and may have other autistic-like symptoms such as stereotypies and repetitive routines (Blank, 1975; Fay, 1973; Freedman, 1971; Keeler, 1958; Wing, 1969).

The question is: why? Why on earth should blind children be echolalic, for example? Although in some cases the constellation of abnormalities might be explicable in terms of "comorbidity" between blindness and autism, with each condition arising from a common underlying organic cause such as Leber's amaurosis (Rogers & Newhart-Larson, 1989), there is often little independent evidence to substantiate this suggestion or to indicate the presence of other neuropsychological impairment. As we have seen, the picture may arise in blind children who seem remarkably normal in other respects. My colleagues Rachel Brown and Maggie Minter have recently collected teacher reports which suggest that a high proportion (more than half) of three- and four-year-old congenitally blind children have multiple problems in the areas of symbolic play, "sharing", echolalia, and personal pronoun use. Only a few of these children would justify a diagnosis of autism. It is also notable that in the majority of the blind children, most of the problems appear to resolve by the age of seven. Blindness seems to delay rather than prevent development in these respects.

I think the most plausible hypothesis to account for all this centres on the relatedness triangle. Recall the importance of vision for enabling the sighted child to see, literally to "see", the outer-directedness of other people's psychological attitudes. Vision enables children to triangulate their own and others' divergent attitudes towards visually-specified objects and events in the world. Recall, too, the significance of such experience for differentiating the respective and potentially transferable roles of participants in communication. The blind child is therefore deprived of a principal means to achieve psychological co-orientation and co-reference with others. As Mulford (1983) discusses, one of the problems is for blind children to determine to whom and to what other people are attending or what others have in mind, a particular problem in the preverbal period. The developmental implications are just those one would expect to arise from impoverished experience of the relatedness triangle, especially deficits in creative symbolic play where one thing is supposed to stand for another, and delays in appreciating the speech-role-dependent aspects of language. Andersen, Dunlea, and Kekelis (1984) have also drawn attention to blind children's impairments in using symbols flexibly, in personal pronoun use, and in understanding deictic terms, and they too have attributed such difficulties to a lack of perspective-taking ability.

Thus we can see how for different reasons, blind and autistic children share a difficulty in both discerning and assuming a variety of co-referential attitudes towards a shared, objective world. They each suffer handicap in deriving role structures that can be applied in a flexible, creative manner. In the terms of Fraiberg and Adelson, blind as well as autistic children have a problem in representing the self as an "I" in a universe of "I's" (Fraiberg & Adelson, 1977: p. 249). This problem with self-representation has an intimate connection with the children's accompanying limitations in attributing alternative meanings to the materials of symbolic play. Moreover for blind and autistic children alike, echolalia and the misuse of personal pronouns reveal a relative failure to anchor utterances in the respective points of view and speech roles of speakers and listeners.

Earlier, I emphasised how a normal one-year-old can perceive the "mental" quality of attitudes in other people's bodily and vocal expressions. The infant can also perceive the directedness of such attitudes in a variety of bodily "cues" such as direction of eye gaze, orientation of action, and so on. In general, autism seems to involve an impairment in the former respect; blindness is an obstacle to achieving the latter. If blind children have some additional impediment to achieving or sustaining intersubjective contact, then the full syndrome of autism may result. On the other hand, vision is only one of several routes to shared reference, and compensatory tactics to augment communication between blind children and other people, together with the influence of language once it evolves, may overcome the developmental obstacles (Urwin, 1983).

In summary, I believe that certain of the phenomena of congenitally blind children lend support to a particular social-developmental account of the emergence of symbolic play and aspects of self-reflective awareness. It is just the kind of account that we need to understand "autism" as a constellation of impairments arising out of a fundamental disorder in a child's experience of co-ordinated, intersubjective personal relations.

EPILOGUE

As I indicated in the Preface to this book, my intention has been to present the outline of a developmental theory that has relevance not only for an understanding of early childhood autism, but also for our perspective on certain facets of normal cognitive as well as socio-emotional functioning in early childhood. I have suggested that in normal children, the emergence of certain distinctive capacities of mind, perhaps most notably the abilities to symbolise in a creative manner, to acquire self-reflective thought, and to communicate in flexible and context-sensitive ways, are dependent upon advances in *inter*personal understanding that require a background of specific forms of interpersonal relatedness with perceptual–affective–conative as well as cognitive underpinnings. It is for this reason that my title refers to the "development of mind", not merely to development in a child's understanding of the mind. The aim has been to articulate certain themes that are central to my approach, as clearly as I can.

There is an obvious limitation to this undertaking. What I have not attempted to do, except in a piecemeal and partial way, is to examine each of my suggestions in relation to overlapping or competing accounts of cognitive and social development. Thus I should have liked to review the many links between the theory I have presented, and the theoretical writings of other authors—perhaps especially (to cite just one reference for each, and including some that I *have* discussed) Alvarez (1992), Baron-Cohen (1988), Bosch (1970), Boucher (1989), Butterworth and Jarrett (1991), Cohen (1980), Dawson and Galpert (1986), Fein, Pennington, Markowitz, Braverman, and Waterhouse (1986), Frith, (1989a), Garfin and Lord (1984), Gomez, Sarria, and Tamarit (1993), Harris (1991), Hermelin and O'Connor, (1985), R.F. Hobson (1985), Kanner (1943), Leslie and Happé, (1989), Loveland (1991), Mahler (1968), Meltzoff and Gopnik (1993), Mundy and Sigman (1989), Newson (1984), Paul (1987), Perner, (1991), Prizant and Wetherby (1986), Rogers and Pennington

(1991), Rutter and Schopler (1987), Tager-Flusberg (1989b), Tomasello, Kruger and Ratner (1993), Trevarthen, (1989), Tustin (1981), Ungerer (1989), Volkmar (1987), Wellman (1990), Wing (1981b), Wolff and Barlow (1979), and Wright (1991). However, this book is long enough already. In these authors' papers and chapters, as indeed in papers of my own that I have cited in the text, the interested reader may find a more detailed or somewhat different treatment of the theoretical issues with which I have been most concerned.

Yet I should not let the matter rest there. At the end of the day, theories stand or fall according to their success in accounting for a sufficiently broad range of phenomena in an adequately detailed and comprehensive way—and according to whether in these respects, they fare better than alternative theoretical proposals. In my defence, I would point out that in other publications I have attempted to characterise, analyse, and argue with alternative explanations of the young child's earliest understandings of the mind, and specifically those influential approaches that posit a developing Theory of Mind (especially Hobson, 1990b,d, 1991b; also Hobson, 1993a,b). Instead of rehearsing the details of those arguments here, I shall conclude this essay by highlighting some broad contrasts between my own approach and that of a leading "cognitivist", Alan Leslie (especially 1987, 1991, 1993).

Notwithstanding the criticisms I have made of Leslie's early theoretical work (for example, in Hobson, 1990b), I owe a great deal to his formulation about the intrinsic connection between the young child's capacity for pretend play, and his or her ability to understand mental states. Moreover as time has passed, it has become apparent to each of us that we share a number of concerns about current notions of the infant-as-little-scientist, and that to some degree my account is complementary to, rather than antithetical to, Leslie's own. Leslie is trying to formalise a description of early information processing in computational terms, and my criticism is more about what his scheme leaves out of the developmental picture, than what it specifies. Much of the social–developmental story that I have suggested to lie behind the 18-month-old's new-found capacities for understanding persons, for self-reflection, for symbolic play, and so on, is sidelined if not wholly contradicted by Leslie's proposal that an innate "decoupling mechanism" is responsible for the child's ability to represent mental representations.

Rather than attempting to summarise Leslie's lines of thinking (for which, see Leslie, 1987, 1988a,b and Hobson, 1991b), I shall present the barest outline of his explanatory scheme and then note specific points in contention. Leslie (1988 and personal communication) defines "metarepresentation" as a particular form of internal representation that consists of the following parts: an agent (typically, a person), an informational relation ("pretend", "think", "believe"), an "anchor", and a decoupled expression which comprises a primary veridical representation of the world that is no longer tied to the reality it represents (a child representing mother as pretending that a cup contains water in an imaginary, playful context). This yields a characterisation of symbolic pretend play, of the form: Mother—pretend—(of)this cup—(that) "it contains water". Thus we are led to see how such play involves recognising and manipulating attitudes to information.

Although I am uneasy about the way that Leslie calls all this a form of "representation" and supposes that "informational relations can be looked at as computational functions" (Leslie, 1988a: p. 28), I believe that in its own terms, his formal description is both accurate and helpful. The major issue is whether those terms presuppose *additional* developmental influences that are denied a role in the theory. For Leslie, it is an innately determined "decoupling mechanism" and the metarepresentational capacity to which this contributes, which determine "the human mind's ability to characterize and manipulate its own attitudes to information" (Leslie, 1987: p. 416). The "decoupling mechanism" is innate; it does not develop through social experience; it has nothing to do with feelings; and it leads to (rather than derives from) the ability to recognise the nature of mental states. Leslie has found it "hard to see how perceptual evidence could ever force an adult, let alone a young child, to invent the idea of unobservable mental states"(Leslie, 1987: p. 422)—although he does not explain how it is that the young child ascribes "mental representations" to bodily-endowed people. In addition, Leslie suggests that pretence reveals a child's ability to represent *beliefs* (Leslie, 1988a: p. 35), and considers that developments in the second to fourth year of life concern the child's growth in understanding of how beliefs relate causally to situations in the world (especially how they are caused by what someone perceives, and how they can cause behaviour). He sees pretend play as "issuing from the attitude of pretending the truth of a proposition that describes a fictional state of affairs" (Leslie, in press: p. 39 of prepublished manuscript).

This scheme maps on to Leslie's explanation of autism, in so far as he attributes autistic children's impairments in symbolic play and "theory of mind" to an absence or malfunction of the decoupling mechanism and to difficulties in forming and/or processing metarepresentations. He has adopted the position (for example in Leslie, 1991) that autistic individuals' affective disorder and impairment in social and communicative behaviour are "secondary consequences" of the basic cognitive deficit.

In which respects, then, is my own account in conflict with that of Alan Leslie? The most fundamental difference is in the importance I give to perceptually-anchored intersubjective communication in the first one and a half years of life, for a young child's emergent understanding of persons-with-minds. I believe there is a great deal in an infant's capacities to perceive and react to the bodily-expressed *attitudes* of other people, that leads the infant towards an understanding of what it means to communicate and to share, what it is to be a self with attitudes of one's own, and what are the implications for a human being's capacity to "represent" the world in different ways. Affective co-ordination is critical for interpersonal engagement; interpersonal engagement is necessary for a child to register how persons differ from things in affording experiences of sharing, conflict, and so on; such experience underpins the child's awareness of persons as having attitudes that co-ordinate with her own; and the interpersonal co-ordination of attitudes *vis-à-vis* the world is what *effects* the "decoupling" of the things or events in the world, from the descriptions under which those things or events may fall for different persons. A developmental sequence that concerns the linkage and differentiation between self and other has intrinsic connections with a growing awareness of the potential linkages and modes of differentiation between "thought" and "thing". The twelve-month-old who can both recognise the separateness of another person-with-attitudes and identify with those person-anchored attitudes, is already well-placed to acquire the insight of what it means to *be* a person who can adopt alternative attitudes to given objects and events.

I have sometimes shifted my emphasis from a person's attitude to something, towards a concern with the description under which the something falls for that person. These approaches are complementary; a fearful person is related to a something-that-is-frightening. Loosely speaking, this "description" amounts to the "representation" with which that something corresponds in the mind of the beholder. However, it is not so much representations and metarepresentations, but rather attitudes and meta-attitudes that hold centre-stage in my developmental account. Nor is it merely that towards the end of the first year, an infant *perceives* the nature and directedness of another person's psychological attitudes—it is also that on the basis of mechanisms that have been operative for several months already, the infant is psychologically *engaged with* the other person's attitudes. Indeed, the child can only come to understand what it means to share and to communicate (and *a fortiori*, what it means to intend to communicate), by having the experience of primitive forms of sharing and communicating. Moreover, it is only through these processes that a child comes to acquire the concept of persons who have a range of qualitatively distinct subjective experiences, related to but also differentiated from those of the child herself. Therefore to return to Leslie's account of metarepresentation, I believe that the concept of "agent" with *attitudes* could only be acquired on the basis of the interpersonal–affective experiences I have outlined, and the concept of "informational relation" is distilled out of a range of observed and experienced person-to-world attitudes. A child ascribes attitudes (and "representations") to bodily-endowed persons, for the reason that *certain* attitudes are perceived *in* bodily expressive behaviour.

This brings me to the third part of Leslie's scheme, the notion of the "expression" that is "decoupled" in metarepresentation. I have already indicated my preferred terminology here, *viz,* the child's awareness of objects and events as having descriptions-for-persons. It may seem a point of technical nicety, but I do not accept that pretence reveals how a child can represent *beliefs.* What the child engaged in symbolic play *does* appreciate, is the distinction between a pretend attitude and a "for-serious" attitude. She also recognises how a person may hold a given description of the world to apply "pretendingly" as opposed to "seriously". Moreover, advances in the child's language around the middle of the second year reveal a deeper understanding of what a language-user may be intending to mean. This adds up to a great deal, but it does not yet amount to an awareness of what is "correct" according to a *privileged* description-for-persons, namely what is real or "truly the case". As Leslie (1988) emphasises, it is not until the age of around four years that children become accurate in considering mental states as both causes of behaviour and effects of perceptual exposure to a situation; but in addition to this, the child has been learning that "reality" is that description of the world concerning which inter-personal agreement is (in principle) attainable. I think that it is only when children come to understand that this is what knowledge is—an account of the facts that is transpersonal, in the sense that it would be agreed by anyone who was not distracted or misled by considerations peculiar to individual viewpoints—that they fully grasp what it is to entertain a false belief (i.e. mistakenly to hold as true of reality), or what it means to distinguish appearances from reality.

It will be clear from all this, as indeed from the remainder of my essay, that I believe Alan Leslie has underestimated the importance of primary interpersonal–affective disorder in the pathogenesis of autism. One of the difficulties in resolving this divergence of opinion on empirical grounds, is that Leslie and I agree on the pivotal significance of the autistic child's relative inability to conceptualise the nature of psychological attitudes. I believe this conceptual deficit is accompanied and indeed caused by the child's relative lack of patterned intersubjective engagement *with* the attitudes of others, a lack of engagement that we feel when we try to relate to and with autistic individuals. The dispute is over the way to characterise the source rather than the far-reaching implications of this disorder, in psychological terms. The development of autistic-like features in congenitally blind children might offer support for my approach, at least in suggesting that failures in "decoupling" can arise from deficient experience of person–person–world relations. The abnormal patterns of relatedness in very young and/or very retarded autistic children might also suggest a deficit that occurs well before a child is at the stage of "metarepresenting", but Leslie acknowledges that infant-level precursors to full-blown metarepresentational capacities might be abnormal in autism. It is here that I believe a rapprochement between our differing viewpoints may be achieved.

I anticipate that as the components of personal relatedness and interpersonal engagement are disentangled, we shall arrive at a more adequate picture of the emergence of a child's understanding of other persons with minds, and of herself as a person who can exercise creative capacities of mind. I believe that at this point we shall also recognise the need for a truly interpersonal and developmental account of the pathogenesis of autism.

References

Adamson, L., & Bakeman, R. (1982). Affectivity and reference: Concepts, methods, and techniques in the study of communication development of 6- to 18-month-old infants. In T. Field & A. Fogel (Eds.), *Emotion and early interaction* (pp. 213–236). Hillsdale, NJ: Lawrence Erlbaum Associates Inc.

Aitken, S. (1977). Psychological sex differentiation as related to the emergence of a self-concept in infancy. Honours thesis, Edinburgh University.

Ainsworth, M.B., & Wittig, B.A. (1969). Attachment and exploratory behaviour of one-year-olds in a strange situation. In B.M. Foss (Ed.), *Determinants of infant behaviour IV* (pp. 111–136). London: Methuen.

Ainsworth, M.D.S., Blehar, M.C., Waters, E., & Wall, S. (1978). *Patterns of attachment*. Hillsdale, NJ: Lawrence Erlbaum Associates Inc.

Alvarez, A. (1992). *Live Company*. London: Tavistock/Routledge.

American Psychiatric Association (1987). *Diagnostic and statistical manual of mental disorders* (3rd ed. rev.) [DSM-III-R]. Washington, DC: APA.

Amsterdam, B. (1972). Mirror self-image reactions before age two. *Developmental Psychobiology, 5,* 297–305.

Andersen, E.S., Dunlea A., & Kekelis, L.S. (1984). Blind children's language: Resolving some differences. *Journal of Child Language, 11,* 645–664.

Anderson, J.R. ((1984). The development of self-recognition: A review. *Developmental Psychobiology, 17,* 35–49.

Attwood, A., Frith, U., & Hermelin, B.(1988). The understanding and use of interpersonal gestures by autistic and Down's syndrome children. *Journal of Autism and Developmental Disorders, 18,* 241–257.

August, G.J., Stewart, M.A., & Tsai, L. (1981). The incidence of cognitive disabilities in the siblings of autistic children. *British Journal of Psychiatry, 138,* 416–422.

Bakeman, R., & Adamson, L.B. (1982). Coordinating attention to people and objects in mother–infant and peer–infant interaction. *Child Development, 55,* 1278–1289.

Baldwin, D.A. (1991). Infants' contribution to the achievement of joint reference. *Child Development, 62,* 875–890.

Baltaxe, C.A.M. (1977). Pragmatic deficits in the language of autistic adolescents. *Journal of Pediatric Psychology, 2, 176–180.*

Baltaxe, C.A.M., & Simmons, J.Q. (1977). Bedtime soliloquies and linguistic competence in autism. Journal of Speech and Hearing Disorders, *42,* 376–393.

Baron-Cohen, S. (1987). Autism and symbolic play. *British Journal of Developmental Psychology, 5,* 139–148.

Baron-Cohen, S. (1988). Social and pragmatic deficits in autism: Cognitive or affective? *Journal of Autism and Developmental Disorders, 18,* 379–402.

Baron-Cohen, S. (1989a). Perceptual role-taking and protodeclarative pointing in autism. *British Journal of Developmental Psychology, 7,* 113–127.

Baron-Cohen, S. (1989b). Are autistic children "behaviourists"? An examination of their mental-physical and appearance-reality distinctions. *Journal of Autism and Developmental Disorders, 19,* 579–600.

Baron-Cohen, S. (1989c). The autistic child's theory of mind: A case of specific developmental delay. *Journal of Child Psychology and Psychiatry, 30,* 285–297.

Baron-Cohen, S. (1991). The development of a theory of mind in autism: Deviance and delay? In M. Konstantareas and J. Beitchman (Eds.), *Psychiatric Clinics of North America, 14,* 33–51.

Baron-Cohen, S., Allen, J., & Gillberg, C. (1992). Can autism be detected at 18 months? The needle, the haystack, and the CHAT. *British Journal of Psychiatry, 161,* 839–843.

Baron-Cohen, S., & Cross, P. (1992). Reading the eyes: Evidence for the role of perception in the development of a theory of mind. *Mind and Language, 7,* 172–186.

Baron-Cohen, S., Leslie, A.M., & Frith, U. (1985). Does the autistic child have a "theory of mind"? *Cognition, 21,* 37–46.

Baron-Cohen, S., Leslie, A.M., & Frith, U. (1986). Mechanical, behavioural and Intentional understanding of picture stories in autistic children. *British Journal of Developmental Psychology, 4,* 113–125.

Bartak, L., Rutter, M., & Cox, A. (1975). A comparative study of infantile autism and specific developmental receptive language disorder: I. The children. *British Journal of Psychiatry, 126,* 127–145.

Bartak, L., Rutter, M., & Cox A. (1977). A comparative study of infantile autism and specific developmental receptive language disorder: III Discriminant function analysis. *Journal of Autism and Developmental Disorders, 7,* 383–396.

Barrett, M.D. (1985). Issues in the study of children's single–word speech: An overview of the book. In M.D. Barrett (Ed.), *Children's single-word speech* (pp. 1–19). Chichester: Wiley.

Bartsch, K., & Wellman, H.M. (1989). Young children's attribution of action to beliefs and desires. Child Development, *60,* 946–964.

Bates, E. (1976). Pragmatics and sociolinguistics in child language. In D.M. Morehead and A.E. Morehead (Eds.), *Normal and deficient child language* (pp. 411–463). Baltimore: University Park Press.

Bates, E. (1979). The emergence of symbols: Ontogeny and phylogeny. In W.A. Collins (Ed.), Children's language and communication, *Minnesota Symposia on Child Psychology, Vol. 12* (pp. 121–155). Hillsdale, NJ: Lawrence Erlbaum Associates Inc.

Bates, E., Camaioni L., & Volterra, V. (1975). The acquisition of performatives prior to speech. Merrill-Palmer Quarterly, *21*, 205–226.

Bates, E., Benigni, L., Bretherton, I., Camaioni, L., & Volterra, V. (1979). Cognition and communication from nine to thirteen months: Correlational findings. In E. Bates (Ed.), *The emergence of symbols: Cognition and communication in infancy* (pp. 69–140). New York: Academic Press.

Bechtel, W. (1988). *Philosophy of mind: An overview for cognitive science.* Hillsdale, NJ: Lawrence Erlbaum Associates Inc.

Bemporad, J.R. (1979). Adult recollections of a formerly autistic child. *Journal of Autism and Developmental Disorders, 9*, 179–197.

Bernard-Opitz, V. (1982). Pragmatic analysis of the communicative behavior of an autistic child. *Journal of Speech and Hearing Disorders, 47*, 99–109.

Bion, W.R. (1962). A theory of thinking. *International Journal of Psycho-Analysis, 43*, 306–310.

Blank, H.R. (1975). Reflections on the special senses in relation to the development of affect with special emphasis on blindness. *Journal of the American Psychoanalytic Association, 23,* 32–50.

Blocker, H. (1969). Physiognomic perception. Philosophy and Phenomenological Research, *29*, 377–390.

Boden, M. (1979). *Piaget.* London: Fontana.

Bolton, N. (1972). *The psychology of thinking.* London: Methuen.

Bolton, N. (1977). *Concept formation.* Oxford: Pergamon Press

Bolton, P., & Rutter, M. (1990). Genetic influences in autism. *International Review of Psychiatry, 2*, 67–80.

Bosch, G. (1970). *Infantile autism* (D. Jordan & I. Jordan, Trans.). New York: Springer-Verlag.

Boucher, J. (1989). The theory of mind hypothesis of autism: Explanation, evidence and assessment. *British Journal of Disorders of Communication, 24,* 181–198.

Boucher, J., & Lewis, V. (1989). Memory impairments and communication in relatively able autistic children. *Journal of Child Psychology and Psychiatry, 30*, 99–122.

Boucher, J., & Lewis, V. (1990). Guessing or creating? A reply to Baron-Cohen. *British Journal of Developmental Psychology, 8*, 205–206.

Boucher, J., & Warrington, E.K. (1976). Memory deficits in early infantile autism: Some similarities to the amnesic syndrome. *British Journal of Psychology, 69*, 73–87.

Bower, T.G.R. (1979). *Human development.* San Francisco: W.H. Freeman.

Bowlby, J. (1969). *Attachment and loss. Volume 1: Attachment.* London: Hogarth.

Bowlby, J. (1973). *Attachment and loss. Volume 2: Separation.* London: Hogarth.

Brazelton, T.B., Koslowski, B., & Main, M. (1974). The origins of reciprocity: The early mother–infant interaction. In M. Lewis & L.A. Rosenblum (Eds.), *The effect of the infant on its caregiver* (pp. 49–76). New York: Wiley.

Brentano, F. (1874/1973). *Psychology from an empirical standpoint* (A.C. Rancurello, D.B. Terrell, & L.L. McAlister, Trans.). London: Routledge & Kegan Paul.

Bretherton, I. (1985). Attachment theory: retrospect and prospect. In I. Bretherton & E. Waters (Eds.), Growing points of attachment theory and research. *Monographs of the Society for Research in Child Development, serial No. 209, 50*, 3–35.

Bretherton, I. (1992). Social referencing, intentional communication, and the interfacing of minds in infancy. In S. Feinman (Ed.), *Social referencing and the social construction of reality in infancy* (pp. 57–77). New York: Plenum.

Bretherton, I., & Beeghly, M. (1982). Talking about internal states: The acquisition of an explicit theory of mind. *Developmental Psychology, 18*, 906–921.

Bretherton, I., McNew, S., & Beeghly-Smith, M. (1981). Early person knowledge as expressed in gestural and verbal communication: When do infants acquire a "theory of mind"? In M.E. Lamb & L.R. Sherrod (Eds.), *Infant social cognition: Empirical and theoretical considerations* (pp. 333–373). Hillsdale, NJ: Lawrence Erlbaum Associates Inc.

Brooks, J., & Lewis, M. (1976). Infants' responses to strangers: Midget, adult and child. *Child Development, 47*, 323–332.

Bruner, J.S. (1975a). From communication to language—A psychological perspective. *Cognition, 3*, 255–287.

Bruner, J.S. (1975b). The ontogenesis of speech acts. *Journal of Child Language, 2*, 1–19.

Bruner, J.S. (1978). Learning how to do things with words. In J.S. Bruner and A. Garton (Eds.), *Human growth and development* (pp. 62–84). Oxford: Clarendon.

Bruner, J.S. (1983). *Child's talk*. Oxford: Oxford University Press.

Buber, M. (1958). *I and thou* (2nd ed.). (R.G.Smith, Trans.). Edinburgh: Clark. (Original work published 1937).

Buhler, C. (1937). *From birth to maturity*. London: Kegan Paul.

Butterworth, G. (Ed.) (1981). *Infancy and epistemology*. Brighton: Harvester.

Butterworth, G., & Jarrett, N. (1991). What minds have in common is space: Spatial mechanisms serving joint visual attention in infancy. *British Journal of Developmental Psychology, 9*, 55–72.

Camaioni, L. (1992). Mind knowledge in infancy: The emergence of intentional communication. *Early Development and Parenting, 1*, 15–22.

Campos, J.J., & Stenberg, C.R. (1981). Perception, appraisal and emotion: The onset of social referencing. In M. E. Lamb & L. R. Sherrod (Eds.), *Infant social cognition: Empirical and theoretical considerations* (pp. 273–314). Hillsdale, NJ: Lawrence Erlbaum Associates Inc.

Cantwell, D., Baker, L., & Rutter, M. (1978). A comparative study of infantile autism and specific developmental receptive language disorder. IV. Analysis of syntax and language function. *Journal of Child Psychology and Psychiatry, 19*, 351–362.

Capps, L., Yirmiya, N., & Sigman, M. (1992). Understanding of simple and complex emotions in non-retarded children with autism. *Journal of Child Psychology and Psychiatry, 33*, 1169–1182.

Caron, A.J., Caron, R.F., & Myers, R.S. (1982). Abstraction of invariant face expressions in infancy. *Child Development, 53*, 1008–1015.

Carpenter, G.C., Tecce J.J., Stechler, G., & Friedman, S. (1970). Differential visual behaviour to human and humanoid faces in early infancy. *Merrill-Palmer Quarterly of Behavior and Development, 16*, 91–108.

Chapman, M. (1988). *Constructive evolution: Origins and development of Piaget's thought*. Cambridge: Cambridge University Press

Charney, R. (1980). Speech roles and the development of personal pronouns. *Journal of Child Language, 7*, 509–528.

Charney, R. (1981). Pronoun errors in autistic children: Support for a social explanation. *British Journal of Disorders of Communication, 15*, 39–43.

Chiat, S. (1981). Context-specificity and generalization in the acquisition of pronominal distinctions. *Journal of Child Language, 8*, 75–91.

Chiat, S. (1982). If I were you and you were me: The analysis of pronouns in a pronoun-reversing child. *Journal of Child Language, 9*, 359–379.

Churchill, D.W. (1972). The relation of infantile autism and early childhood schizophrenia to developmental language disorders of childhood. *Journal of Autism and Childhood Schizophrenia, 2*, 182–197.

Clark, P., & Rutter, M. (1981). Autistic children's responses to structure and to interpersonal demands. *Journal of Autism and Developmental Disorders, 11*, 201–217.

Cohen, D.J. (1980). The pathology of the self in primary childhood autism and Gilles de la Tourette syndrome. *Psychiatric Clinics of North America, 3*, 383–402.

Cohn, J.F., & Tronick, E.Z. (1983). Three-month-old infants' reaction to simulated maternal depression. *Child Development, 54*, 185–193.

Cooley, C.H. (1902). *Human nature and the social order*. New York: Scribner.

Corbett, J., Harris, R., Taylor, E., & Trimble, M. (1977). Progressive disintegrative psychosis of childhood. *Journal of Child Psychology and Psychiatry, 18*, 211–219.

Costall, A. (1981). On how so much information controls so much behaviour: James Gibson's theory of direct perception. In G. Butterworth (Ed.), *Infancy and epistemology: An evaluation of Piaget's theory* (pp. 30–51). Brighton: Harvester.

Cummings, E.M., Zahn-Waxler, C., & Radke-Yarrow, M. (1981). Young children's responses to expressions of anger and affection by others in the family. *Child Development, 52*, 1274–1282.

Curcio, F. (1978). Sensorimotor functioning and communication in mute autistic children. *Journal of Autism and Childhood Schizophrenia, 8*, 281–292.

Dahlgren, S.O., & Gillberg, C. (1989). Symptoms in the first two years of life: A preliminary population study of infantile autism. *European Archives of Psychiatry and Neurological Sciences, 238*, 169–174.

Damasio, A.R., & Maurer, R.G. (1978). A neurological model for childhood autism. *Archives of Neurology, 35*, 777–786.

Dawson, G. (Ed.). (1989). *Autism: Nature, diagnosis and treatment*. New York: Guilford.

Dawson, G., & Adams, A. (1984). Imitation and social responsiveness in autistic children. *Journal of Abnormal Child Psychology, 12*, 209–226.

Dawson, G., & Galpert, L. (1986). A developmental model for facilitating the social behavior of autistic children. In E. Schopler & G. Mesibov (Eds.), *Social problems in autism* (pp. 237–261). New York: Plenum.

Dawson, G., Hill, D., Spencer, A., Galpert, L., & Watson, L. (1990). Affective exchanges between young autistic children and their mothers. *Journal of Abnormal Child Psychology, 18*, 335–345.

Dawson, G., & Lewy, A. (1989). Reciprocal subcortical–cortical influences in autism: The role of attentional mechanisms. In G. Dawson (Ed.), *Autism: Nature, diagnosis and treatment* (pp. 144–173). New York: Guilford.

Dawson, G., & McKissick, F.C. (1984). Self-recognition in autistic children. *Journal of Autism and Developmental Disorders, 14*, 383–394.

Decarie, T.G. (1978). Affect development and cognition in a Piagetian context. In M. Lewis & L. Rosenblum (Eds.), *The development of affect* (pp. 183–204). New York: Plenum.

DeMyer, M.K. (1975). The nature of the neuropsychological disability in autistic children. *Journal of Autism and Childhood Schizophrenia, 5*, 109–128.

DeMyer, M.K., Alpern, G.D., Barton, S., DeMyer, W.E., Churchill, D.W., Hingtgen, J.N., Bryson, C.Q., Pontius, W., & Kimberlin, C. (1972). Imitation in autistic, early schizophrenic, and non-psychotic subnormal children. *Journal of Autism and Childhood Schizophrenia, 2*, 264–287.

Dennett, D.C. (1985). Conditions of personhood. *Brainstorms* (pp. 267–285). Brighton: Harvester. (Original work published 1976).

de Villiers, P.A., & de Villiers, J.G. (1974). On this, that, and the other: Nonegocentrism in very young children. *Journal of Experimental Child Psychology, 18*, 438–447.

Dewey, M.A., & Everard, M.P. (1974). The near-normal autistic adolescent. *Journal of Autism and Childhood Schizophrenia, 4*, 348–356.

Donaldson, M. (1978). *Children's minds*. London: Fontana/Collins.

Dore, J. (1985). Holophrases revisted: their 'logical' development from dialog. In M. Barrett (Ed.), *Children's single word speech* (pp. 23–58). Chichester: Wiley.

Dunn, J. (1988). *The beginnings of social understanding*. Oxford: Blackwell.

Dunn, J., Bretherton, I., & Munn, P. (1987). Conversations about feeling states between mothers and their young children. *Developmental Psychology, 23*, 132–139.

Dunn, L.M. (1965). *Expanded manual for the Peabody Picture Vocabulary Test*. Circle Pines, MN: American Guidance Service.

Dunn, L.M., Dunn, L.M., & Whetton, C. (1982). *British Picture Vocabulary Scale*. Windsor: NFER - Nelson.

Ekman, P. (1984). Expression and the nature of emotion. In K.R. Scherer & P. Ekman (Eds.), *Approaches to emotion* (pp. 319–343). Hillsdale, NJ: Lawrence Erlbaum Associates Inc.

Ekman, P., & Friesen, V.W. (1975). *Unmasking the face. A guide to recognizing emotions from facial cues*. Englewood Cliffs, NJ: Prentice-Hall.

Fagan, J.F. (1972). Infants' recognition memory for faces. *Journal of Experimental Child Psychology, 14*, 453–476

Fagan, J.F. (1976). Infants' recognition of invariant features of faces. *Child Development, 47*, 627–638.

Fagan, J.F., & Singer, L.T. (1979). The role of simple feature differences in infants' recognition of faces. *Infant Behavior and Development, 2*, 39–45.

Fay, W.H. (1973). On the echolalia of the blind and of the autistic child. *Journal of Speech and Hearing Disorders, 38*, 478–489.

Fay, W.H. (1979). Personal pronouns and the autistic child. *Journal of Autism and Developmental Disorders, 9*, 247–260.

Fein, D., Pennington, B., Markowitz, P., Braverman, M., & Waterhouse, L. (1986). Toward a neuropsychological model of infantile autism: Are the social deficits primary? *Journal of the American Academy of Child Psychiatry, 25*, 198–212.

Feinman, S. (1982). Social referencing in infancy. *Merrill-Palmer Quarterly*, *28*, 445–470.

Feinman, S., & Lewis, M. (1983). Social referencing at ten months: A second-order effect on infants' responses to strangers. *Child Development*, *54*, 878–887.

Feinman, S., Roberts, D., Hsieh, K.-F., Sawyer, D., & Swanson, D. (1992). A critical review of social referencing in infancy. In S. Feinman (Ed.), *Social referencing and the social construction of reality in infancy* (pp. 15–54). NY: Plenum.

Fernyhough, C. (1992). Ideology and dialogue in the development of higher mental functioning. Unpublished manuscript, Department of Experimental Psychology, University of Cambridge.

Field, T.M. (1985). Neonatal perception of people: Maturational and individual differences. In T.M. Field & N.A. Fox (Eds.), *Social perception in infants* (pp. 31–52). Norwood, NJ: Ablex.

Field, T.M., & Fox, N.A. (Eds.) (1985). *Social perception in infants*. Norwood, NJ: Ablex.

Field, T.M., Woodson, R., Greenberg, R., & Cohen, D. (1982). Discrimination and imitation of facial expressions by neonates. *Science*, *218*, 179–181.

Field, T.M., Woodson, R., Cohen, D., Greenberg, R., Garcia, R., & Collins, K. (1983). Discrimination and imitation of facial expressions by term and preterm neonates. *Infant Behavior and Development*, *6*, 485–489.

Flavell, J.H. (1963). *The developmental psychology of Jean Piaget*. Princeton, NJ: Van Nostrand.

Flavell, J.H. (1974). The development of inferences about others. In T. Mischel (Ed.), *Understanding other persons* (pp. 66–116). Oxford: Blackwell.

Flavell, J.H. (1988). The development of children's knowledge about the mind: From cognitive connections to mental representations. In J.W. Astington, P.L. Harris, & D.R. Olson (Eds.), *Developing theories of mind* (pp. 244–267). Cambridge: Cambridge University Press.

Flavell, J.H., Botkin, P.T., Fry, C.L., Wright, J.W., & Jarvis P.E. (1968). *The development of role-taking and communication skills of children*. New York: Wiley.

Flavell, J.H., Flavell, E.R., & Green, F.L. (1983). Development of the appearance–reality distinction. *Cognitive Psychology*, *15*, 95–120.

Flavell, J.H. Green F.L., & Flavell, E.R. (1986). Development of knowledge about the appearance–reality distinction. *Monographs of the Society for Research in Child Development*, *51*, 1 (Serial Number 202).

Folstein, S., & Rutter, M. (1977). Infantile autism: A genetic study of 21 twin pairs. *Journal of Child Psychology and Psychiatry*, *18*, 297–321.

Forguson, L., & Gopnik, A. (1988). The ontogeny of common sense. In J.W. Astington, P.L. Harris, & D.R. Olson (Eds.), *Developing theories of mind* (pp. 226–243). Cambridge: Cambridge University Press.

Fraiberg, S., & Adelson, E. (1977). Self-representation in language and play. In S. Fraiberg (Ed.), *Insights from the blind* (pp. 248–270). London: Souvenir.

Freedman, D.A. (1971). Congenital and perinatal sensory deprivation: Some studies in early development. *American Journal of Psychiatry*, *127*, 1539–1545.

Frege, G. (1892/1960). On sense and reference. In P. Geach & M. Black (Eds.), *Philosophical writings of Gottlob Frege* (pp. 56–78). Oxford: Blackwell.

Freud, S. (1925). Negation. In J. Strachey (Ed.), *The standard edition of the complete psychological works of Sigmund Freud* (Vol. XIX) (pp. 233–239). London: Hogarth.

Frith, U. (1989a). *Autism: Explaining the enigma*. Oxford: Blackwell.

Frith, U. (1989b). A new look at language and communication in autism. *British Journal of Disorders of Communication, 24*, 123–150.

Frith, U. (Ed.) (1991). *Autism and Asperger syndrome*. Cambridge: Cambridge University Press.

Frye, D., Rawling, P., Moore, C., & Myers, I. (1983). Object-person discrimination and communication at 3 and 10 months. *Developmental Psychology, 19*, 303–309.

Furth, H.G. (1969). *Piaget and knowledge*. Englewood Cliffs, NJ: Prentice-Hall.

Gajzago, C., & Prior, M. (1974). Two cases of 'recovery' in Kanner Syndrome. *Archives of General Psychiatry, 31*, 264–268.

Gallup, G.G. (1968). Mirror-image stimulation. *Psychological Bulletin, 70*, 782–793.

Gallup, G.G. (1982). Self-awareness and the emergence of mind in primates. *American Journal of Primatology, 2*, 237–248.

Garfin, D.G. & Lord, C. (1984). Communication as a social problem in autism. In E. Schopler & G.B. Mesibov, (Eds.), *Social behavior in autism* (pp. 133–151). New York: Plenum.

Gelman, R., & Spelke, E. (1981). The development of thoughts about animate and inanimate objects: implications for research on social cognition. In J.H. Flavell & L. Ross (Eds.), *Social cognitive development* (pp. 43–66). Cambridge: Cambridge University Press.

Gillberg, C., Ehlers, S., Schaumann, H., Jakobsson, G., Dahlgren, S.O., Lindblom, R., Bagenholm, A., Tjuus, T., & Blidner, E. (1990). Autism under age 3 years: A clinical study of 28 cases referred for autistic symptoms in infancy. *Journal of Child Psychology and Psychiatry, 31*, 921–934.

Gomez, J.-C. (1991). Visual behaviour as a window for reading the mind of others in primates. In A. Whiten (Ed.), *Natural theories of mind* (pp. 195–207). Oxford: Blackwell.

Gomez, J.-C., Sarria, E., & Tamarit, J. (1993). The comparative study of early communication and theories of mind: Ontogeny, phylogeny, and pathology. In S. Baron-Cohen, H. Tager-Flusberg, & D. Cohen (Eds.), *Understanding other minds: Perspectives from autism* (pp. 397–426). Oxford: Oxford University Press.

Goodenough, F. (1931). *Anger in young children*. Minneapolis: University of Minnesota Press.

Goodman, R. (1989). Infantile autism: A syndrome of multiple primary deficits? *Journal of Autism and Developmental Disorders, 19*, 409–424.

Gopnik, A., & Slaughter, V. (1991). Young children's understanding of changes in their mental states. *Child Development, 62*, 98–110.

Gould, J. (1986). The Lowe and Costello Symbolic Play Test in socially impaired children. *Journal of Autism and Developmental Disorders, 16*, 199–213.

Grandin, T. (1984). My experience as an autistic child and review of selected literature. *Journal of Orthomolecular Psychiatry, 13*, 144–174.

Grandin, T. (1992). An inside view of autism. In E. Schopler & G.B. Mesibov (Eds.), *High-functioning individuals with autism* (pp. 105–126). New York, Plenum.

Grice, H.P. (1957). Meaning. *Philosophical Review, 66*, 377–388.

Hamlyn, D.W. (1974). Person-perception and our understanding of others. In T. Mischel (Ed.), *Understanding other persons* (pp. 1–36). Oxford: Blackwell.

Hamlyn, D.W. (1978). *Experience and the growth of understanding.* London: Routledge & Kegan Paul.

Hamlyn, D.W. (1982). What exactly is social about the origin of understanding? In G. Butterworth & P. Light (Eds.), *Social Cognition* (pp. 17–31). Brighton: Harvester.

Hamlyn, D.W. (1983). The logical and psychological aspects of learning. In *Perception, learning and the self* (pp. 71–90). London: Routledge and Kegan Paul. (Original work published 1967).

Hamlyn, D.W. (1990). *In and out of the black box.* Oxford: Blackwell.

Hammes, J.G.W., & Langdell, T. (1981). Precursors of symbol formation and childhood autism. *Journal of Autism and Developmental Disorders, 11*, 331–346.

Happé, F.G.E. (1991). The autobiographical writings of three Asperger syndrome adults: Problems of interpretation and implications for theory. In U. Frith (Ed.), *Autism and Asperger syndrome* (pp. 207–242). Cambridge: Cambridge University Press.

Happé, F.G.E. (1993). Communicative competence and theory of mind in autism: A test of relevance theory. *Cognition* (in press).

Harris, P.L. (1991). The work of the imagination. In A. Whiten (Ed.), *Natural theories of mind* (pp. 283–304). Oxford: Blackwell.

Haviland, J.M., & Lelwica, M. (1987). The induced affect response: 10-week-old infants' responses to three emotion expressions. *Developmental Psychology, 23*, 97–104.

Hermelin, B., & O'Connor, N. (1967). Remembering of words by psychotic and subnormal children. *British Journal of Psychology, 58*, 213–218.

Hermelin, B., & O'Connor, N. (1985). Logico-affective states and non-verbal language. In E. Schopler & G.B. Mesibov (Eds.), *Communication problems in autism* (pp. 283–310). New York: Plenum.

Hermelin, B., & O'Connor, N. (1986). Idiot savant calendrical calculators: rules and regularities. *Psychological Medicine, 16*, 885–893.

Hermelin, B., & O'Connor, N. (1990a). Factors and primes: a specific numerical ability. *Psychological Medicine, 20*, 163–169.

Hermelin, B., & O'Connor, N. (1990b). Art and accuracy: The drawing ability of idiot savants. *Journal of Child Psychology and Psychiatry, 31*, 217–228.

Hermelin, B., O'Connor, N., Lee, S., & Treffert, D. (1989). Intelligence and musical improvisation. *Psychological Medicine, 19*, 447–457.

Hess, E.H. (1970). Ethology and developmental psychology. In P. Mussen, (Ed.), *Carmichael's manual of child psychology* (Vol. 1) (3rd ed.) (pp. 1–38). New York: Wiley.

Hiatt, S.W., Campos, J.J., & Emde, R.N. (1979). Facial patterning and infant emotional expression: Happiness, surprise, and fear. *Child Development, 50*, 1020–1035.

Hobson, R.F. (1985). *Forms of feeling.* London: Tavistock.

Hobson, R.P. (1980). The question of egocentrism: The young child's competence in the coordination of perspectives. *Journal of Child Psychology and Psychiatry, 21*, 325–331.

Hobson, R.P. (1982a). The autistic child's concept of persons. In D. Park (Ed.), *Proceedings of the 1981 International Conference on Autism, Boston, USA* (pp. 97–102). Washington, DC: National Society for Children and Adults with Autism.

Hobson, R.P. (1982b). The question of childhood egocentrism: The coordination of perspectives in relation to operational thinking. *Journal of Child Psychology and Psychiatry, 23*, 43–60.

Hobson, R.P. (1983a). *Origins of the personal relation, and the strange case of autism.* Paper presented to the Association for Child Psychology and Psychiatry, London.

Hobson, R.P. (1983b). The autistic child's recognition of age-related features of people, animals and things. *British Journal of Developmental Psychology, 4*, 343–352.

Hobson, R.P. (1984). Early childhood autism and the question of egocentrism. *Journal of Autism and Developmental Disorders, 14*, 85–104.

Hobson, R.P. (1987). The autistic child's recognition of age- and sex-related characteristics of people. *Journal of Autism and Developmental Disorders, 17*, 63–79.

Hobson, R.P. (1989a). Beyond cognition: A theory of autism. In G. Dawson (Ed.), *Autism: Nature, diagnosis, and treatment* (pp. 22–48). New York: Guilford.

Hobson, R.P. (1989b). On sharing experiences. *Development and Psychopathology, 1*, 197–203.

Hobson, R.P. (1990a). On the origins of self and the case of autism. *Development and Psychopathology, 2*, 163–181.

Hobson, R.P. (1990b). On acquiring knowledge about people and the capacity to pretend: Response to Leslie. *Psychological Review, 97*, 114–121.

Hobson, R.P. (1990c). On psychoanalytic approaches to autism. *American Journal of Orthopsychiatry, 60*, 324–336.

Hobson, R.P. (1990d). Concerning knowledge of mental states. *British Journal of Medical Psychology, 63*, 199–213.

Hobson, R.P. (1991a). Methodological issues for experiments on autistic individuals' perception and understanding of emotion. *Journal of Child Psychology and Psychiatry, 32*, 1135–1158.

Hobson, R.P. (1991b). Against the theory of 'Theory of Mind'. *British Journal of Developmental Psychology, 9*, 33–51.

Hobson, R.P. (1991c). What is autism? In M. Konstantareas & J. Beitchman (Eds.), *Psychiatric Clinics of North America, 14*, 1–17.

Hobson, R.P. (1992). Social perception in high-level autism. In E. Schopler & G. Mesibov (Eds.), *High-functioning individuals with autism* (pp. 157–184). New York: Plenum.

Hobson, R.P. (1993a). Through feeling and sight to self and symbol. In U. Neisser (Ed.), *Ecological and interpersonal knowledge of the self.* New York: I.U.P.

Hobson, R.P. (1993b). The emotional origins of social understanding. *Philosophical Psychology.* (In press).

Hobson, R.P. (1993c). Understanding persons: The role of affect. In S. Baron-Cohen, H. Tager-Flusberg, & D. Cohen (Eds.), *Understanding other minds: Perspectives from autism* (pp. 204–227). Oxford: Oxford University Press.

Hobson, R.P. (1993d). Perceiving attitudes, conceiving minds. In C. Lewis and P. Mitchell (Eds.), *Origins of an understanding of mind.* Hillsdale, NJ: Lawrence Erlbaum Associates Inc. (In press).

Hobson, R.P. (1993e). The intersubjective domain: Approaches from developmental psychopathology. *Journal of the American Psychoanalytic Association.* (In press).

Hobson, R.P., & Lee, A. (1989). Emotion-related and abstract concepts in autistic people: Evidence from the British Picture Vocabulary Scale. *Journal of Autism and Developmental Disorders, 19,* 601–623.

Hobson, R.P., Ouston, J., & Lee, A. (1988a). What's in a face? The case of autism. *British Journal of Psychology, 79,* 441–453.

Hobson, R.P., Ouston, J., & Lee, A. (1988b). Emotion recognition in autism: Co-ordinating faces and voices. *Psychological Medicine, 18,* 911–923.

Hobson, R.P., Ouston, J., & Lee, A. (1989). Naming emotion in faces and voices: Abilities and disabilities in autism and mental retardation. *British Journal of Developmental Psychology, 7,* 237–250.

Hoffman, M.L. (1975). Developmental synthesis of affect and cognition and its implications for altruistic motivation. *Developmental Psychology, 11,* 607–622.

Hoffman, M.L. (1984). Interaction of affect and cognition in empathy. In C.E. Izard, J. Kagan, & R.B. Zajonc (Eds.), *Emotions, cognition and behaviour* (pp. 103–131). Cambridge: Cambridge University Press.

Hornik, R., Risenhoover, N., & Gunnar, M. (1987). The effects of maternal positive, neutral and negative affective communications on infant responses to new toys. *Child Development, 58,* 937–944.

Hughes, C., & Russell, J. (1993). Autistic children's difficulty with mental disengagement from an object: Its implications for theories of autism. *Developmental Psychology, 29,* 498–510.

Hurtig, R., Ensrud, S., & Tomblin, J.B. (1982). The communicative function of question production in autistic children. *Journal of Autism and Developmental Disorders, 12,* 57–69.

Husserl, E. (1901). *Logische Untersuchungen (Vol 2).* Halle, Germany: Niemeyer.

Huttenlocher, J., & Higgins, E.T. (1978). Issues in the study of symbolic development. In W.A. Collins (Ed.), *Minnesota Symposia on Child Psychology (Vol. 11)* (pp. 98–140). Hillsdale, NJ: Lawrence Erlbaum Associates Inc.

Izard, C.E. (1977). *Human emotions.* New York: Plenum.

Izard, C.E. (1979). *The maximally discriminative facial movement coding system (MAX).* Newark, DE: University of Delaware Instructional Resources Center.

Jennings, W.B. (1973). *A study of the preference for affective cues in autistic children.* Unpublished doctoral dissertation, Memphis State University.

Johnson, C.M., & Wellman, H.M. (1982). Children's developing conceptions of the mind and brain. *Child Development, 53,* 222–234.

Jordan, R.R. (1989). An experimental comparison of the understanding and use of speaker-addressee personal pronouns in autistic children. *British Journal of Disorders of Communication, 24,* 169–179.

Kagan, J. (1982). The emergence of self. *Journal of Child Psychology and Psychiatry, 23,* 363–381.

Kanner, L. (1943). Autistic disturbances of affective contact. *Nervous Child, 2,* 217–250.

Kanner, L. (1971). Follow-up study of eleven autistic children originally reported in 1943. *Journal of Autism and Childhood Schizophrenia, 1,* 119–145.

Kanner, L., & Lesser, L. (1958). Early infantile autism. *Pediatric Clinics of North America, 51,* 711–730.

Kanner, L., Rodriguez, A., & Ashenden, B. (1972). How far can autistic children go in matters of social adaptation? *Journal of Autism and Childhood Schizophrenia, 2*, 9–33.

Kasari, C., Sigman, M., Mundy, P., & Yirmiya, N. (1990). Affective sharing in the context of joint attention interactions of normal, autistic and mentally retarded children. *Journal of Autism and Developmental Disorders, 20*, 87–100.

Kasari, C., Sigman, M.D., Baumgartner, P., & Stipek, D.J. (1993). Pride and mastery in children with autism. *Journal of Child Psychology and Psychiatry, 34*, 352–362.

Kaye, K. (1982). *The mental and social life of babies*. London: Methuen.

Keeler, W.R. (1958). Autistic patterns and defective communication in blind children with retrolental fibroplasia. In P.H. Hoch & J. Zubin (Eds.), *Psychopathology of communication* (pp. 64–83). New York: Grune and Stratton.

Kernberg, O. (1976). *Object relations theory and clinical psychoanalysis*. Northvale, NJ: Aronson.

Klein, M. (1930, reprinted 1975). The importance of symbol formation in the development of the ego. In M. Klein, *Love, guilt, reparation and other works, 1921–1945* (pp. 219–232). London: Hogarth.

Klin, A., Volkmar, F.R., & Sparrow, S.S. (1992). Autistic social dysfunction: Some limitations of the theory of mind hypothesis. *Journal of Child Psychology and Psychiatry, 33*, 861–876.

Klinnert, M.D., Campos, J.J., Sorce, J.F., Emde, R.N., & Svejda, M. (1983). Emotions as behavior regulators: Social referencing in infancy. In R. Plutchik, & H. Kellerman (Eds.), *Emotion: Theory, research and experience. Vol. 2: Emotions in early development* (pp. 57–86). New York: Academic Press.

Kolvin, I. Humphrey, M., & McNay, A. (1971). Studies in childhood psychoses: VI. Cognitive factors in childhood psychoses. *British Journal of Psychiatry, 118*, 415–420.

Kujawski, J. (1985). *The origins of gender identity*. Doctoral dissertation. University of Edinburgh.

La Barbera, J.D., Izard, C.E., Vietze, P., & Parisi, S.A. (1976). Four- and six-month-old infants' visual responses to joy, anger, and neutral expressions. *Child Development, 47*, 535–538.

Lamb, M.E., & Sherrod, L.R. (Eds.) (1981). *Infant social cognition*. Hillsdale, NJ: Lawrence Erlbaum Associates Inc.

Landry, S.H., & Loveland, K.A. (1988). Communication behaviors in autism and developmental language delay. *Journal of Child Psychology and Psychiatry, 29*, 621–634.

Landry, S.H., & Loveland, K.A. (1989). The effect of social context on the functional communication skills of autistic children. *Journal of Autism and Developmental Disorders, 19*, 283–299.

Langdell, T. (1978). Recognition of faces: An approach to the study of autism. *Journal of Child Psychology and Psychiatry, 19*, 255–268.

Langdell, T. (1981). *Face perception: An approach to the study of autism.* Unpublished doctoral dissertation, University College, London.

Langer, S.K. (1957). *Philosophy in a new key* (3rd ed.). Cambridge, MA: Harvard University Press.

Leal, M.R.M. (Ed.) (1993). *Psychotherapy as mutually contingent intercourse*. Coleccao 'Temas de Psicologia', Associacao dos Psicologos Portugeses, Portugal.

Lee, A., Hobson, R.P., & Chiat, S. (1993). I, you, me and autism: An experimental study. *Journal of Autism and Developmental Disorders* (In press).

Leslie, A.M. (1987). Pretense and representation: The origins of "theory of mind". *Psychological Review*, *94*, 412–426.

Leslie, A.M. (1988a). Some implications of pretense for mechanisms underlying the child's theory of mind. In J.W. Astington, P.L. Harris, & D. Olson (Eds.), *Developing theories of mind* (pp. 19–46) Cambridge: Cambridge University Press.

Leslie, A.M. (1988b). The necessity of illusion: Perception and thought in infancy. In L. Weiskrantz (Ed.), *Thought without language* (pp. 185–210). Oxford: Oxford University Press.

Leslie, A.M. (1991). The theory of mind impairment in autism: Evidence for a modular mechanism of development? In A. Whiten (Ed.), *Natural theories of mind* (pp. 63–78). Oxford: Blackwell.

Leslie, A.M. (1993). ToMM, ToBy, and agency: Core architecture and domain specificity. In L. Hirschfield & S. Gelman (Eds.), Domain specificity in cognition and culture. New York: Cambridge University Press.

Leslie, A.M., & Frith, U. (1988). Autistic children's understanding of seeing, knowing and believing. *British Journal of Developmental Psychology*, *6*, 315–324.

Leslie, A.M., & Happé, F. (1989). Autism and ostensive communication: The relevance of metarepresentation. *Development and Psychopathology*, *1*, 205–212.

Lewis, M., & Brooks-Gunn, J. (1979). *Social cognition and the acquisition of self*. New York: Plenum.

Lewis, V., & Boucher, J (1988). Spontaneous, instructed and elicited play in relatively able autistic children. *British Journal of Developmental Psychology*, *6*, 325–339.

Liben, L.S. (Ed.) (1983). *Piaget and the foundations of knowledge*. Hillsdale, NJ: Lawrence Erlbaum Associates Inc.

Lockyer, L., & Rutter, M. (1969). A five to fifteen year follow-up study of infantile psychosis: III. Psychological aspects. *British Journal of Psychiatry*, *115*, 865–882.

Lockyer, L., & Rutter, M. (1970). A five to fifteen year follow-up study of infantile psychosis: IV. Patterns of cognitive ability. *British Journal of Social and Clinical Psychology*, *9*, 152–163.

Lord, C. (1984). The development of peer relations in children with autism. In F.J. Morrison, C. Lord, & D.P. Keating (Eds.), *Advances in applied developmental psychology* (pp. 165–229). New York: Academic Press.

Lord, C., & Garfin, D. (1986). Facilitating peer-directed communication in autistic children and adolescents. *Australian Journal of Human Communication Disorders*, *14*, 33–49.

Lord, C., & Hopkins, J.M. (1986). The social behavior of autistic children with younger and same-age nonhandicapped peers. *Journal of Autism and Developmental Disorders*, *16*, 249–262.

Lord, C., & Magill, J. (1989). Methodological and theoretical issues in studying peer-directed behavior and autism. In G. Dawson (Ed.), *Autism: Nature, diagnosis, and treatment* (pp. 326–345). New York: Guilford.

Lotter, V. (1966). Epidemiology of autistic conditions in young children: I. Prevalence. *Social Psychiatry*, *1*, 124–137.

Lotter, V. (1967). Epidemiology of autistic conditions in young children: II. Some characteristics of the parents and children. *Social Psychiatry*, *1*, 163–173.

Lotter, V. (1978). Follow-up studies. In M. Rutter & E. Schopler (Eds.), *Autism: A reappraisal of concepts and treatments* (pp. 475–495). London: Plenum.

Loveland, K.A. (1984). Learning about points of view: spatial perspective and the acquisition of 'I/you'. *Journal of Child Language*, *11*, 535–556.

Loveland, K.A. (1986). Discovering the affordances of a reflecting surface. *Developmental Review*, *6*, 1–24.

Loveland, K.A. (1991). Social affordances and interaction II: Autism and the affordances of the human environment. *Ecological Psychology*, *3*, 99–119.

Loveland, K.A., & Landry, S.H. (1986). Joint attention and language in autism and developmental language delay. *Journal of Autism and Developmental Disorders*, *16*, 335–349.

Loveland, K.A., & Tunali, B. (1991). Social scripts for conversational interactions in autism and Down syndrome. *Journal of Autism and Development Disorders*, *21*, 177–186.

Loveland, K.A., & Tunali, B. (1993). Narrative language in autism and the theory of mind hypothesis: A wider perspective. In S. Baron-Cohen, H. Tager-Flusberg, & D.J. Cohen (Eds.), *Understanding other minds: Perspectives from autism* (pp. 247–266). Oxford: Oxford University Press.

Loveland, K.A., Tunali, B., Kelley, M.L., & McEvoy, R.E. (1989). Referential communication and response adequacy in autism and Down's syndrome. *Applied Psycholinguistics*, *10*, 301–313.

Loveland, K.A., McEvoy, R.E., Tunali, B., & Kelley, M.L. (1990). Narrative story-telling in autism and Down's syndrome. *British Journal of Developmental Psychology*, *8*, 9–23.

McArthur, L.Z., & Baron, R.M. (1983). Toward an ecological theory of social perception. *Psychological Review*, *90*, 215–238.

Macdonald, H., Rutter, M., Howlin, P., Rios, P., LeCouteur, A., Evered, C., & Folstein, S. (1989). Recognition and expression of emotional cues by autistic and normal adults. *Journal of Child Psychology and Psychiatry*, *30*, 865–877.

McHale, S.M., Simeonsson, R.J., Marcus, L.M., & Olley, J.G. (1980). The social and symbolic quality of autistic children's communication. *Journal of Autism and Developmental Disorders*, *10*, 299–310.

Macmurray, J. (1961). *Persons in relation*. London: Faber & Faber.

McShane, J. (1980). *Learning to talk*. Cambridge: Cambridge University Press.

Mahler, M.S. (1968). On human symbiosis and the vicissitudes of individuation: Infantile psychosis. New York: International Universities Press.

Malatesta, C.Z. (1981). Infant emotion and the vocal affect lexicon. *Motivation and Emotion*, *5*, 1–23.

Malcolm, N. (1962). Wittgenstein's philosophical investigations. In V.C. Chappell (Ed.), The philosophy of mind (pp. 74–100). Englewood Cliffs, NJ: Prentice-Hall.

Mans, L., Cichetti, D., & Sroufe, L.A. (1978). Mirror reactions of Down's syndrome infants and toddlers: Cognitive underpinnings of self-recognition. *Child Development*, *49*, 1247–1250.

Mead, G.H. (1934). *Mind, self and society* (C.W. Morris, Ed.). Chicago: University of Chicago Press.

Meltzoff, A.N. (1990). Foundations for developing a concept of self: The role of imitation in relating self to other and the value of social mirroring, social modeling, and self-practice in infancy. In D. Cicchetti & M. Beeghly (Eds.), *The self in transition* (pp. 139–164). Chicago: University of Chicago Press.

Meltzoff, A.N., & Gopnik, A. (1993). The role of imitation in understanding persons and developing theories of mind. In S. Baron-Cohen, H. Tager-Flusberg, & D. Cohen (Eds.), *Understanding other minds: Perspectives from autism* (pp. 335–366). Oxford: Oxford University Press.

Meltzoff, A.N., & Moore, M.K. (1977). Imitation of facial and manual gestures by human neonates. *Science, 198,* 75–78.

Meltzoff, A.N., & Moore, M.K. (1983). Newborn infants imitate adult facial gestures. *Child Development, 54,* 702–709.

Merleau-Ponty, M. (1964). The child's relations with others (W. Cobb, Trans.). In M. Merleau-Ponty, *The primacy of perception* (pp. 96–155). Evanston, IL: Northwestern University Press.

Miedzianik, D. (1986). My autobiography. Nottingham: Child Development Research Unit, University of Nottingham.

Miller, C.L. (1983). Developmental changes in male/female voice classification by infants. *Infant Behavior and Development, 1,* 173–183.

Morris, C.W. (1938). *Foundations of the Theory of Signs,* (International Encyclopaedia of Unified Science, Vol. 1). Chicago: University of Chicago Press. Reprinted as: C. Morris (1971). Writings on the general theory of signs. In T.A. Sebeok (Ed.), *Approaches to semiotics.* The Hague: Mouton.

Mulford, R. (1983). Referential development in blind children. In A.E. Mills (Ed.), *Language acquisition in the blind child: Normal and deficient* (pp. 89–132). London: Croom Helm.

Mundy, P., & Sigman, M. (1989). The theoretical implication of joint-attention deficits in autism. *Development and Psychopathology, 6,* 313–330.

Mundy, P., Sigman, M., & Kasari, C. (1990). A longitudinal study of joint attention and language development in autistic children. *Journal of Autism and Developmental Disorders, 20,* 115–128.

Mundy, P., Sigman, M., & Kasari, C. (1993). The theory of mind and joint-attention deficits in autism. In S. Baron-Cohen, H. Tager- Flusberg, & D. Cohen (Eds.), *Understanding other minds: Perspectives from autism* (pp. 181–203). Oxford: Oxford University Press.

Mundy, P., Sigman, M., Ungerer, J., & Sherman, T. (1986). Defining the social deficits of autism: The contribution of non-verbal communication measures. *Journal of Child Psychology and Psychiatry, 27,* 657–669.

Mundy, P., Sigman, M., Ungerer, J., & Sherman, T. (1987). Nonverbal communication and play correlates of language development in autistic children. *Journal of Autism and Developmental Disorders, 17,* 349–364.

Murray, L., & Trevarthen, C. (1985). Emotional regulation of interactions between two-month-olds and their mothers. In T. M. Field & N. A. Fox (Eds.), *Social perception in infants* (pp. 177–197). Norwood, NJ: Ablex.

Neisser, U. (1988). Five kinds of self-knowledge. *Philosophical Psychology, 1,* 35–59.

Nelson, C.A. (1987). The recognition of facial expressions in the first two years of life: Mechanisms of development. *Child Development, 58,* 889–909.

Neuman, C.J., & Hill, S.D. (1978). Self-recognition and stimulus preference in autistic children. *Developmental Psychobiology, 11,* 571–578.

Newson, E. (1984). The able autistic child: persisting barriers. *Communication, 18,* 30–38.

Newson, E., Dawson, M., & Everard, P. (1984). The natural history of able autistic people: Their management in social context. Summary of the the report to the DHSS in four parts. Part 1. *Communication, 18,* 16–22.

Newson, J., & Newson, E. (1976). On the social origins of symbolic functioning. In V.P. Varma & P. Williams (Eds.), *Piaget, psychology and education* (pp. 84–96). London: Hodder and Stoughton

O'Connor, N., & Hermelin, B. (1963). Measures of distance and motility in psychotic children and severely subnormal controls. *British Journal of Social and Clinical Psychology, 3,* 29–33.

O'Connor, N., & Hermelin, B. (1967a). Auditory and visual memory in autistic and normal children. *Journal of Mental Deficiency Research, 11,* 126–131.

O'Connor, N., & Hermelin, B. (1967b). The selective visual attention of psychotic children. *Journal of Child Psychology and Psychiatry, 8,* 167–179.

O'Connor, N., & Hermelin, B. (1989). The memory structure of autistic idiot-savant mnemonists. *British Journal of Psychology, 80,* 97–111.

Ogden, T.H. (1983). The concept of internal object relations. *International Journal of Psycho-Analysis, 64,* 227–241.

Ogden, C.K., & Richards, I.A. (1923/1985). *The meaning of meaning.* London: Routledge.

Ohta, M. (1987). Cognitive disorders of infantile autism: A study employing the WISC, spatial relationship conceptualization, and gesture imitations. *Journal of Autism and Developmental Disorders, 17,* 45–62.

O'Neil, W.M. (1968). *The beginnings of modern psychology.* Harmondsworth, Middlesex: Penguin.

Ornitz, E.M., Guthrie, D., & Farley, A.H. (1977). The early development of autistic children. *Journal of Autism and Childhood Schizophrenia, 7,* 207–230.

Oster, H. (1981). "Recognition" of emotional expression in infancy? In M.E.Lamb & L.R. Sherrod (Eds.), Infant social cognition: Empirical and theoretical issues. Hillsdale, NJ: Lawrence Erlbaum Associates Inc.

Ozonoff, S., Pennington, B.F., & Rogers, S.J. (1991a). Executive function deficits in high-functioning autistic individuals: Relationship to Theory of Mind. *Journal of Child Psychology and Psychiatry, 32,* 1081–1105.

Ozonoff, S., Pennington, B.F., & Rogers, S.J. (1991b). Asperger's syndrome: Evidence of an empirical distinction from high-functioning autism. *Journal of Child Psychology and Psychiatry, 32,* 1107–1122.

Paivio, A., Yuille, J.C., & Madigan, S.A. (1968). Concreteness, imagery and meaningfulness values for 925 nouns. *Journal of Experimental Psychology Monograph Supplement, 76,* 1–25.

Park, C.C. (1986). Social growth in autism: A parent's perspective. In E. Schopler & G.B. Mesibov (Eds.), *Social behavior in autism* (pp. 81–99). New York: Plenum.

Paul, R. (1987). Communication. In D.J. Cohen, A.M. Donnellan, & R. Paul (Eds.), *Handbook of autism and pervasive developmental disorders* (pp. 61–84). New York: Wiley.

Paul, R., & Cohen, D.J. (1985). Comprehension of indirect requests in adults with autistic disorders and mental retardation. *Journal of Speech and Hearing Research, 28,* 475–479.

Perner, J. (1988). Developing semantics for theories of mind: From propositional attitudes to mental representation. In J.W. Astington, P.L. Harris, & D.R. Olson (Eds.), *Developing theories of mind* (pp. 141–172). Cambridge: Cambridge University Press.

Perner, J. (1990). Understanding the representational mind. Cambridge, MA: MIT/Bradford.

Perner, J. (1991). Discussant's contribution to the Symposium on Intention in the Child's Theory of Mind. *The 1991 Biennial Meeting of the Society for Research in Child Development*. Seattle, WA.

Perner, J. (1993). The theory of mind deficit in autism: Rethinking the metarepresentation theory. In S. Baron-Cohen, H. Tager-Flusberg, & D.J. Cohen (Eds.), *Understanding other minds: Perspectives from autism* (pp. 112–137). Oxford: Oxford University Press.

Perner, J., Frith, U., Leslie, A.M., & Leekam, S.R. (1989). Exploration of the autistic child's theory of mind: Knowledge, belief and communication. *Child Development, 60*, 689–700.

Perner, J., Ruffman, E., & Leekam, S.R. (1993). Theory of mind is contagious: You catch it from your sibs. Submitted for publication.

Piaget, J. (1953). *The origin of intelligence in the child*. Harmondsworth, Middlesex: Penguin Books.

Piaget, J. (1954). *The construction of reality in the child*. New York: Basic Books.

Piaget, J. (1970). *Genetic epistemology* (E. Duckworth, Trans.). New York: Columbia University Press.

Piaget, J. (1972). *The principles of genetic epistemology* (W. Mays, Trans.). London: Routledge & Kegan Paul.

Piaget, J., & Inhelder, B. (1969). *The psychology of the child* (H. Weaver, Trans.). London: Routledge & Kegan Paul.

Premack, D., & Woodruff, G. (1978). Does the chimpanzee have a theory of mind? *Behavioral and Brain Sciences, 4*, 515–526.

Prizant, B., & Duchan, J. (1981). The functions of immediate echolalia in autistic children. *Journal of Speech and Hearing Disorders, 46*, 241–249.

Prizant, B., & Rydell, P. (1984). Analysis of functions of delayed echolalia in autistic children. *Journal of Speech and Hearing Research, 27*, 183–192.

Prizant, B.M., & Wetherby, A.M. (1987). Communicative intent: A framework for understanding social-communicative behavior in autism. *Journal of the American Academy of Child & Adolescent Psychiatry, 26*, 472–479.

Pronovost, W., Wakstein, M.P., & Wakstein, D.J. (1966). A longitudinal study of the speech behavior and language comprehension of fourteen children diagnosed atypical or autistic. *Exceptional Children, 33*, 19–26.

Reddy, V. (1991). Playing with others' expectations: Teasing and mucking about in the first year. In A. Whiten (Ed.), *Natural theories of mind* (pp. 143–158). Oxford: Blackwell.

Renfrew, L. (1972). *The Action Picture Test*. Oxford: North Place.

Ricks, D.M. (1975). Vocal communication in pre-verbal normal and autistic children. In N. O'Connor (Ed.), *Language, cognitive deficits, and retardation* (pp. 75–80). London: Butterworths.

Ricks, D.M. (1979). Making sense of experience to make sensible sounds. In M. Bullowa (Ed.), *Before speech* (pp. 245–268). Cambridge: Cambridge University Press.

Ricks, D.M., & Wing, L. (1975). Language, communication and the use of symbols in normal and autistic children. *Journal of Autism and Childhood Schizophrenia, 5*, 191–221.

Riguet, C.B., Taylor, N.D., Benaroya, S., & Klein, L.S. (1981). Symbolic play in autistic, Down's, and normal children of equivalent mental age. *Journal of Autism and Developmental Disorders, 11*, 439–448.

Rogers, S.J., & Newhart-Larson, S. (1989). Characteristics of infantile autism in five children with Leber's congenital amaurosis. *Developmental Medicine and Child Neurology, 31*, 598–608.

Rogers, S.J., Ozonoff, S., & Maslin-Cole, C. (1991). A comparative study of attachment behavior in young children with autism or other psychiatric disorders. *Journal of the American Academy of Child and Adolescent Psychiatry, 30*, 483–488.

Rogers, S.J., & Pennington, B.F. (1991). A theoretical approach to the deficits in infantile autism. *Development and Psychopathology, 3*, 137–162.

Roth, D., & Leslie, A.M. (1991). The recognition of attitude conveyed by utterance: A study of preschool and autistic children. *British Journal of Developmental Psychology, 9*, 315–330.

Rowland, C. (1983). Patterns of interaction between three blind infants and their mothers. In A.E. Mills (Ed.), *Language acquisition in the blind child: Normal and deficient* (pp. 114–132). London: Croom Helm.

Rumsey, J.M., Andreasen, N.C., & Rapoport, J.L. (1986). Thought, language, communication and affective flattening in autistic adults. *Archives of General Psychiatry, 43*, 771–777.

Rumsey, J.M., Rapoport, J.L., & Sceery, W.R. (1985). Autistic children as adults: Psychiatric, social, and behavioral outcomes. *Journal of the American Academy of Child and Adolescent Psychiatry, 24*, 465–473.

Runeson, S., & Frykholm, G. (1986). Kinematic specification of gender and gender expression. In V. McCabe & G.J. Balzano (Eds.), *Event cognition: An ecological perspective* (pp. 259–273). Hillsdale, NJ: Lawrence Erlbaum Associates Inc.

Russell, B. (1940). *An inquiry into meaning and truth*. London: Allen and Unwin.

Russell, J. (1981). Piaget's theory of sensorimotor development: Outline, assumptions and problems. In G. Butterworth (Ed.), *Infancy and epistemology* (pp. 3–29). Brighton: Harvester.

Russell, J. (1984). The subject-object division in language acquisition and ego development. *New Ideas in Psychology, 2*, 57–74.

Russell, J., Mauthner, N., Sharpe, S., & Tidswell, T. (1991). The 'windows task' as a measure of strategic deception in preschoolers and autistic subjects,. *British Journal of Developmental Psychology, 9*, 331–349.

Rutter, M. (1970). Autistic children: Infancy to adulthood. *Seminars in Psychiatry, 2*, 435–450.

Rutter, M., Bartak, L., & Newman, S. (1971). Autism—a central disorder of cognition and language? In M. Rutter (Ed.), *Infantile autism: Concepts, characteristics and treatment* (pp. 148–171). London: Churchill Livingstone.

Rutter, M., Greenfeld, D., & Lockyer, L. (1967). A five to fifteen year follow-up study of infantile psychosis II: Social and behavioural outcome. *British Journal of Psychiatry, 113*, 1183–1199.

Rutter, M., & Schopler, E. (1987). Autism and pervasive developmental disorders: Concepts and diagnostic issues. *Journal of Autism and Developmental Disorders*, *17*, 159–186.

Sagi, A., & Hoffman, M.L. (1976). Empathic distress in the newborn. *Developmental Psychology*, *12*, 175–176.

Sandler, J., & Sandler, A-M. (1978). On the development of object relationships and affects. *International Journal of Psycho-Analysis*, *59*, 285–296.

Schaffer, H.R. (1966). The onset of fear of strangers and the incongruity hypothesis. *Journal of Child Psychology and Psychiatry*, *7*, 95–106.

Schaffer, H.R. (1984). *The child's entry into a social world*. London: Academic Press.

Schaffer, H.R. (1989). Early social development. In A. Slater & G. Bremner (Eds.), *Infant development* (pp. 189–210). Hillsdale, NJ: Lawrence Erlbaum Associates Inc.

Scheerer, M., Rothmann, E., & Goldstein, K. (1945). A case of "idiot savant" : An experimental study of personality organisation. *Psychological Monographs*, *58*, (whole no. 269), 1–63.

Scheler, M. (1954). *The nature of sympathy* (P. Heath, Trans.). London: Routledge & Kegan Paul.

Searle, J.R. (1969). *Speech acts*. Cambridge: Cambridge University Press.

Seibert, J.M., Hogan, A.E., & Mundy, P.C. (1982). Assessing interactional competencies: The Early Social-Communication Scales. *Infant Mental Health Journal*, *3*, 244–258.

Shantz, C.U. (1975). The development of social cognition. In E.M. Hetherington (Ed.), *Review of child development research, Vol. 5* (pp. 257–323). Chicago: University of Chicago Press.

Shapiro, T. (1977). The quest for a linguistic model to study the speech of autistic children. *Journal of the American Academy of Child Psychiatry*, *16*, 608–619.

Shapiro, T., Roberts, A., & Fish, B. (1970). Imitation and echoing in young schizophrenic children. *Journal of the American Academy of Child and Adolescent Psychiatry*, *9*, 548–567.

Shapiro, T., Sherman, M., Calamari, G., & Koch, D. (1987). Attachment in autism and other developmental disorders. *Journal of the American Academy of Child and Adolescent Psychiatry*, *26*, 485–490.

Sharpless, E.A. (1985). Identity formation as reflected in the acquisition of personal pronouns. *Journal of the American Psychoanalytic Association*, *33*, 861–885.

Shatz, M., Wellman, H.M., & Silber, S. (1983). The acquisition of mental verbs: A systematic investigation of the first reference to mental states. *Cognition*, *14*, 301–321.

Shaw, R., & Pittenger, J. (1977). Perceiving the face of change in changing faces: Implications for a theory of object perception. In R. Shaw & J. Bransford (Eds.), *Perceiving, acting and knowing: Toward an ecological psychology* (pp. 103–132). Hillsdale, NJ: Lawrence Erlbaum Associates Inc.

Sigman, M.D., Kasari, C., Kwon, J.-H., & Yirmiya, N. (1992). Responses to the negative emotions of others by autistic, mentally retarded, and normal children. Child Development, *63*, 796–807.

Sigman, M., & Mundy, P. (1987). Symbolic processes in young autistic children. In D. Ciccheti & M. Beeghly (Eds.), Symbolic development in atypical children. *New directions for child development, No. 36* (pp. 31–46). San Francisco: Jossey Bass.

Sigman, M., & Mundy, P. (1989). Social attachments in autistic children. *Journal of the American Academy of Child and Adolescent Psychiatry, 28,* 74–81.

Sigman, M., Mundy, P., Sherman, T., & Ungerer, J.A. (1986). Social interactions of autistic, mentally retarded and normal children and their caregivers. *Journal of Child Psychology and Psychiatry, 27,* 647–656.

Sigman, M., & Ungerer, J.A. (1984a). Attachment behaviors in autistic children. *Journal of Autism and Developmental Disorders, 14,* 231–243.

Sigman, M., & Ungerer, J.A. (1984b). Cognitive and language skills in autistic, mentally retarded, and normal children. *Developmental Psychology, 20,* 293–302.

Silberg, J.L. (1978). The development of pronoun usage in the psychotic child. *Journal of Autism and Childhood Schizophrenia, 8,* 413–425.

Simner, M.L. (1971). Newborn's response to the cry of another infant. *Developmental Psychology, 5,* 136–150.

Snow, M.E., Hertzig, M.E., & Shapiro, T. (1987). Expression of emotion in young autistic children. *Journal of the American Academy of Child and Adolescent Psychiatry, 26,* 836–838.

Sodian, B., & Frith, U. (1992). Deception and sabotage in autistic, retarded, and normal children. *Journal of Child Psychology and Psychiatry, 33,* 591–605.

Sorce, J.F., & Emde, R. (1981). Mother's presence is not enough. *Developmental Psychology, 17,* 737–745.

Sorce, J.F., Emde, R.N., Campos, J., & Klinnert, M.D. (1985). Maternal emotional signaling: Its effect on the visual cliff behavior of 1-year-olds. *Developmental Psychology, 21,* 195–200.

Sperber, D., & Wilson, D. (1986). *Relevance: Communication and cognition.* Oxford: Blackwell.

Spiker, D., & Ricks, M. (1984). Visual self-recognition in autistic children: Developmental relationships. *Child Development, 55,* 214–225.

Sroufe, L.A. (1986). Appraisal: Bowlby's contribution to psychoanalytic theory and developmental psychology; Attachment: Separation: Loss. *Journal of Child Psychology and Psychiatry, 27,* 841–849.

Stern, D.N. (1985). *The interpersonal world of the infant.* New York: Basic Books.

Stone, W.L., & Lemanek, K.L. (1990). Parental report of social behaviors in autistic preschoolers. *Journal of Autism and Developmental Disorders, 20,* 513–522.

Strawson, P.F. (1962). Persons. In V.C. Chappell (Ed.), *The philosophy of mind* (pp. 127–146). Englewood Cliffs, NJ: Prentice-Hall. (Original work published 1958).

Sugarman, S. (1983). Why talk? Comment on Savage-Rumbaugh et al. *Journal of Experimental Psychology: General, 112,* 493–497.

Sugarman, S. (1984). The development of preverbal communication. In R.F. Schiefelbusch & J. Pickar (Eds.), *The acquisition of communicative competence* (pp. 23–67). Baltimore: University Park Press.

Sugarman, S. (1987). *Piaget's construction of the child's reality.* Cambridge: Cambridge University Press.

Sylvester-Bradley, B. (1985). Failure to distinguish between people and things in early infancy. *British Journal of Developmental Psychology, 3,* 281–292.

Tager-Flusberg, H. (1981). On the nature of linguistic functioning in early infantile autism. *Journal of Autism and Developmental Disorders, 11,* 45–56.

Tager-Flusberg, H. (1985). The conceptual basis for referential word meaning in children with autism. *Child Development, 56*, 1167–1178.

Tager-Flusberg, H. (1989a). *An analysis of discourse ability and internal state lexicons in a longitudinal study of autistic children.* Paper presented at the Biennial Meeting of the Society for Research in Child Development, Kansas City, April.

Tager-Flusberg, H. (1989b). A psycholinguistic perspective on language development in the autistic child. In G. Dawson (Ed.), *Autism: Nature, diagnosis and treatment* (pp. 92–115). New York: Guilford.

Tager-Flusberg, H. (1991). Semantic processing in the free recall of autistic children: Further evidence for a cognitive deficit. *British Journal of Developmental Psychology, 9*, 417–430.

Tager-Flusberg, H. (1992). Autistic children's talk about psychological states: Deficits in the early acquisition of a theory of mind. *Child Development, 63*, 161–172.

Tager-Flusberg, H. (1993). What language reveals about the understanding of minds in children with autism. In S. Baron-Cohen, H. Tager-Flusberg, & D.J. Cohen (Eds.), *Understanding other minds: Perspectives from autism* (pp. 138–157). Oxford: Oxford University Press.

Tager-Flusberg, H., & Anderson, M. (1991). The development of contingent discourse ability in autistic children. *Journal of Child Psychology and Psychiatry, 32*, 1123–1134.

Tan, J., & Harris, P.L. (1991). Autistic children understand seeing and wanting. *Development and Psychopathology, 3*, 163–174.

Tantam, D. (1991). Asperger syndrome in adulthood. In U. Frith (Ed.), *Autism and Asperger syndrome* (pp. 147–183). Cambridge: Cambridge University Press.

Tiegerman, E., & Primavera, L. (1981). Object manipulation: an interactional strategy with autistic children. *Journal of Autism and Developmental Disorders, 11*, 427–438.

Tomasello, M. (1992). The social bases of language acquisition. *Social Development, 1*, 67–87.

Tomasello, M., & Farrar, M.J. (1986). Joint attention and early language. *Child Development, 57*, 1454–1463.

Tomasello, M., Kruger, A.C., & Ratner, H.H. (1993). Cultural learning. *Behavioral and Brain Sciences* (In press).

Trevarthen, C. (1979). Communication and cooperation in early infancy: A description of primary intersubjectivity. In M. Bullowa (Ed.), *Before speech* (pp. 321–347). Cambridge: Cambridge University Press.

Trevarthen, C. (1982). The primary motives for cooperative understanding. In G. Butterworth and P. Light (Eds.), *Social Cognition* (pp. 77–109). Brighton: Harvester.

Trevarthen, C. (1989). The relation of autism to normal socio-cultural development: The case for a primary disorder in regulation of cognitive growth by emotions. [Published in French as: "Les relations entre autisme et developpement socioculturel normal: Arguments en faveur d'un trouble primaire de la regulation du developpement cognitif par les emotions"]. In G. Lelord, J.P. Muk, M. Petit, & D. Sauvage (Eds.), *Autisme et troubles du developpement global de l'enfant.* Paris: Expansion Scientifique Francais.

Trevarthen, C., & Hubley, P. (1978). Secondary intersubjectivity: Confidence, confiding and acts of meaning in the first year. In A. Lock (Ed.), *Action, gesture and symbol: The emergence of language* (pp. 183–229). London: Academic Press.

Tronick, E., Als, H. Adamson, L., Wise S., & Brazelton, T.B. (1978). The infant's response to entrapment between contradictory messages in face-to-face interaction. *Journal of the American Academy of Child and Adolescent Psychiatry, 17*, 1–13.

Tustin, F. (1981). *Autistic states in children*. London: Routledge & Kegan Paul.

Tymchuk, A.J., Simmons, J.Q., & Neafsey, S. (1977). Intellectual characteristics of adolescent childhood psychotics with high verbal ability. *Journal of Mental Deficiency Research, 21*, 133–138.

Ungerer, J.A. (1989). The early development of autistic children: Implications for defining primary deficits. In G. Dawson (Ed.), *Autism, diagnosis and treatment* (pp. 75–91). New York: Guilford.

Ungerer, J.A., & Sigman, M. (1981). Symbolic play and language comprehension in autistic children. *Journal of the American Academy of Child Psychiatry, 20*, 318–337.

Urwin, C. (1983). Dialogue and cognitive functioning in the early language development of three blind children. In A.E. Mills (Ed.), *Language acquisiton in the blind: Normal and deficient* (pp. 142–161). London: Croom Helm.

Volkmar, F.R. (1987). Social development. In D.J. Cohen & A.M. Donnellan (Eds.), *Handbook of autism and pervasive developmental disorders* (pp. 41–60). New York: Wiley.

Volkmar, F.R., Sparrow, S.S., Goudreau, D., Cicchetti, D.V., Paul, R., & Cohen, D.J. (1987). Social deficits in autism: An operational approach using the Vineland Adaptive Behavior Scales. *Journal of the American Academy of Child and Adolescent Psychiatry, 26*, 156–161.

Vygotsky, L.S. (1962). *Thought and language.* (E. Hanfmann & G. Vakar, Trans.). Cambridge, MA: MIT Press

Vygotsky, L.S. (1978). Internalization of higher psychological functions. In M. Cole, V. John-Steiner, S. Scribner, & E. Souberman (Eds.), *Mind in Society: The development of higher psychological processes* (pp. 52–57). Cambridge, MA: Harvard University Press.

Walden, T.A., & Ogan, T.A. (1988). The development of social referencing. *Child Development, 59*, 1230–1240.

Walker, A.S. (1982). Intermodal perception of expressive behaviors by human infants. *Journal of Experimental Child Psychology, 33*, 514–535.

Walker-Andrews, A.S. (1988). Infants' perception of the affordances of expressive behaviors. In C. Rovee-Collier (Ed.), *Advances in infancy research, Vol. 5* (pp. 173–221). Norwood, NJ: Ablex.

Weeks, S.J., & Hobson, R.P. (1987). The salience of facial expression for autistic children. *Journal of Child Psychology and Psychiatry, 28*, 137–152.

Weigl, E. (1941). On the psychology of so-called processes of abstraction (M.J. Rioch, Trans.). *Journal of Abnormal and Social Psychology, 36*, 3–33.

Wellman, H.M. (1990). *The child's theory of mind.* Cambridge, MA: MIT Bradford.

Wellman, H.M. (1991). From desires to beliefs: Acquisition of a theory of mind. In A. Whiten (Ed.), *Natural theories of mind* (pp. 19–38). Oxford: Blackwell.

Wellman, H.M., & Bartsch, K. (1988). Young children's reasoning about beliefs. *Cognition, 30*, 239–277.

Wellman, H.M., & Estes, D. (1986). Early understanding of mental entities: A reexamination of childhood realism. *Child Development, 57*, 910–923.

Wellman, H.M., & Woolley, J.D. (1990). From simple desires to ordinary beliefs: The early development of everyday psychology. *Cognition, 35*, 910–923.

Werner, H. (1948). *Comparative psychology of mental development.* Chicago: Follett.

Werner, H., & Kaplan, B. (1984). *Symbol formation.* Hillsdale, NJ: Lawrence Erlbaum Associates Inc. (Original work published 1963).

Wetherby, A.M. (1986). Ontogeny of communicative functions in autism. *Journal of Autism and Developmental Disorders, 16*, 295–316.

Wetherby, A.M., & Gaines, B.H. (1982). Cognition and language development in autism. *Journal of Speech and Hearing Disorders, 47,* 63–70.

Wetherby, A.M., & Prutting, C.A. (1984). Profiles of communicative and cognitive-social abilities in autistic children. *Journal of Speech and Hearing Research, 27*, 364–377.

Wimmer, H., & Perner, J. (1983). Beliefs about beliefs: Representation and constraining function of wrong beliefs in young children's understanding of deception. *Cognition, 13*, 103–128.

Wimpory, D. (1986). *Developing sociability in preverbal autistic children.* Paper presented to the BPS Developmental Section Conference, 1986, Exeter.

Wing, L. (1969). The handicaps of autistic children—A comparative study. *Journal of Child Psychology and Psychiatry, 10*, 1–40.

Wing, L. (1981a). Asperger's syndrome: a clinical account. *Psychological Medicine, 11*, 115–129.

Wing, L. (1981b). Language, social and cognitive impairments in autism and severe mental retardation. *Journal of Autism and Developmental Disorders, 11*, 31–44.

Wing, L. (1988a). Possible clues to the underlying pathology—1. Clinical facts. In L. Wing (Ed.), *Aspects of autism: Biological research* (pp. 1–10). London: Gaskell/The National Autistic Society.

Wing, L. (1988b). The continuum of autistic characteristics. In E. Schopler & G.B. Mesibov (Eds.), *Diagnosis and assessment in autism* (pp. 91–110). New York: Plenum.

Wing, L., & Gould, J. (1979). Severe impairments of social interaction and associated abnormalities in children: Epidemiology and classification. *Journal of Autism and Developmental Disorders, 9*, 11–29.

Wing, L., Gould, J., Yeates, S.R., & Brierley, L.M. (1977). Symbolic play in severely mentally retarded and in autistic children. *Journal of Child Psychology and Psychiatry, 18*, 167–178.

Wing, L., & Wing, J.K. (1971). Multiple impairments in early childhood autism. *Journal of Autism and Childhood Schizophrenia, 1*, 256–266.

Wittgenstein, L. (1958). *Philosophical investigations* (G.E.M. Anscombe, Trans. 2nd ed.). Oxford: Blackwell.

Wittgenstein, L. (1980). In G. H. von Wright & H. Nyman (Eds.), *Remarks on the philosophy of psychology*, Vol. 2 (C. G. Luckhardt & M.A.E. Aue, Trans.). Oxford: Blackwell.

Wolf, D., & Gardner, H. (1981). On the structure of early symbolization. In R.L. Schiefelbusch & D.D. Bricker (Eds.), *Early language: Acquisition and intervention* (pp. 287–327). Baltimore: University Park Press.

Wolff, P.H. (1969). The natural history of crying and other vocalizations in early infancy. In B.M. Foss, (Ed.), *Determinants of infant behaviour, Vol IV* (pp. 81–109). London: Methuen.

Wolff, S., & Barlow, A. (1979). Schizoid personality in childhood: A comparative study of schizoid, autistic and normal children. *Journal of Child Psychology and Psychiatry, 20,* 29–46.

Woodruff Smith, D. (1989). *The circle of acquaintance.* Dordrecht: Kluwer Academic.

Wright, K. (1991). *Vision and separation: Between mother and baby.* London: Free Association Books.

Wulff, S.B. (1985). The symbolic and object play of children with autism: A review. *Journal of Autism and Developmental Disorder, 15,* 139–148.

Yirmiya, N., Kasari, C., Sigman, M., & Mundy, P. (1989). Facial expressions of affect in autistic, mentally retarded and normal children. *Journal of Child Psychology and Psychiatry, 30,* 725–735.

Yirmiya, N., Sigman, M.D., Kasari, C., & Mundy, P. (1992). Empathy and cognition in high-functioning children with autism. *Child Development, 63,* 150–160.

Young-Browne, G., Rosenfeld, H.M., & Horowitz, F.D. (1977). Infant discrimination of facial expressions. *Child Development, 48,* 555–562.

Zahn-Waxler, C., Radke-Yarrow, M., & King, R.A. (1979). Child rearing and children's prosocial initiations towards victims of distress. *Child Development, 50,* 319–330.

Zucker, K.J. (1985). The infant's construction of his parents in the first six months of life. In T.M. Field & N.A. Fox (Eds.), *Social perception in infants* (pp. 127–156). Norwood, NJ: Ablex.

Zukow, P.G. (1984). Criteria for the emergence of symbolic conduct: When words refer and play is symbolic. In L. Feagans, C. Garvey, & R. Golinkoff (Eds.), *The origins and growth of communication* (pp. 162–175). Norwood, NJ: Ablex.

Author Index

Subject Index